Eeky parky

THE MOST UNNATURAL ACT OF ALL

INSIDE THE ART OF

De-Escalation

MODERN SURVIVAL SKILLS

For Law Enforcement, Security, Correction & Citizens-At-Risk

Hammer Says –

"IT'S TIME TO CONSIDER A SAFER WAY TO DEAL WITH THE HUMAN PREDATORS WHO WALK AMONG US. DON'T YOU THINK?"

By Harry Hammer, PPCT Instructor Trainer (IT), Advanced Verbal Judo and De-Escalation Techniques Instructor.

LIMITS OF LIABILITY/DISCLAIMER

OF WARRANTY

The author and publisher of this book and the accompanying materials have used their best efforts in preparing this program. The author and publisher make no representation or warranties with respect to the accuracy, applicability, fitness, or completeness of the contents of this work. They disclaim any warranties (expressed or implied), merchantability, of fitness for any particular purpose.

The author and publisher shall in no event be held liable for any loss or damages. As always, the advise of competent, legal, tax, accounting, or other professional counsel should be sought.

This book contains material protected under International or Federal Copyright Laws and Treaties. Any unauthorized

THIS GREAT COP

A TRUE STORY

Several years back, a great cop dispatched himself from his cruiser to trek his beat on foot. He was tracking a bad guy wanted for aggravated assault. Before long, he walked smack into a giant of a man who looked all pissed off at the world and ready to fight, to boot. As the beast arranged himself into an impressive boxer's stance, the great cop recognized that the guy matched the description of the fugitive he happened to be hunting.

With no hesitation, the cop smiled his sincerest smile and greeted the huge fugitive. "How you doing today, sir?"

The big man dropped his fists and stepped out of character. A look of surprise replaced the hostility on his face and he looked around, as if to see if the cop was addressing someone else. "Ahh, well, none too sporty, officer, none too sporty. I just threw a cash register through a store window, and to top that off, tossed me a couple people through that same window."

The great cop maintained that smile and shrugged his shoulders. "Well heck, you seem like a nice enough fellah to me. Willing to own up to things."

4

"Not really, but thanks anyway," the fugitive said, and then, without too much more ado, the fugitive offered both hands to the cop, who, acting as if a violent fugitive with a rap sheet the size of Altoona volunteering to be handcuffed was exactly what he had expected the entire time, hooked him up and escorted him the block and a half to his black and white.

This great cop is the personification of **Generating Voluntary Compliance, which is a central theme of De-escalation and should be the goal** of all law enforcement interactions!

THE LEGAL CONSIDERATIONS OF DE-ESCALATION

Let's start by addressing something every police, corrections, security, probation and parole or law enforcement officer should know about the legal considerations when dealing with **verbal hostility and blatant disrespect.**

Throughout this book, we will be discussing actions and attitudes of both citizens and police. I think, therefore, the below court decision concerning officers and **verbal abuse,** and especially how police react to that abuse, makes the *Fighting Words Doctrine* important.

It is not just the *crap or blatant disrespect in the way of profanity and insults* that citizens hurl at police that is at issue here. Often, it is little more than a person's *piss-poor attitude* that initiates a forceful reaction by an officer(s). That reaction could be in the form of profanity, threats, physical retribution and/or incarceration. Doesn't matter. Today, as 2016 comes to an end, it is a problem for police and citizens alike.

We will talk about *attitude* in a pursuant chapter. Attitude of both police and citizens. For now, however, let's examine **words.** Specifically, words of disrespect and/or hatred of authority uttered at an officer or an entire group of officers. The courts have long debated issues surrounding what they considered *"Fighting Words."* This is a word(s) that *"actually disrupts or obstructs police officers in the performance of their duties."*

"THE FIGHTING WORDS DOCTRINE"

As articulated in **Houston V Hill** and other related court decisions.

A police officer is expected... to overcome verbal attacks, profanity, et al. , as long as these words and/or actions do not constitute a threat to that officer's safety..."

The Supreme Court went on to propound that, a **properly trained officer may reasonably be expected to exercise a higher degree of restraint...and should be...less likely to respond belligerently to words and attitudes that do not meet the definition of "fighting words...."**

These words uttered by Justice Powell in *Lewis v. City of New Orleans,* declared that "*profanity, name calling and obscene gestures directed at police officers **do not constitute fighting words!**"*

Additionally, in *Duran v. City of Douglas,* the courts decided that a subject who was arrested after verbally attacking an officer "was acting and speaking within his First Amendment rights, and excoriated the (arresting) officers because *officers are expected to be **professional** and to rise above mere thuggery and to show restraint.*"

Again, in *The City of Bismarck, North Dakota v. Shoppert,* another seminal decision regarding how police must respond to verbal abuse: *"Police are expected to rise above the average citizen...and are expected to be trained to restrain themselves and to divorce themselves from (reacting to) anger..."*

There have been other similar court decisions, but I am sure you get the picture. Police, because of their status as *professionals, the training they receive,* and their mission of protecting society, must rise above the flaws and frailties of the average citizens, and to also rise above the verbal attacks often launched in their direction.

This is not easy to do. But, once you accept the mantle of professionalism, strap on the gun and pin on the badge, that is exactly what you must do.

One problem. The courts point out the training police receive. The courts also point to the *professionalism* of our police. However, I think it apropos to note that there is still a crying need for more and better de-escalation and crisis-intervention training. My research reveals that many police administrations across the country acknowledge the need for more de-escalation training, and the closer I look at some of the problems and issues involved, I see police still reacting poorly and aggressively to perceived disrespect and the initial resistance to commands.

Gary Kluglewics, a highly-regarded law enforcement and Verbal Judo instructor, in an ILEETA presentation in April, 2010, stated that *"most law enforcement agencies teach some form of professional communications skills, but many departments never incorporate this training paradigm in their decision-making, nor do they incorporate it in their defensive tactics and/or weapons training."*

And so long as this is true, their training and professionalism must be questioned. With these legal issues evident, one of the purposes of this book is to encourage law enforcement and others to begin looking at some of the key issues that will help upgrade their ability to deflect verbal abuse and to adequately communicate with everybody. I have little doubt that, achieving these two goals will maximize both their safety and the safety of the citizens with whom they must work.

MEET THE AUTHOR, HARRY HAMMER.

Harry Hammer, with wife Sandra, toasting the year 2016.

*HARRY HAMMER IS AN AWARD-WINNING PPCT (PRESSURE POINT CONTROL TACTICS) INSTRUCTOR TRAINER (IT) AND ADVANCED DE-ESCALATION TECHNIQUES INSTRUCTOR. HAMMER IS ALSO ONE OF ONLY A DOZEN OR SO (FORMER) ADVANCED VERBAL JUDO INSTRUCTORS IN THE WORLD. THE LIST OF TRAININGS HAMMER HAS RESEARCHED, CREATED AND CONDUCTED THROUGHOUT THE UNITED STATES IS LEGION, INCLUDING PPCT DEFENSIVE TACTICS (DT) INSTRUCTOR CERTIFICATION; SPONTANEOUS KNIFE DEFENSE (SKD); GROUND AVOIDANCE & GROUND ESCAPES (GAGE); TACTICAL HANDCUFFING; SEXUAL HARASSMENT ASSAULT & RAPE PREVENTION (SHARP); ADVANCED FIGHTING ARTS FOR GIRLS AND WOMEN; VIOLENT PATIENT MANAGEMENT (VPM); DISRUPTIVE STUDENT MANAGEMENT (DSM); ESCAPE & EVASION; INMATE CONTROL; COUNTER-ABDUCTION TACTICS (CAT) FOR CHILDREN AND MANAGEMENT OF WORKPLACE VIOLENCE, PLUS, OF COURSE, **ADVANCED DE-ESCALATION TECHNIQUES; VERBAL JUDO AND THE MANAGEMENT OF AGGRESSION.***

HARRY HAMMER IS PICTURED HERE (RED HAT) AT A PPCT INSTRUCTOR TRAINER CONFERENCE IN ST. LOUIS WITH TWO LONGTIME, SUCCESSFUL PPCT IT'S – PERRY HARRIS OF SOUTH CAROLINA, IN THE MIDDLE, AND DANGEROUS DAN SOLLA, DIRECTOR OF RED SCORPION OUT OF THE PHILLY AREA, ON THE FAR LEFT.

HARRY IS ALSO THE AUTHOR OF TWO SUCCESSFUL BOOKS. BARS, BOUNCERS, BAD GUYS AND BEYOND IS NUMBER ONE IN ITS GENRE ON AMAZON. BOUNCERS ADDRESSES THE ROLE OF BOUNCERS, SECURITY POLICE AND BAR MANAGERS IN ENTERTAINMENT VENUE (BARS, NIGHTCLUBS, ENTERTAINMENT CONCERTS, ETC.). HIS SECOND OPUS - SUPER- SECRET POLICE SHIT THAT CAN SAVE YOUR LIFE - IS AN AMAZING COMPENDIUM OF LIFE PRESERVING SELF-DEFENSE SKILLS, CONCEPTS, PRINCIPLES, TECHNIQUES AND STRATEGIES DESIGNED TO MAXIMIZE THE PERSONAL AND PROFESSIONAL SAFETY OF TODAY'S CITIZENS IN AN INCREASINGLY-DANGEROUS WORLD.

HAMMER IS A FORMER MARINE WHO RETIRED FROM THE PA. BOARD OF PROBATION AND PAROLE (PBPP) IN 2004 AFTER OVER 34-YEARS AS AN (PAROLE) AGENT, SUPERVISOR AND LEAD TRAINER AND TRAINING MANAGER. HE STARTED ACTION FIGHTING ARTS, HIS OWN TRAINING AND CONSULTING ENTERPRISE EARLY THAT YEAR. SINCE THEN, HAMMER HAS TRAINED AND/OR CERTIFIED (AS INSTRUCTORS) NEARLY 1000 PROBATION/PAROLE, CORRECTIONS, POLICE, SECURITY, MILITARY, AND LAY CITIZENS (AT RISK), INCLUDING HEALTH CARE PROFESSIONALS, EDUCATIONAL STAFF, COURTHOUSE EMPLOYEES AND OTHERS.

HARRY FIRST INTRODUCED BASIC AND ADVANCED DE-ESCALATION TECHNIQUES (BASIC DE-ESCALATION SKILLS AS PART OF HIS BASIC PROBATION AND PAROLE ACADEMY AND **ADVANCED DE-ESCALATION AS PART OF THE REGULAR TRAINING CURRICULUM FOR ALL COUNTY AND STATE STAFF)** *IN* **1989** *AS A STAFF DEVELOPMENT SPECIALIST, THE FIRST TRAINING OF ITS KIND IN EITHER THE STATE, COUNTY OR FEDERAL PROBATION SYSTEM(S). HARRY CREDITS* **JAMES O. SMITH,** *THEN THE DIRECTOR OF THE STAFF DEVELOPMENT UNIT (OF THE PBPP), AS THE PROGENITOR OF DE-ESCALATION AS A TRAINING PARADIGM. SMITH, HARRY MAINTAINS, FIRST RECOGNIZED THE NEED FOR "SOME KIND OF TRAINING PROGRAM THAT WOULD ADDRESS THE WIDE GAP BETWEEN OFFICER PRESENCE AND VERBAL DIRECTIONS - THE FIRST TWO LEVELS OF CONTROL ON OUR CONTINUUM OF CONTROL- AND THE USE OF PHYSICAL FORCE (SOFT AND HARD EMPTY HAND CONTROL) AND DEADLY FORCE ACTIONS WHEN DEALING WITH THE WIDE-CONTINUUM OF RESISTANCE PROBATION AND PAROLE STAFF CONFRONT ON THE STREET EVERY DAY."*

SMITH WAS THE FIRST TO RECOGNIZE A NEED AFTER SCOURING SCORES OF USE- OF- FORCE REPORTS AND CONCLUDING THAT MANY OF THE INCIDENTS — SOME OF WHICH RESULTED IN INJURIES TO BOTH OFFICER AND PAROLEE — SEVERAL OF WHICH HAD GENERATED LAW SUITS (AGAINST THE PBPP), NOT TO MENTION UNWANTED PUBLICITY, THAT **THE USE OF PROVOCATIVE LANGUAGE** **_PRODUCED RATHER THAN REDUCED ANIMOSITY AND RESISTANCE_.** *SMITH, THEN, HARRY ALWAYS INSISTS, IS THE FATHER OF DE-ESCALATION, IN NOT ONLY THE PA. PAROLE BOARD AND ALL 67 COUNTIES, BUT IN MANY STATES, SINCE THERE EXISTED NO SUCH PROGRAM UNTIL THEN.*

SINCE THAT DATE IN 1987 OR 88 (HAMMER IS NOT SURE. NOR IS SMITH), HARRY HAS CONDUCTED SEMINARS AT THE ASLET (AMERICAN SOCIETY OF LAW ENFORCEMENT TRAINERS) INTERNATIONAL TRAINING CONFERENCES IN ALBUQUERQUE, NEW MEXICO AND ORLANDO, FLORIDA. HE HAS ALSO CONDUCTED PROGRAMS FOR THE PA. DISTRICT ATTORNEY CONFERENCE

(LANCASTER) AND THE PA. AND NJ WARDENS' CONFERENCES (ALTOONA, PA. AND ATLANTIC CITY, N.J. HE HAS ALSO BEEN THE FEATURED SPEAKER AT NUMEROUS D & A TREATMENT CONFERENCES, INCLUDING GUADENZIA HOUSE CENTERS IN PHILADELPHIA, NORRISTOWN, HARRISBURG AND BALTIMORE, MD., TREATMENT TRENDS, INC., IN ALLENTOWN, ST. LUKE'S MEDICAL CENTER UNIVERSITY (ALLENTOWN, BETHLEHEM AND EASTON), AND THE POCONO MEDICAL `, EAST STROUDSBURG, PA.

WHY YOU SHOULD READ THIS BOOK.

- *RESEARCH SHOWS THAT 97 TO 98% OF ALL CONFLICTS CAN BE RESOLVED WITH NON-VIOLENT DE-ESCALATION TECHNIQUES. IN THIS BOOK, YOU WILL LEARN JUST ABOUT EVERYTHING YOU WILL EVER NEED TO KNOW TO RESOLVE ALMOST EVERY TYPE OF CONFLICT, THAT LEFT UNIMPEDED, COULD LEAD TO VIOLENCE OR ANOTHER TYPE OF TRAGEDY.*

- *LEARN HOW TO PREDICT, PREVENT, AND/OR DEFUSE SUICIDE BY COP (SBC) INCIDENTS. SBC INCIDENTS ARE UNFORTUNATELY ON THE INCREASE ACROSS THE COUNTRY. THESE ARE TRAGIC SCENARIOS CAUSING SUFFERING AND OTHER CATASTROPHIC PREDICAMENTS FOR BOTH THE "VICTIM (THE SUICIDAL SUBJECT)" AND THE OFFICER(S) INVOLVED.*

- *IN THIS BOOK, YOU WILL LEARN SKILLS, TACTICS, TECHNIQUES, AND PRINCIPLES THAT WILL MAXIMIZE YOUR CHANCES OF STAYING SAFE THROUGH THE MASTERY OF WORDS.*

  THE NUMBER ONE GOAL OF (MY) DE-ESCALATION PROGRAM IS OFFICER OR STAFF SAFETY!

- *RELATIVE TO THE GOAL OF OFFICER SAFETY, POLICE KILLED ON DUTY IN 2016 HAS INCREASED BY OVER 50% OVER 2015!*

- *IN THIS BOOK, YOU WILL UNDERSTAND HOW TO DE-ESCALATE ANYONE, ANYTIME, ANYWHERE! SKEPTICAL? I DON'T BLAME YOU. READ ON AND LET ME CONVINCE AND REASSURE YOU.*

- *LEARN AND MASTER THE ANCIENT AND FORMIDABLE ART OF MUSHIN TO STAY CENTERED AND UNDER CONTROL IN ALL STRESSFUL SITUATIONS.* MUSHIN IS A JAPANESE TERM LITERALLY MEANING NO MIND (TACTICAL INDIFFERENCE), NO FEAR, NO JUDGMENTS.

- *TOM BARNOWSKI, DIRECTOR OF THE NORTHAMPTON COMMUNITY COLLEGE'S SCHOOL OF BUSINESS AND INDUSTRY (BETHLEHEM, PA.) PROCLAIMS THAT IT IS INEVITABLE THAT THE TREND TOWARD COMMUNITY POLICING WILL CONTINUE INTO 2017 AND BEYOND. BARNOWSKI GOES A STEP FURTHER EVEN, PREDICTING THAT THE CONCEPT OF COMMUNITY POLICING WILL EVENTUALLY BECOME A CRITICAL MOVEMENT IN MODERN LAW ENFORCEMENT! DE-ESCALATION SKILLS AND PRINCIPLES WILL BE A MUST-HAVE SKILL TO ANY AGENCY OR INDIVIDUAL SEEKING TO ENHANCE ITS, OR HIS, PUBLIC INDIVIDUAL SEEKING TO ENHANCE ITS OR HIS PUBLIC IMAGE AND THE CAPABILITY TO SUCCEED AT COMMUNITY POLICING!*

- *MASTER THE ABILITY TO DEFLECT VERBAL ABUSE WHILE STILL ACHIEVING YOUR PROFESSIONAL OBJECTIVES. SKEPTICAL AGAIN? READ ON. THERE IS A SURPRISINGLY EASY FORMULA FOR MANAGING ALL TYPES OF VERBAL HOSTILITY, THE MOST COMMON TYPE OF ATTACK AGAINST OFFICERS AND CITIZENS! THE ABILITY TO DEFLECT RATHER THAN TO ABSORB VERBAL ABUSE WILL, IF YOU ALLOW IT, BE A CRUCIAL COMPONENT OF THE PROFESSIONAL COMMUNICATIONS SKILL SET THAT CAN PREVENT YOU FROM GOING FROM "HERO-TO-ZERO!"*

- *EMPOWER YOURSELF AND DISEMPOWER YOUR ATTACKER. AVOID TIPPING OVER THE DIGNITY*

14

DOMINOES BY MASTERING THE STRIP PHRASE AND THE ART OF DEFLECTION.

- *IN THIS BOOK, YOU WILL LEARN ONE OF THE GREATEST SKILLS IN HUMAN INTERACTIONS:* HOW TO *STAY COOL WHEN EVERYONE ELSE IS HOT AND OUT OF CONTROL!*

- *THE GOAL OF VERBAL JUDO IS ONE ANYONE WORKING WITH AGGRESSIVE, POTENTIALLY VIOLENT PEOPLE SHOULD STRIVE FOR: "TO GENERATE VOLUNTARY COMPLIANCE!" INFLUENCE THE EMOTIONALLY DISTURBED OR PATHOLOGICALLY-RESISTANT SUBJECT (OR, ANYBODY) TO DO WHAT YOU WANT OR NEED HIM TO DO WHILE MAKING HIM BELIEVE IT WAS HIS IDEA IN THE FIRST PLACE!*

- *LEARN WIN/WIN SKILLS INSTEAD OF PROFESSIONAL-IMAGE-BUSTING WIN/LOSE TACTICS! I-STATEMENTS OVER ACCUSATORY YOU-STATEMENTS; EMPATHY; TACTICAL RESPECT; EMPATHIC, AND/OR REFLECTIVE LISTENING/THE TACTICAL-TEN (CAR) STOP AND MANY OTHER SKILLS.*

- *LEARN CRITICAL SKILLS, TACTICS, AND TECHNIQUES CRUCIAL TO CALMING MENTALLY ILL, EMOTIONALLY DISTURBED, AND EXTREMELY VIOLENT "BRAIN DAMAGED" PEOPLE. ONE OF THE MOST DIFFICULT AND TOO-OFTEN CATASTROPHIC PROBLEMS CONFRONTED BY POLICE – AND ONE THAT LOOKS TO EVEN GET MORE VEXING IN THE FUTURE – IS HOW POLICE DEAL WITH THE SEVERELY MENTALLY ILL AND EMOTIONALLY DISTURBED, ESPECIALLY WHEN CONFRONTED BY BIZARRE BEHAVIOR AND POTENTIALLY THREATENING BEHAVIORS!*

- *IN SUMMARY, THE GOALS OF DE-ESCALATION AND THIS BOOK ARE TO MAXIMIZE OFFICER AND STAFF SAFETY; TO ENHANCE PROFESSIONAL IMAGE; TO GREATLY REDUCE VICARIOUS LIABILITY; DECREASE PERSONAL AND PROFESSIONAL STRESS; MAXIMIZE COURTROOM POWER; IMPROVE COMMUNITY RELATIONS AND TO ESTABLISH JUSTIFICATION OF ALL USE OF FORCE (PRECLUSION).*

AN INTRODUCTION TO DE-ESCALATION OF AGGRESSION

"DE-ESCALATION IS A DELIBERATE PROCESS THAT RECOGNIZES AND PRESERVES THE RIGHTS OF OTHERS...AFTER ALL, AT THE END OF THE DAY, ARE WE NOT THE KEEPERS OF THE PEACE?"

Central Winology Philosophy

THIS IS MY THIRD IN A SERIES OF NON-FICTION BOOKS CENTERED AROUND PSYCHOLOGICAL, VERBAL AND PHYSICAL (SUBJECT-CONTROL AND SELF-DEFENSE) SKILLS, PRINCIPLES, AND TACTICS FOCUSING ON MAXIMIZING SUBJECT CONTROL OR SELF-DEFENSE. MY FIRST (BARS, BOUNCERS, BAD GUYS AND BEYOND) WAS DESIGNED TO PROMOTE SKILLS THAT WOULD ENABLE BOUNCERS AND SECURITY POLICE TO VERBALLY DEFUSE PATRONS WHO WERE UNDER THE INFLUENCE OF DRUGS, ALCOHOL, TESTOSTERONE, AND/OR ANGER. MY SECOND – SUPER SECRET POLICE SHIT THAT CAN SAVE YOUR LIFE – ADVOCATED A CLUSTER OF PHYSICAL, MENTAL, AND EMOTIONAL LIFE PRESERVING SKILLS, TECHNIQUES, AND PRINCIPLES, CULLED FROM A LIFETIME OF EXPERIENCE AS A MARINE, A P.O., AND MORE SPECIFICALLY, A PPCT INSTRUCTOR TRAINER, TO BE USED AGAINST THOSE MISCREANTS WHO WOULD, IF ALLOWED, TAKE AN INNOCENT CITIZEN'S LIFE, OR AT THE VERY LEAST, SEVERELY INJURE HIM OR HER.

AUTHOR'S NOTE. *TO ENHANCE YOUR READING EXPERIENCE, OR AT THE LEAST TO MINIMIZE THE TEDIUM, I WILL BE ELIMINATING THE CONFUSING, DISTRACTING AND MIND NUMBING LANGUAGE OF DUAL GENDER REFERENCES. EVEN THOUGH MANY OFFICERS*

AND CITIZENS ARE FEMALE, I AM GOING TO REFER ONLY TO MALES, ELIMINATING THE CONFUSING AND MUDDLED REFERENCES SUCH AS "HE/SHE, HIM/HER," ETC. I REFER TO THE END OF THE PREVIOUS PARAGRAPH WHEREIN I WROTE, "...TAKE AN INNOCENT CITIZEN'S LIFE, OR AT THE VERY LEAST, SEVERELY INJURE HIM OR HER."

"JESUS, HARRY, THE WORLD IS ON FIRE!"

A NEW YORK POLICE OFFICER COMMENTING DURING A BREAK AT ONE OF MY PPCT SPONTANEOUS KNIFE DEFENSE INSTRUCTOR CERTIFICATION SEMINARS. AT HIS REQUEST, I AM KEEPING HIM ANONYMOUS. THE COMMENT CAME AFTER THREE OFFICERS WERE AMBUSHED AND SHOT IN BATON ROUGE, LOUISIANA. OTHER OFFICERS COMMISERATED, NOTING THAT THEY FELT THE SAME WAY AFTER OFFICERS WERE AMBUSHED AND KILLED IN DALLAS, TEXAS

THIS BOOK IS DIFFERENT. IT IS ONE I'VE WANTED TO PEN FOR YEARS. DECADES, EVEN. THE MOST UNNATURAL ACT OF ALL – INSIDE THE ART OF DE-ESCALATION IS INSPIRED BY CURRENT EVENTS. EVENTS THAT ARE STILL GOING ON ALL OVER OUR COUNTRY. AMBUSHES AND KILLING OF DOZENS OF INNOCENT POLICE OFFICERS. CONTROVERSIAL POLICE SHOOTINGS OF ARMED AND UNARMED BLACK CITIZENS. MANY DEEMED TO BE JUSTIFIED, BUT IN SOME CASES, PUBLIC PERCEPTION DIFFERED DRAMATICALLY. SOME SHOOTING NOT CONSIDERED JUSTIFIED BY THE MEDIA, COURTS AND AGENCY ADMINISTRATIONS.

IN SOME SHOOTINGS, POLICE TRANSPARENCY WAS QUESTIONED.

THEN, IN WHAT APPEARS TO BE OUTRIGHT RETALIATION, CITIZENS HAVE AMBUSHED AND KILLED SCORES OF INNOCENT POLICE OFFICERS IN VARIOUS CITIES ACROSS OUR COUNTRY. JUST THE OTHER DAY – NOVEMBER 21, 2016 – THREE OFFICERS WERE AMBUSHED AND SHOT -ONE FATALLY – IN THREE DIFFERENT CITIES IN THE UNITED STATES.

As several officers have stated during and after my training(s). "Jesus, The World is on Fire (paraphrasing)!"

Speculation by pundits on CBS, CNN and other channels indicate that these are coincidental and unrelated events performed by mentally ill or emotionally disturbed individuals. Others have speculated that these events are related only because they are the result of blossoming resentment and hatred of anything smacking of authority.

And then there are those who opine that, whether these acts of violence are related or not, whether they involve killers with severe mental issues, or whether they involve hate groups targeting police, there is a need for de-escalation trainings. Now more than ever.

In a recent article – "De-escalation Training, Learning to Back-Off," featured in "Police-The Law Enforcement Magazine, *David Griffith reported that, after* "Ferguson" and other controversial encounters with "unarmed" citizens, knife-wielding perps, and others who seemed resistant but far from harmful, a "spotlight has been focused on police tactics and training that has led to implementation of policy changes and training in de-escalation..."

Griffith noted that a report by a Washington-based criminal justice think-tank, the Police Executive Research Forum (PERF), lists thirty guiding principles for law enforcement use-of-force policy and training. Nine of these guidelines directly mention de-escalation, and/or discuss aspects of how officers can reduce force by backing-off in situations where immediate action is not mandated by law or required for officer safety.

WHICH IMPELS US TO CONSIDER THE QUESTION, "WHAT EXACTLY IS DE-ESCALATION?" WHILE I SAY THERE IS NO ONE PRECISE DEFINITION THAT WORKS FOR EVERYONE, GRIFFITH, WHO POSED THAT QUESTION TO VETERAN OFFICERS AND TRAINERS, ARRIVED AT AS SATISFACTORY A DEFINITION AS ANYONE WHEN HE CONCLUDED:

"DE-ESCALATION COMES DOWN TO A COMBINATION OF COMMUNICATIONS, EMPATHY, INSTINCT(S), AND SOUND OFFICER SAFETY TACTICS, THE GOAL OF WHICH IS TO HELP OFFICERS ACHIEVE A POSITIVE OUTCOME WHERE NEITHER THE OFFICER NOR THE CITIZEN IS HURT. AND, WHEN IT COMES TO DE-ESCALATION TRAINING, THE PHILOSOPHY (WINOLOGY) BEHIND THE TRAINING IS THAT OFFICERS NEED TO TAKE EVERY OPPORTUNITY TO SLOW DOWN SITUATIONS AND EMOTIONS WHENEVER POSSIBLE."

IN SUM, "WORDS MATTER." FOR CONTEXT, I AM PENNING THIS IN EARLY DECEMBER, 2016, AFTER A DIRTY AND CONTENTIOUS PRESIDENTIAL CAMPAIGN. EVERYTHING SEEMS INTENSIFIED AND EMOTIONS ARE ESCALATED. PLUS, MILWAUKEE IS LITERALLY BURNING DUE TO PROTESTS OVER THE SHOOTING OF AN ARMED BLACK MAN. OUR COUNTRY HAD JUST WITNESSED WEEKS OF DISRUPTIONS AND VIOLENCE IN DALLAS, TEXAS, BATON ROUGE, LOUISIANA, IN THE STATE OF MINNESOTA, AS WELL AS OTHER CITIES, SUCH AS BALTIMORE, ST. LOUIS AND PHILADELPHIA.

SO, YOU CAN IMAGINE HOW PLEASED I AM THAT DEPARTMENTS ACROSS THE COUNTRY ARE FINALLY COMING TO GRIPS WITH THE "NECESSARY" USE OF FORCE IN MANY SITUATIONS AND THE URGENT NEED TO MANAGE THE ILL-FEELINGS IN THOSE COMMUNITIES OVER THE INJURY, DEATHS AND RELATED TRAUMA INCIDENTAL TO THAT USE OF FORCE. OBVIOUSLY, I APPLAUD THE ATTENTION ON AVOIDING THE **UNNECESSARY USE OF FORCE** *AND* INSTILLING A VALUE SYSTEM ON *LEARNING HOW TO DISENGAGE AND/OR SHIFTING FROM* HARD-ASS COP MODE (MY WORDS) TO CONCERNED PROBLEM-SOLVING MODE.

HOWEVER, IT IS MY CONTENTION THAT WHAT WE ARE SEEING HERE ARE JUST WORDS. NOT REAL AND BONA FIDE ACTIONS THAT WILL MAKE A DIFFERENCE. AND THAT, MY FRIENDS, IS WHAT THE REST OF THIS BOOK IS ABOUT!

THE NEED FOR DE-ESCALATION TECHNIQUES TRAINING FOR ALL LAW ENFORCEMENT?

"MUSHIN (STAYING CENTERED AND BALANCED) IS A STATE OF MIND THAT ESTABLISHES AN OFFICER'S PROFESSIONAL PRESENCE, THE NUMBER ONE TOOL IN BEING ABLE TO GENERATE VOLUNTARY COMPLIANCE – WHAT I HOPE SOMEDAY WILL BE THE GOAL OF ALL LAW ENFORCEMENT..."

ANYONE WHO QUESTIONS THE NEED FOR OUR LAW ENFORCEMENT AGENCIES TO ADOPT DE-ESCALATION TRAINING FOR THEIR STAFF PROBABLY NEEDS TO LOOK NO FURTHER THAN THE DALLAS POLICE DEPT. BY MANY ACCOUNTS, THE DALLAS POLICE DEPARTMENT IS A NATIONAL EXAMPLE FOR OTHER CITIES LOOKING TO WORK EFFECTIVELY WITH ALL CITIZENS AS WELL AS AGITATED PROTESTORS.

ACCORDING TO (FORMER) DALLAS POLICE CHIEF DAVID BROWN, AFTER IMPLEMENTING DE-ESCALATION TACTICS TRAINING, EXCESSIVE FORCE COMPLAINTS PLUMMETED FROM 147 IN 2009 TO 53 IN 2014. NOTES FROM BUZZ FEED NEWS WROTE THAT, "DALLAS' OVERALL RATE OF ARRESTS HAS DROPPED, ALONG WITH THE MURDER RATE, WHICH HIT AN 80-YEAR LOW IN 2014. ALSO, ALTHOUGH IMPOSSIBLE TO MEASURE OBJECTIVELY, STAFF MORALE HAS IMPROVED GREATLY AND THE DPD IS IN A CLASS BY ITSELF...."

CHIEF BROWN TOLD THE DALLAS MORNING NEWS THAT WHAT WAS RESPONSIBLE FOR THE MANY IMPROVEMENTS COULD BE ACCREDITED TO "MAKING AN IMPACT THROUGH TRAINING, COMMUNITY POLICING (PRINCIPLES AND TACTICS) AND HOLDING OFFICERS ACCOUNTABLE. BROWN CONCLUDED WITH, "THIS IS THE MOST DRAMATIC DEVELOPMENT IN POLICING ANYWHERE IN AMERICA."

MAJOR MAX GERON, A SECURITY STUDIES SCHOLAR, WHO NOW HEADS THE DALLAS POLICE DEPARTMENT'S MEDIA RELATIONS DEPARTMENT, RELATED THE DPD'S DE-ESCALATION FUELED SYSTEM TO THE PROBLEM OF DEALING WITH MASS PROTESTS WITH **MASS FORCE AND UNRELENTING POWER.** ACCORDINGLY, HE TOLD THE WASHINGTON POST FOLLOWING PROTESTS IN FERGUSON, MISSOURI:

"THE IDEAL POLICE RESPONSE TO THIS KIND OF PROTEST IS NO RESPONSE AT ALL."

YOU MIGHT DISAGREE WITH THAT PHILOSOPHY AND I CAN UNDERSTAND IF YOU DO. HOWEVER, THIS PHILOSOPHY IS ONE THAT IS RIGHT IN STEP WITH MY DE-ESCALATION PHILOSOPHY. HOPEFULLY, I CAN CONVINCE YOU OF THAT IN THIS BOOK. IF I CANNOT SUCCEED AT THAT, I CAN OFFER ONE MORE NUGGET ABOUT DE-ESCALATION AND THE DALLAS POLICE DEPARTMENT.

SINCE DE-ESCALATION TRAINING HAS BEEN INCEPTED BY THE DPD, THERE HAVE BEEN FEWER POLICE-INVOLVED SHOOTINGS THAN ANY OTHER (AMERICAN) CITY.

ONE MORE QUOTE FROM CHIEF BROWN: "TRUST IS HARD TO EARN AND EASY TO LOSE."

FORMER NEW YORK CITY POLICE COMMISSIONER WILLIAM BRATTON (JULY, 2014) EMPHASIZED RESTORING TRUST IN POLICE AS THE DEBATE OVER POLICE BRUTALITY ESCALATED FOLLOWING THE CONTROVERSIAL CHOKE-HOLD RELATED DEATH OF ERIC GARDNER IN STATEN ISLAND. BRATTON BOLSTERED TRAINING IN DE-ESCALATION SKILLS IN WHAT HE TERMED, "A HOPEFUL TRANSITION FROM BEING 'THE POLICE' *TO BEING* 'YOUR POLICE...'*

"NEW YORK CITY POLICE DEPT. NEEDS PROBLEM-ORIENTED POLICING, WHICH REQUIRES NOT JUST VIGILANCE, BUT ALSO NIMBLENESS, OPEN-MINDEDNESS, FLEXIBILITY, COMPASSION..."

PHILADELPHIA POLICE DEPT. COMMISSIONER CHARLES RAMSEY AND SAN DIEGO P.D. CHIEF WILLIAM LANSDOWNE RECENTLY AGREED (AT AN INTERNATIONAL CONFERENCE OF POLICE COMMISSIONERS) THAT THE NEW GOAL IS TO BRING WHATEVER RESOURCES ARE NEEDED – INCLUDING ADDITIONAL EMPHASIS ON DE-ESCALATION PROGRAMS – "TO GIVE OFFICERS THE ABILITY TO **SLOW DOWN (THEIR REACTION DURING) POTENTIALLY VIOLENT SITUATIONS."**

PHILADELPHIA PD CAPTAIN FRAN HEALY WENT A STEP FURTHER. HEALY SUGGESTED THAT TODAY'S COPS MUST LEARN HOW TO SHIFT OUT OF "COP MODE" AND INTO "SOCIAL WORKER MODE" WHEN SITUATIONS AND SCENARIOS DEMAND SUCH A MIND-SHIFT, SUCH AS TACTICS TO DEAL WITH PEOPLE IN CRISIS.

PART OF THAT "MIND-SHIFT" MIGHT INCLUDE AVOIDING TACTICS LIKE BOXING A SUSPECT OR CITIZEN IN (TRAPPING, WHICH WE WILL ADDRESS LATER), MAKING DIRECT AND CHALLENGING EYE CONTACT, AND/OR LEARNING HOW AND WHEN TO **DISENGAGE** *FROM CERTAIN SITUATIONS INSTEAD OF PENETRATING AND ESCALATING THAT SCENARIO. HEALY NOTED THAT "OFTEN, TENSE ENCOUNTERS DEVELOP OVER*

NOTHING MORE THAN A PERSON'S REFUSAL TO COMPLY WITH AN ORDER (OR, POOR ATTITUDE), WITHOUT ANY ACTIVELY AGGRESSIVE OR HOSTILE ACTIONS TOWARD AN OFFICER."

COMMISSIONER RAMSEY ALSO SUGGESTED THAT "IT IS CRUCIAL (FOR OUR OFFICERS) TO SLOW THINGS DOWN SO THEY CAN THINK THROUGH TACTICS..."

RAMSEY STATED THAT IT WAS HIS INTENTION TO TRAIN OFFICERS TO UNDERSTAND THAT NOT ALL SITUATIONS REQUIRED (POLICE) ACTION, AND IN THOSE SCENARIOS (SURRENDER THEIR EGO), TO DISENGAGE...

AFTER FERGUSON

SINCE THE CONTROVERSIAL SHOOTING OF MICHAEL BROWN ON AUGUST 9, 2014, POLICE DEPARTMENTS AROUND THE COUNTRY HAVE STEPPED UP THEIR TRAINING IN DE-ESCALATION, FOCUSING ON "DEFUSING TENSE SITUATIONS WITH WORDS OR GESTURES INSTEAD OF BEING CONFRONTATIONAL OR REACHING FOR A WEAPON," *ACCORDING TO GENE JOHNSON AND ERIC TUCKER OF THE ASSOCIATED PRESS (NOVEMBER 29, 2014).*

JOHNSON AND TUCKER ALSO POINT OUT IN THEIR ARTICLES THAT THE DEPARTMENT OF JUSTICE BELIEVES THIS APPROACH **"CAN IMPROVE THE TRUST BETWEEN POLICE AND RESIDENTS, AND CURTAIL THE UNNECESSARY USE OF FORCE, WHICH CAN IMPROVE THE SAFETY OF OFFICERS AND CIVILIANS ALIKE."**

WHICH IS IMPORTANT. COMMISSIONER RAMSEY. "THERE IS ANOTHER TYPE OF **DE-ESCALATION THAT I BELIEVE IS CRUCIAL. AND THAT IS HOW WE MANAGE DURING AND ESPECIALLY** <u>AFTER</u> **USE OF FORCE SCENARIOS. I BELIEVE WE MUST LEARN HOW TO DE-ESCALATE AND DEFUSE TENSIONS IN THE COMMUNITY** <u>AFTER</u> *A USE OF FORCE INCIDENT..."*

I BELIEVE IT IS IMPORTANT TO POINT OUT HERE THAT I BELIEVE THIS PUSH TOWARD MANDATORY DE-ESCALATION TRAINING IMMEDIATELY AFTER FERGUSON SHOULD NOT IMPLY GUILT ON THE PART OF OFFICER DARREN WILSON, THE FERGUSON OFFICER WHO SHOT MICHAEL BROWN. INVESTIGATIONS AND A PURSUANT GRAND JURY RULING EXONERATED WILSON, PLUS EYE WITNESSES WHO EARLIER HAD TESTIFIED THAT BROWN HAD HIS HANDS UP AND WAS IN THE PROCESS OF SURRENDERING WHEN HE WAS "EXECUTED," *RECANTED IMMEDIATELY AFTER PHYSICAL EVIDENCE TO THE CONTRARY EMERGED.*

MOREOVER, SIMILAR MOVEMENTS DEMANDING ENHANCED DE-ESCALATION TRAINING FOLLOWING OTHER SHOOTINGS, WHICH I HAVE ALREADY MENTIONED OR WILL MENTION IN PURSUANT CHAPTERS, INCLUDING THOSE OF SEVERELY MENTALLY DISTURBED PEOPLE, TO ME, SHOULD NOT BE AN INDICTMENT AGAINST ALL OR EVEN MOST POLICE OFFICERS.

IN MOST CASES, LAW ENFORCEMENT PERSONNEL ARE GOOD PEOPLE TRYING TO DO THE RIGHT THING UNDER STRESSFUL CIRCUMSTANCES. IN THE SCORE OF INCIDENTS I HAVE STUDIED, TO BE HONEST, DE-ESCALATION TRAINING MIGHT NOT HAVE PREVENTED MAYBE FIVE OR SIX OF THE SHOOTING DEATHS. FOR INSTANCE, I DOUBT THAT TACTICAL COMMUNICATIONS, THE ABILITY TO CONNECT, AND MIRRORING CALM COULD HAVE INTERVENED ON WILSON'S USE OF FINAL FORCE AGAINST BROWN. I WAS NOT THERE, BUT THE CHAIN OF EVENTS AS I KNOW THEM INDICATES TO ME THAT THINGS WENT SOUTH AWFULLY FAST. TOO FAST, PROBABLY, FOR THE USE OF WORDS TO CAUSE A CHANGE OF EVENTS.

YET, THERE ARE THE OTHER 90% OF EVENTS THAT WENT SOUTH. EVENTS THAT ENDED UP RUINING THE LIVES OF CITIZENS, THEIR FAMILIES, OTHER MEMBERS OF A COMMUNITY, AND THE POLICE OFFICERS INVOLVED. THESE ARE THE CATASTROPHIC EVENTS THAT I BELIEVE DE-ESCALATION TRAINING CAN PREVENT.

WHERE THIS BOOK AND MY DE-ESCALATION SYSTEM COMES IN?

I ALWAYS ADVOCATE A WARRIOR STATE OF MIND. HAVE DONE SO FOR LITERALLY DECADES. THIS STATE OF MIND IS 'A HABIT OF MIND' KNOW AS MUSHIN, WHICH IS A JAPANESE TERM , LITERALLY MEANING, NO MIND, NO BIAS, NO JUDGMENT. IN MUSHIN, WE ACT LIKE A NEUTRAL, DISINTERESTED REFEREE WHOSE EGO IS NOT AT STAKE...
HAMMER'S BASIC WINOLOGY PHILOSOPHY

FOR ME, CONVINCING POLICE, CORRECTIONS, SECURITY AND OTHER CRIMINAL JUSTICE AGENCIES TO BRING THEIR STAFF INTO THE WORLD OF TACTICAL COMMUNICATIONS, WHICH IS CENTRAL TO THE (ADVANCED) DE-ESCALATION TRAINING SYSTEM IS A CRUCIAL REASON FOR WRITING THIS BOOK.

SO.....

WHETHER YOU HAVE HEARD THE ADAGE (WORDS MATTER) OR NOT, TRUST ME. I CERTAINLY HAVE. MAYBE MORE. WHY? BECAUSE I HAVE FOREVER BELIEVED THAT WORDS AND HOW WE USE THEM MATTER. AND, FOLKS, WHEN I SAY, "MATTER," I MEAN, BIG TIME "MATTER!"

VERBAL JUDO, INC., PROBABLY THE LEADING VERBAL-SKILLS TRAINING SYSTEM IN THE WORLD, ESTIMATES THAT 98% OF ALL CONFLICTS CAN BE MANAGED BY REDUCTIVE TACTICAL (VERBAL) COMMUNICATIONS. NEITHER I NOR VERBAL JUDO MINIMIZES THE IMPORTANCE AND NEED FOR PHYSICAL FORCE, BUT WE ARE BOTH UNITED IN OUR INSISTENCE THAT OFFICERS AND DEPARTMENTS DEPENDING UPON ONLY PHYSICAL COMBAT

ARE NOT ONLY WRONG-HEADED BUT PLACING THEMSELVES IN A LEGAL, TACTICAL AND EVEN MEDICAL JACKPOT. OVER THE PURSUANT CHAPTERS – ALONG WITH NUMEROUS TALES FROM THE STREET – I WILL DO MY BEST TO CONVINCE YOU – IF YOU EVEN NEED TO BE CONVINCED – THAT BECOMING WHAT THE GREAT GEORGE THOMPSON, FOUNDER OF VERBAL JUDO, CALLED A PEACE WARRIOR WILL MAKE YOU AND YOUR DEPARTMENT A SAFER ENTITY, A DEPARTMENT WITH MEASURABLY LESS (VICARIOUS) LIABILITY OR COURT ROOM ISSUES, AND TRUST ME, GIVE YOU A MEASURABLY ENHANCED PROFESSIONAL IMAGE.

ON THE OTHER HAND, LET'S FACE IT. DE-ESCALATING A POTENTIALLY VIOLENT, EMOTIONALLY DISTURBED OR TOTALLY ANTISOCIAL INDIVIDUAL IS NEVER EASY. MATTER OF FACT, I AM TELLING YOU HERE AND NOW THAT IT IS PROBABLY MORE DIFFICULT THAN ALMOST ANY OTHER TACTICAL UNDERTAKING. I MEAN, USING FORCE AND/OR YOUR ISSUED WEAPONS IS RELATIVELY EASY. SCREAMING, YELLING, USING PROFANITY IS SUPER EASY BECAUSE, AFTER ALL, VIOLENCE, AGGRESSION, CURSING OR THREATENING WHEN FACING RESISTANCE OR VERBAL HOSTILITY COMES NATURALLY!

BUT HERE'S THE POINT: IT IS COUNTER-INTUITIVE AND UNNATURAL TO EXERCISE PATIENCE AND TO USE KIND AND CONSIDERATE WORDS WHEN YOUR NATURAL FEELING IS JUST THE OPPOSITE! NEVERTHELESS, THAT IS EXACTLY WHAT IT TAKES TO RESPOND IN A PROFESSIONAL MANNER UNDER THE COLOR OF LAW. THAT IS WHAT IT TAKES TO ACHIEVE COURTROOM, TACTICAL AND MEDICAL ACCEPTABILITY! AND, THAT IS WHAT IT TAKES TO STAY SAFE!

SOME RESEARCH TELLS US THAT ONLY 90 % OF PEOPLE CAN BE DE-ESCALATED. FOR SURE, THERE ARE BAD GUYS (AND GALS)

OUT THERE THAT YOU NEED TO BE ALL ABOUT TACTICS, BALANCED MOVEMENT, CONTACT AND COVER AND YOUR VERBAL-INTERACTION WILL BE MOSTLY IN COMMANDS AND DIRECTION (I WILL ADDRESS THOSE SCENARIOS IN A LATER CHAPTER). THESE ARE THE ONES WE CALL THE THREE-PERCENTERS. TRUE AND COMMITTED BAD GUYS YOU ARE GOING TO SPEND A MINIMUM TIME WITH APPEALS FOR COOPERATION (ALTHOUGH, YOU STILL MIGHT), TRYING TO CROSS THEIR EXPERIENCES WITH YOURS, EMPATHY, AND ALL THAT.

BUT, IF YOU ADHERE TO THE PRINCIPLES, TACTICS, AND STRATEGIES DISCUSSED IN THE FOLLOWING CHAPTERS, I CAN ALMOST GUARANTEE YOU WILL KEEP YOURSELF UNDER CONTROL, WILL DEPERSONALIZE, AND EVEN DEPRECIATE THE VERBAL ICON. VERBAL HOSTILITY & INSULTS WILL BOUNCE HARMLESSLY OFF YOU, INSTEAD OF YOU ABSORBING THEM AND THEN FREAKING OUT. WHICH, BY THE WAY, WILL ALLOW YOU TO ALLEVIATE YOURSELF OF ALL THE PERSONAL AND PROFESSIONAL STRESS THAT USUALLY ACCOMPANIES DEALING WITH VERBAL ABUSE.

*AND THAT, MY DEAR READER, IS **WHAT DE-ESCALATION IS ALL ABOUT!** THE BAD GUY IS STILL PISSED OFF, IS STILL REFUSING TO COOPERATE, AND MAY EVEN BE THREATENING YOU AND OTHERS. HE IS FAR FROM DE-ESCALATED.*

*BUT THAT IS NOT ON YOU, BECAUSE NOW WHATEVER IT IS YOU DO TO GET HIM INTO CUFFS AND/OR INTO THE CRUISER IS GOOD, NOT ONLY IN THE STREET, BUT IMPORTANTLY, **IN THE MEDIA AND IN THE COURT ROOM!** WHY? **BECAUSE YOU JUST ESTABLISHED JUSTIFICATION AND JUSTIFICATION IS PRECLUSION!***

BUT, WHAT HAPPENS WHEN AN OFFICER REACTS PERSONALLY AND VISCERALLY IN AN EMOTIONALLY-CHARGED SITUATION, AND CANNOT ESTABLISH PRECLUSION? CHANCES ARE, ESPECIALLY WHEN THE INTERACTION GOES TO HELL, HE ENDS UP ON U-TUBE AND SUSPENDED WHILE UNDER INVESTIGATION BY INTERNAL AFFAIRS. NOT ONLY THAT, THE VIDEO, CAPTURED ON CELL PHONE, GOES VIRAL TO MILLIONS OF PEOPLE, RESULTING IN RACIAL UNREST AND PROTESTS. CHANCES ARE THAT THINGS ARE GOING TO GET EVEN WORSE FOR THIS OFFICER (SO FAR, UNNAMED) AND THE FORT WORTH POLICE DEPARTMENT.

LIKE THIS UNSEEMLY EPISODE THAT WENT VIRAL ON WEDNESDAY, DECEMBER 22, 2016:

POLICE IN TEXAS ARE INVESTIGATING A FORT WORTH OFFICER

DECEMBER 22, 2016

AN OFFICER CALLED BY MS. JACQUELINE CRAIG TO HELP HER AND HER FAMILY AFTER A NEIGHBOR ALLEGEDLY ASSAULTED HER 7-YEAR-OLD SON AND THREATENED HIM FOR LITTERING, ENDED UP VIOLENTLY WRESTLING CRAIG AND HER DAUGHTER TO THE GROUND AND HANDCUFFING BOTH. THE INCIDENT ,CAUGHT ON VIDEO BY A NEIGHBOR, HAS GONE VIRAL, AND HAS CAUSED INCREASED RACIAL TENSIONS IN THIS AND OTHER BLACK NEIGHBORHOODS IN THE AREA.

THE EPISODE BEGAN WEDNESDAY IN A FORT WORTH NEIGHBORHOOD WHEN AN OFFICER SUMMONED BY MS. CRAIG ARRIVED ON THE SCENE AND IMMEDIATELY BEGAN QUESTIONING CRAIG ABOUT WHY SHE HADN'T TAUGHT HER SON NOT TO LITTER. THE INTERVENTION QUICKLY ESCALATED IN EMOTIONS AS CRAIG PROTESTED THAT HER PARENTING SHOULDN'T BE THE ISSUE, THAT THE NEIGHBOR'S ASSAULT SHOULD BE THE FOCUS OF THE CONTACT. THE OFFICER AND THE WOMAN EXCHANGED ESCALATING PROFANITY AND AT ONE POINT THE WOMAN STATED THAT THE OFFICER'S QUESTIONING OF HOW SHE PARENTED HER SON WAS NOT THE ISSUE AND WAS STARTING TO "PISS ME OFF," TO WHICH THE OFFICER RESPONDED THAT SHE WAS BEGINNING "TO PISS ME OFF."

At this point, Ms. Craig's daughter stepped in between the officer and her mother, apparently trying to move her mother away from the conflict with the officer. The officer grabbed both women, threw them to the ground and handcuffed them. Several people began to move toward the officer and the officer brandished a taser toward them and threatened them with force and/or arrest(s).

Television reports indicate that emotions are running high in that neighborhood and an attorney for Ms. Craig and her family stated at an impromptu news conference that it appears that the (white) officer had determined, even before his arrival on the scene, that the (black) woman was wrong, that her son had littered, even before any evidence was forthcoming.

The attorney has accused the officer of "obvious racial motives."

Once again, as a long-time instructor trainer and peace officer, I know that the great majority of departments operate efficient and compassionate departments with professional and open-minded officers. But still, this is the latest of scores of incidents. I believe they show the need for a deep and sincere examination by all law enforcement entities of the type of culture-reversing training I am proposing in this work. Not only that, but also changing how they (administrators, et al.)

THINK ABOUT THE CONCEPT OF DE-ESCALATION. BY THAT I MEAN, MAKING THE *IDEA* OF PROFESSIONALLY COMMUNICATING WITH AND RESPECTING **ALL PEOPLE** A CRITICAL PART OF THE WAY THEY MAKE DECISIONS AND THE WAY THEY TRAIN THEIR STAFF(S) ON THE USE OF FORCE.

THE WORLD OF POLICE TRAINING I ENVISION IN THE *"PERFECT WORLD"* INVOLVES TEACHING AND **PRIORITIZING** *TACTICAL (OR PROFESSIONAL) COMMUNICATIONS AND* ADVANCED DE-ESCALATION TECHNIQUES AS A VITAL PART OF DEFENSIVE TACTICS, FIREARMS, AND OTHER TACTICAL TRAINING PROGRAMS. ALSO IN MY *PERFECT POLICE TRAINING WORLD,* OFFICERS WOULD BE HELD ACCOUNTABLE FOR UNACCEPTABLE ACTIONS THAT ESCALATE EMOTIONS AND END WITH UNNECESSARY VIOLENCE, MUCH LIKE THE FORT WORTH INCIDENT I DOCUMENTED EARLIER.

GOING A STEP FURTHER, HOLDING OFFICERS, SUPERVISORS, TRAINERS AND OTHERS ACCOUNTABLE SHOULD NOT MEAN WHEN YOU SCREW UP – LIKE THE FORT WORTH OFFICER DID – THAT HE IS OUSTED UNCEREMONIOUSLY FROM THE DEPARTMENT. ALTHOUGH, IN SOME CATASTROPHIC CASES, THAT MIGHT HAPPEN, BUT FOR THE MOST PART, DEPARTMENTS SHOULD TAKE THAT OFFICER(S) AND "REHABILITATE" THROUGH RETRAINING PROGRAMS LIKE MINE, OR THROUGH THEIR OWN PROGRAMS.

BUT THIS IS JUST THE INTRODUCTION. THAT'S WHAT THE REST OF THIS BOOK IS ALL ABOUT. LIKE, WHAT EXACTLY DO I MEAN BY DE-ESCALATION? WHAT IS/ARE ITS GOAL(S), OBJECTIVES AND WHY IS IT IMPORTANT FOR YOU AND/OR YOUR

DEPARTMENT TO MAKE THE CONCEPT AND ITS PRINCIPLES YOUR OWN?

*BUT THEN, ONCE YOU KNOW EXACTLY WHAT IT IS, **HOW** DO YOU USE THE PRINCIPLES AND STRATEGIES TO DEFUSE A SCENARIO LIKE THE FORT WORTH INCIDENT? OR, HOW WOULD YOU DEFUSE A CONTACT WITH A POTENTIALLY VIOLENT PERSON WHEN IT STARTS GOING SIDEWAYS?*

ARE ALL PEOPLE WE DEAL WITH THE SAME? WILL MY TACTICS WORK ON EVERYBODY? WHAT ABOUT THE SEVERELY MENTALLY ILL, OR AN EMOTIONALLY DISTURBED PERSON? WHAT ABOUT SCENARIOS INVOLVING A SUICIDE BY COP (SBC) "VICTIM," WHEN YOU HAVE MILLISECONDS TO REACT?

YOU LIKELY KNOW THAT NOTHING WORKS ALL THE TIME WITH EVERYBODY. SOME TACTICS WORK EVERY TIME WITH CERTAIN PEOPLE, BUT TRY THAT TACTIC WITH SOMEONE WITH A DIFFERENT MINDSET AND/OR A DIFFERENT PROBLEM AND, KAPOW! THINGS GO TO HELL QUICK LIKE.

LET'S USE THE MYRIAD OF QUESTIONS AND ISSUES AS A MEANS OF SPRING BOARDING INTO THE MAINSTREAM OF THIS BOOK.

*LET'S BEGIN TALKING ABOUT **THE WAY**.*

CHAPTER 1. THIS IS 'THE WAY.'

ON

ACTING NATURALLY

"A SINCERE SMILE IS LIKE A WRECKING BALL.
IT CAN KNOCK DOWN BARRIERS..."

JEFFREY IMBODEN, FORMER BOARD MEMBER, PA. BOARD
OF PROBATION & PAROLE

LET'S **BEGIN WITH THIS:** PROFICIENCY IN DE-ESCALATION ALLOWS US TO
CONTROL EVENTS AND ENCOUNTERS RATHER THAN BEING A VICTIM OF THEM.
RIGHT THERE WE HAVE AN ESSENTIAL CORE OF THE INTERACTIONAL SYSTEM I
AM ADVOCATING HERE.

*MAYBE ANOTHER WAY OF SAYING THIS IS THAT THE UNSKILLED PERSON IS
RULED BY HIS* **ADRENALIN** *AND THE SKILLED PERSON* **USES IT** *TO SAFELY AND
EFFECTIVELY MOVE THROUGH ONE ENCOUNTER OR SCENARIO AFTER
ANOTHER. ADRENALIN WILL ALWAYS BE WITH US. IT IS INHERENT IN ALMOST
EVERYTHING WE DO, ESPECIALLY WHEN WE DO IT WITH AGGRESSIVE PEOPLE.
BUT MY DE-ESCALATION ("WINOLOGY") SYSTEM* **JUMPS OVER IT** *BECAUSE,
FOR IT TO WORK MASTERFULLY, THE SYSTEM MUST ELIMINATE, OR AT LEAST
MINIMIZE REACTING SPONTANEOUSLY AND EMOTIONALLY.*

*FOR INSTANCE, TAKE THE TITLE OF THIS BOOK. "THE MOST UNNATURAL ACT
OF ALL." THE TITLE CONTAINS WORDS THAT ARE CENTRAL TO THE THEME*

OF THIS BOOK. IF WE CAN AVOID REACTING NATURALLY TO WORDS, ATTITUDES, AND OTHER PROBLEMATIC ACTIONS, WE WILL BE ABLE TO CONTROL EVERY ENCOUNTER OR INTERACTION RATHER THAN BEING CONTROLLED BY THEM! AS AN ASIDE, ONE OF THE CENTRAL UNDERSTANDINGS OF SUCCESSFUL TACTICAL COMMUNICATIONS IS, WITHOUT CONTROL, THERE CAN BE NO MUTUAL RESPECT AND RESPECT IS ESSENTIAL FOR MANAGING AGGRESSION.

THE "NATURAL, OR AUTOMATIC" REACTION EXPOSED.

"HERE IS A PRINCIPLE WELL WORTH CONSIDERING: "WE ARE PEACE WARRIORS."
IF A POLICE OFFICER CANNOT HANDLE THAT CONCEPT
PHILOSOPHICALLY, HE CANNOT HANDLE IT TACTICALLY."

GEORGE THOMPSON, VERBAL JUDO

WHEN I SAY "NATURAL REACTION," I MEAN REACTING VISCERALLY AND EMOTIONALLY TO "ATTITUDES", RESISTANCE, AND VERBAL INSULTS AS WELL AS THE ACTIONS OF OTHERS. THE FACT THAT THESE ARE EMOTIONAL REACTIONS TO THE ACTIONS OR ATTITUDES OF OTHERS, TELLS US THAT THESE REACTIONS ARE AUTOMATIC. MEANING THEY OCCUR BEFORE THE OFFICER **HAS THE OPPORTUNITY TO THINK!**

I ASK YOU TO THINK ABOUT THIS FOR A MOMENT. HONESTLY, WHAT ARE YOUR IMMEDIATE AND NATURAL FEELINGS WHEN SOMEONE – ANYONE – SCREAMS IN YOUR FACE, INSULTS YOUR LOVED ONES, INSULTS YOUR RELIGION, YOUR RACE, YOUR LOOKS, MAYBE CALLS YOU AN ASSHOLE OR A COCKSUCKER, OR ANY OTHER TYPE OF "UNACCEPTABLE" EPITHET?

WHAT DO YOU IMMEDIATELY FEEL WHEN SOMEONE RUSHES INTO YOUR PERSONAL SPACE (WITHIN 2-FEET, MAYBE) AND GETS HIS HANDS ALL UP IN YOUR GRILL? HERE IS A BETTER

QUESTION. I CAN GUESS WHAT YOU ARE GOING TO FEEL, BUT WHAT IS MORE IMPORTANT IS WHAT WILL YOU <u>DO</u>?

WELL, IF YOU ARE ANYTHING LIKE ME – AND I BET YOU ARE – WHAT YOU NATURALLY OR AUTOMATICALLY <u>FEEL</u> IS:

- ➤ *ANGER!*

- ➤ *BURNING, SEETHING, HATE!*

- ➤ *RAGE!*

- ➤ *FEAR!*

- ➤ *THE IMMEDIATE URGE TO AVENGE BEING DISRESPECTED AND ATTACKED!*

- ➤ *EMBARRASSMENT!*

- ➤ *HUMILIATION!*

- ➤ *THE URGE TO PHYSICALLY COUNTERSTRIKE!*

- ➤ *THE URGE TO UTTER PROFANITIES AND EVEN DOUBLE-DOWN YOUR ATTACKER'S PROFANITY!*

- ➤ *THE INSTINCT TO GET DEFENSIVE AND JUSTIFYING YOUR COMPETENCY AND INTEGRITY WHEN YOUR COMPETENCY IS QUESTIONED.*

- ➤ *YOUR "TRIGGERS" HAVE BEEN PULLED. YOUR HOT BUTTONS HAVE BEEN PUSHED. YOU COULD KILL!*

*A **<u>NATURAL</u>** REACTION IS A **PERSONAL** AND EMOTIONAL REACTION TO EVENTS AND EPISODES. EACH OF THE ABOVE EMOTIONAL REACTIONS IS UNDERSTANDABLE BECAUSE EACH OF THEM IS A **NATURAL** EMOTION. AND THE FACT THAT IT IS EXPECTED IS IMPORTANT BECAUSE THAT IS EXACTLY WHAT THE*

PROBLEM-PERSON **EXPECTS** (AND HOPES FOR). IT IS EVEN POSSIBLY THE REASON BEHIND HIS INSULT(S), THREAT(S), PROFANITY IN THE FIRST PLACE!

THE BAD GUY IS USING WORDS AS A WEAPON WITH THE GOAL OF INFLUENCING THE OFFICER TO **REACT PERSONALLY AND EMOTIONALLY.** CAUSE THE "PROFESSIONAL" TO SPEAK AND ACT UNPROFESSIONALLY.

A NATURAL OR AUTOMATIC *REACTION CAN BE* **CATASTROPHIC** IN ANY TYPE OF INTERACTION, BUT ESPECIALLY WHEN DEALING WITH MANIPULATIVE, AGGRESSIVE OR POTENTIALLY VIOLENT PEOPLE.

SO, AS I SAID ABOVE, "A BETTER QUESTION THAN WHAT DO YOU FEEL, IS WHAT WOULD YOU <u>DO</u>?" THE ABOVE EMOTIONS ARE NATURAL *REACTIONS TO OFFENSIVE LANGUAGE AND PROVOCATIVE PHYSICAL MOVEMENTS.* HOWEVER, THE ONLY IMPORTANT ISSUE WHEN IT COMES TO EITHER ACTING LIKE A PROFESSIONAL OR REACTING LIKE A THUG, IS **<u>HOW</u>** DO YOU RESPOND.

AND, AS I WROTE AT THE BEGINNING OF THIS BOOK, **WORDS (DO) MATTER.**, *WORDS USED MASTERFULLY, AS I WILL SHOW IN PURSUANT CHAPTERS, CAN SAVE THE DAY.* BUT WORDS USED NATURALLY - WHEN ONE IS IN AN EMOTIONALLY-CHARGED STATE (VISCERALLY) - CAN ALSO GET YOU FIRED, GET YOU SUED, GET YOU ARRESTED, GET YOU DIVORCED, GET YOU PUNCHED, OR EVEN GET YOU KILLED!

OR, AS IN THE FORT WORTH DEBACLE, **WORDS** CAN GET YOU ON THE 11 O'CLOCK NEWS, GET YOU SUSPENDED AND UNDER INVESTIGATION, TO BOOT!

WHY DO WE ACT NATURALLY?

"MORE LIKELY THAN NOT, WHEN A PERSON (OFFICER) IS THREATENED AND/OR INSULTED WITH WORDS, THE SYMPATHETIC NERVOUS SYSTEM (SNS) – FIGHT OR FLIGHT – IS ACTIVATED. WHEN THE SNS IS IN PLAY, THE NEO CORTEX, OR INTELLIGENT BRAIN, IS BYPASSED. ALTHOUGH TIME AND STRENGTH ARE ENHANCED, COGNITIVE SKILLS AND INTELLECT ARE VICTIMS, MAKING THE OFFICER ABLE TO RUN AND FIGHT WELL, BUT MORE OR LESS, BECAUSE OF SNS, WILL REACT WITH ALMOST 98% **EMOTIONS GEARED TO PROTECT HIMSELF, BECAUSE, AFTER ALL, FIGHT OR FLIGHT IS A NATURAL PROTECTIVE INSTINCT..** AT THE END OF THE DAY, HOWEVER, (HE) WILL BE ESSENTIALLY UNABLE TO EXERCISE INTELLIGENT DISCRIMINATION AND TO SEPARATE HIMSELF FROM HIS RUNAWAY EMOTIONS, ETC."

THE DEBILITATING IMPACT OF FIGHT OR FLIGHT AND SNS. QUOTED BY THE AUTHOR.

SOUNDS LIKE A STUPID QUESTION, DOESN'T IT? WE REACT NATURALLY BECAUSE IT IS NATURAL. LIKE THE QUOTE ABOVE ILLUSTRATES, FIGHT OR FLIGHT IS NATURAL, MEANING THAT WITHOUT MANAGING ONE'S EMOTIONS, WE CANNOT HELP BUT REACT WITH AGGRESSION AND MAYBE EVEN VIOLENCE. IT IS THAT SIMPLE. IN MY EARLY YEARS AS A STREET AGENT (PA. STATE PAROLE AGENT), LONG BEFORE I EVER ENCOUNTERED THE CONCEPT OF DE- ESCALATION, I REACTED TO ALMOST ALL EVENTS – ON AND OFF THE JOB – NATURALLY, AS I THINK THIS LITTLE STORY WILL ILLUSTRATE.

A TRUE REAL-LIFE EXAMPLE OF REACTING NATURALLY

"WITHOUT PROPER DE-ESCALATION AND VERBAL COMMUNICATIONS TRAINING, WE HAVE LITTLE HOPE OF REDUCING UNNECESSARY POLICE-CITIZEN VIOLENCE."

JAMES J. FYFE, PROFESSOR OF JUSTICE, AMERICAN UNIVERSITY, LA TIMES

I MAY HAVE BEEN A (PA) STATE PAROLE AGENT FOR FIVE YEARS. GIVE OR TAKE. BACK THEN, THERE WAS NO SUCH THING AS TRAINING. OH, WE HAD A TRAINING DIVISION, OR SOMETHING THAT PASSED FOR ONE, BUT NO ONE COUNSELED US ON SUBJECT CONTROL OR DE-ESCALATION. We just did what we did and reacted "naturally" to whatever went down on the streets, meaning we reacted, more often than not, emotionally. And when we fucked up, which we often did, our training motto was, "Okay, dude, you fucked up, so, here's the dealio. From now on, do not do that, dig?" That's the way it was, back in the seventies.

Until that day, any probationer or parolee whom I told, "Look, you violated the crap out of your (parole) conditions, so you know the drill. Turn around, give me your hands, so I can hook you up, and you and I are going to take a drive to The Wall (county prison)." And that would be it.

But not this day. This parolee, with the street-name of Turk, who looked like an extra in a Hell's Angels movie, just shot me a big, *"Yo, you want to see things go bang look," widened his stance and* made a fist. Then he considered me with a pair of dead black eyes, which panned me from head to foot, as if seeing me for the very first time. I later learned to associate those lifeless eyes with those rare, committed, criminal psychopaths and evil motor scooters, those violent human predators that walked the earth causing havoc wherever they went.

His eyes panned down to my right hand, which held a set of shiny, silver Peerless handcuffs. He smiled without any hint of humor.

"Harry, you try to handcuff me, I'm going to fucking tear you a new asshole. I swear to fucking God. I'll light you up like a fucking KKK rally and send your remains straight to Hell!"

Me, I was unprepared for resistance of any kind. Worse, nobody had ever suggested what I should do in such a situation. Far as I knew, I wasn't allowed to disengage. The equation was set in stone. He had violated the conditions of his parole. A warrant had been issued, I was here to bring him in - to "retrieve him -" So, back he must go!

If I didn't take him in, as far as I knew, I would be in trouble.

That turned out not to be true, but like I said, that was what I believed back then.

Anyway, I said to the parolee, "Look, Sam, you just can't do that. I am your parole agent, you are on parole. You really have no choice. I have to take you back to The Wall, and you have to go."

He looked like he was really enjoying himself with a goofy *this is going to be loads of fun grin* on his face when he spat out these words: "Well, la dee fucking duh, Harry. I say again, touch me and I will light your fucking punk ass up!"

"Punk ass?" Well, now, he had gone too far, I surmised, my emotions heating up. Big time.

Here's the thing. Today, I would have had a little conversation with myself. Told myself that one of my triggers had been pulled and would have taken a deep breath, exhaled (Cycle Breathing) and begun the process of mirroring calm. I would have kept my distance, smiled, looked calm and confident, and maybe uttered a peace phrase or two. No doubt, I would have empathized with his issue(s) concerning going back to prison, followed maybe by a period of tactical silence.

Maybe I would have said something like, "Turk, I can see that you want to fight me, and looking at you, I believe you could do some wicked damage. But, the thing is, even if you do whup me, believe me when I say, there will be four, five, maybe six more officers to replace me, and they will take you down. They may even hurt you pretty bad.

"So, the thing is, Turk, you are going to jail. You can count on that. And, if you go like that – the hard way – you are going for a helluva lot longer than if I take you in. If you go voluntarily. So, it is up to you how you go. So, how about it, Turk? Are you going to work with me here?"

And, if those nice words failed, I would have disengaged, suggesting that, when I returned – with ample backup, of course - he would be arrested and taken to the county prison. But, the last thing I would have done was to roll up my sleeves, curse under my breath and wade in there swinging.

But again, this was back then, and back then, I had yet to hear anything about de-escalation. Not only that, like I said, back then, I took everything **personally**. Worse, back then I was 100% Ego, and after all, he had called me "punk ass," so, the truth be known, I really didn't want a peaceful resolution. He had pissed me off, had called me an offensive name, so, in my mind, Turk had himself an ass-whipping coming.

I gently replaced my cuffs in the black pouch on my waist, stripped off my sports jacket, shrugged my shoulders, stepped toward Sam, and caught a strong roundhouse punch with my lead shoulder, ducked and felt a forearm bounce off the side of my head, and then I plowed in and felt another punch bounce off my back as I grabbed him and tackled him hard and drove a couple knee shots and head butts in there to completely knock the wind out of him.

Unfortunately, my little story didn't end there. I cuffed him and patted him down for weapons. "I ain't got no weapons, Harry," he spat. "If I did, you'd be fucking dead by now."

I think I uttered a few curse words toward the parolee as I led him out of his house toward my state car. I was almost through the front door when Sam's mother intervened.

"Where you taking my boy?" she asked, not unkindly. A reasonable question for a mother to ask, don't you think? But I was still triggered, filled with anger and self-righteousness, so I was not in a reasonable mood. I replied like a jerk.

"Where does it look like I'm taking your boy. He's all beat up and he's wearing my cuffs?" With that, I turned and started dragging her son toward the door.

"I won't never forget this, you bald, fat motherfucker," she yelled.

And, I stopped dead in my tracks. My professional objective was to retrieve the parolee, and yet, the woman's insults caused me to stop. Worse, I let go of my prisoner and turned to face the woman.

Encouraged now that her insults had "foot swept" me to the point I had let go of her son, she took another shot. "Yeah, you heard me. You are a fat, bald motherfucker, and I hear you are a total, stupid asshole also!"

Fortunately, Turk just stood there and just watched the exvhange between me and his mother, mesmerized. He was enraged by the blatant disrespect I was showing her, and in the transport vehicle on our way to the county prison, he told me so. Promised to get his revenge someday. Nevertheless, instead of escaping while I lost my focus on my professional objectives and engaged in an eg—scuffle with his mother, he stood there, transfixed, so at least I didn't lose my prisoner.

But, the thing is, by reacting emotionally and "naturally," I lost much more than a prisoner. In the exchange I lost my professionalism, the respect of both Turk and his mother, and jeopardized my safety because of my lack of understanding of how to manage my emotions in stressful situations. I allowed my ego stand in the way of my professional duty. Took a meaningless insult (I wasn't bald) personally, and jeopardized not only my safety, but career.

REACTING NATURALLY MEANT IN MY CASE, TAKING INSULTS AND INNUENDOES PERSONALLY, REACTING ANGRILY TO PERCEIVED DISRESPECT, AND EVEN REACTING ALMOST VIOLENTLY TO VERBAL HOSTILITY. REACTING NATURALLY ALSO MEANT – UNFORTUNATELY – BEING HAULED BEFORE ONE OR MORE SUPERVISORS TO BE CAUTIONED ABOUT MY INAPPROPRIATE ATTITUDE CONCERNING PROBATIONERS AND PAROLEES, NOT TO MENTION ALMOST GETTING SUSPENDED FOR THAT AND OTHER VERBAL SCUFFLES IN WHICH I WAS INVOLVED, AGAIN FOR TAKING INSULTS PERSONALLY (UNPROFESSIONAL ACTIONS) TO VERBAL HOSTILITY AND OTHER PERCEIVED ATTACKS ON MY PERSONALITY.

REACTING NATURALLY IS AN ISSUE THAT NEEDS TO BE ADDRESSED HERE BECAUSE IT IS ESSENTIALLY UNSAFE. DANGEROUS TO OFFICERS, CITIZENS, EVEN EVILDOERS. WHY? BECAUSE WHEN YOU REACT EMOTIONALLY IN STRESSFUL SITUATIONS, YOU CREATE MISSTEPS THAT ALL TOO OFTEN RESULT IN CHAOS OR VIOLENCE. IN OTHER WORDS, REACTING "NATURALLY" MEANS THAT:

THE OFFICER IS 98% CONCERNED WITH PROTECTING EGO (GEORGE THOMPSON, FOUNDER OF VERBAL JUDO, CALLED EGO, ALONG WITH "TONE," THE MOST DANGEROUS WORD(S) IN A COP'S VERNACULAR.

TACTICALLY UNSAFE BECAUSE EGO MAKES OFFICERS CONCENTRATE INSIDE INSTEAD OF 360 DEGREES OUTSIDE OF OURSELVES, WHERE POTENTIAL DANGER MAY EXIST. EGO-

46

CENTRIC TACTICS (WHICH IS BASICALLY NO TACTICS) ARE CENTERED OFTEN ON LOOKING INSIDE TO COME UP WITH AN INSULT TO COUNTERATTACK VERBAL HOSTILITY, ETC.

EASY FOR A BAD GUY TO COAX INTO BECOMING ANGRY FOR PERCEIVED DISRESPECT, OR EVEN MINOR RESISTANCE. THIS IS IMPORTANT BECAUSE *SHOWING ANGER, OR ACTING WITH (PERSONAL) RAGE TENDS TO CHIP AWAY AT THE OFFICER'S AUTHORITY, POWER AND INFLUENCE.* WHICH IS OFTEN THE MOTIVATION FOR TAUNTING AN OFFICER IN THE FIRST PLACE.

AND, IN THE ABOVE REAL-LIFE SCENARIO, I WAS INVESTIGATED, NEARLY SUSPENDED, AND THE MOTHER APPEARED AT THE PAROLE HEARING AND TESTIFIED AS TO MY "UNPROFESSIONAL ATTITUDE AND ACTIONS." I SURVIVED THE SITUATION, AND IMPORTANTLY, LEARNED A VALUABLE LESSON ABOUT DEALING WITH INSULTS, THREATS AND EVEN PHYSICAL INTIMIDATION.

I SUGGEST THAT YOU EXAMINE MY DEFUSE EQUATION IN A PURSUANT CHAPTER, WHICH ADDRESSES UNIVERSAL PRINCIPLES OF DE-ESCALATION AND MANAGING AGGRESSIVE PEOPLE.

SNS ACTIVATION AND THE "NATURAL REACTION."

"PERCEPTIONS THAT CAN TRIGGER SNS ACTIVATION INCLUDE OBJECTIVE THREAT PERCEPTION; OBJECTIVE FEAR PERCEPTION; UNEXPECTED LOUD NOISES OR TOUCHING (SURPRISES) AND EXHAUSTION. ANY OF THESE CAN CAUSE US TO SPIN INTO A WORLD WHERE OUR VERY SURVIVAL IS SEEMINGLY THREATENED..."

PPCT DEFENSIVE TACTICS HUMAN FACTORS.

YES, WE REACT HOW WE REACT BECAUSE IT IS **NATURAL**. BUT THERE IS A SECOND AND MORE PROFOUND REASON WE REACT THIS WAY: OUR SYMPATHETIC NERVOUS SYSTEM (SNS), WHEN IT IS ACTIVATED BY SURVIVAL STRESS CAUSED BY PERCEIVED DANGER.

THE SNS IS A BRANCH OF OUR AUTONOMIC NERVOUS SYSTEM (ANS), WHICH IS IN CHARGE OF ALL VOLUNTARY AND INVOLUNTARY FUNCTIONS OF THE BODY. THE ANS IS DIVIDED INTO THE PARASYMPATHETIC AND SYMPATHETIC BRANCHES. THE PARASYMPATHETIC NERVOUS SYSTEM (PNS) IS DOMINANT DURING NON-STRESSFUL ENVIRONMENTS WHERE A PERSON PERCEIVES HE IS SAFE. THE PNS CONTROLS CRITICAL SURVIVAL FUNCTIONS, SUCH AS VISUAL ACUITY, COGNITIVE PROCESSING, AND FINE OR COMPLEX MOTOR SKILL EXECUTION.

ESSENTIALLY, PNS CAN BE CHARACTERIZED AS THE **SMART, PRECISE AND DELIBERATE** NERVOUS SYSTEM.

THE SNS, HOWEVER, IS A POWERFUL SURVIVAL MECHANISM SHARED BY ALL MAMMALS ENABLING THEM TO COMPLETELY FOCUS THE BODY'S RESOURCES ON EITHER CHARGING TOWARD OR RUNNING AWAY FROM AN OPPONENT (FIGHT OR FLIGHT).

THE SNS HELPS US TUNE OUT PERIPHERAL INFORMATION, FOCUS ON THE THREAT AT HAND, AND INCREASE BLOOD FLOW TO MUSCLE GROUPS THAT SUPPORT GROSS MOTOR SKILLS (RUNNING, JUMPING, STABBING, PUNCHING, ETC.).

THE SNS PROCESS IS AUTOMATIC, VIRTUALLY UNCONTROLLABLE, AND IT DOMINATES ALL VOLUNTARY AND INVOLUNTARY SYSTEMS UNTIL THE THREAT HAS BEEN ELIMINATED.

HOWEVER, ACTIVATION OF SNS OVERRIDES THE BENEFITS OF THE PNS AND WE PAY A PRICE IN TERMS OF PERCEPTION, COGNITIVE PROCESSING, AND THE ABILITY TO PERFORM CERTAIN SKILLS.

THE THING IS, THE IMPACT OF SNS ACTIVATION APPEARS TO BE EXCEPTIONALLY DESTRUCTIVE TO COGNITIVE PROCESSING, WHICH IS ESSENTIAL TO COMMUNICATION SKILLS AND CRISIS INTERVENTION. SCIENTISTS (JOSEPH LEDOUX, NEUROSCIENTIST, AND OTHERS) HAVE FOUND THAT RECOGNITION, ANALYSIS, DECISION MAKING, LOGIC AND DISCRETION ARE SERIOUSLY COMPROMISED WHEN THE SNS IS FULLY ACTIVATED.

ALL OF THIS MEANS THAT OFFICERS ARE NOT NATURALLY PREDISPOSED TO DE-ESCALATING HOSTILE AND AGGRESSIVE PEOPLE, SINCE WHEN UNDER THE INFLUENCE OF SNS ACTIVATION, THEY ARE ACTING OUT OF THEIR PRIMITIVE BRAIN, NOT THEIR NEO CORTEX, OR INTELLIGENT BRAIN.

I THINK THIS IS IMPORTANT TO UNDERSTAND. JOSEPH LEDOUX FOUND THAT UNDER NON-STRESS CONDITIONS, INFORMATION IS PROCESSED FROM OUR PERCEPTUAL SENSES TO OUR THALAMUS AREA OF THE BRAIN, WHICH ACTS LIKE A RELAY STATION. THE THALAMUS THEN SENDS THE INFORMATION TO OUR SENSORY

CORTEX WHERE IT IS PROCESSED AND FORWARDED TO THE NEOCORTEX (OUR SMART, OR THINKING BRAIN). THE NEOCORTEX CROSS-COMPARES THE INFORMATION WITH THE HIPPOCAMPUS (THE SOURCE OF STATIC MEMORY) AND WITH THE AMYGDALA (WHICH HOLDS ALL EMOTIONAL MEMORY). A RESPONSE IS EVENTUALLY FORMULATED AND SENT BACK DOWN THROUGH THE AMYGDALA TO THE MOTOR PORTIONS OF THE LOWER BRAIN AND FINALLY, THE SPINAL CORD.

HERE, I BELIEVE, IS THE CRUCIAL PART OF THIS ENTIRE PNS AND SNS CYCLE THAT AFFECTS OUR ABILITY OR INABILITY TO PERCEIVE, ANALYZE AND EVALUATE, FORMULATE A STRATEGY (TO MANAGE AGGRESSION, ETC.) OR TO INITIATE APPROPRIATE FORCE. WHEN OUR BRAIN IS PRESENTED WITH AN SNS TRIGGER – ANGER, FEAR, A SERIOUS THREAT PERCEPTION, MAYBE A STARTLE RESPONSE – A SIGNAL IS SENT FROM THE THALAMUS DIRECTLY TO THE AMYGDALA AND A **RESPONSE IS OFTEN INITIATED <u>BEFORE</u> THE THINKING BRAIN – THE NEO CORTEX – CAN PROCESS THE INITIAL PERCEPTION.**

THE ADVANTAGE OF THIS THALAMUS-AMYGDALA CIRCUIT IS TIME, FOR IT TAKES TWICE AS LONG FOR A SIGNAL TO BE PROCESSED THROUGH THE NEOCORTEX. HOWEVER, THE SPEED ADVANTAGE IS A TRADEOFF FOR ACCURACY IN PROCESSING AND THE **DEVELOPMENT OF A MORE REFINED PLAN.** AS LEDOUX POINTED OUT, SOME EMOTIONAL REACTIONS CAN BE FORMED WITHOUT ANY CONSCIOUS OR COGNITIVE PARTICIPATION.

WHAT DOES ALL THIS MEAN? IT MEANS THAT IT IS **NATURAL** FOR US -ESPECIALLY WITHOUT CORRECTIVE TRAINING OR COUNSELING – TO RELY ON OUR EMOTIONS IN A CRISIS OR CONFRONTATION OF SOME SORT WHEN OUR SNS IS TRIGGERED. REMEMBER, WHEN THE PNS IS DOMINANT – WHEN WE FEEL SAFE – WE CAN RELY ON OUR **THINKING BRAIN** (THE NEO

CORTEX). UNDER PNS, THEN, WE CAN REACT NATURALLY OR EVEN EMOTIONALLY BECAUSE THE NEOCORTEX IS AVAILABLE AND ACTIVE.

WHEN THE NEO CORTEX IS ON THE JOB, YOU ARE GOING TO HAVE THE TIME AND THE ABILITY TO THINK THROUGH DIFFICULT SITUATIONS WITH DIFFICULT PEOPLE. BUT WE ARE TALKING SNS-SCENARIOS HERE. WITHOUT SOME SORT OF "FIREBREAK" OR TIME-OUT PROGRAM (DE-ESCALATION) DESIGNED TO MINIMIZE THE THALAMUS-AMYGDALA CIRCUIT WHEN IT IS SAFE TO MINIMIZE IT, WE ARE GOING TO BE PRONE TO OVERREACT, UNDERREACT, OR ACT IN SUCH A WAY AND IN SUCH A MANNER THAT WE PROVOKE AND ALIENATE THE PEOPLE WITH WHOM WE ARE WORKING (THE BAD GUY, WITNESSES, THE PUBLIC, THE MEDIA, AND THE COURT SYSTEM).

IN COMING CHAPTERS, WE WILL ADDRESS BITS AND PIECES OF WHAT I HAVE CALLED, FOR YEARS, THE UNNATURAL ACT, WHICH IS ESSENTIAL FOR OFFICERS AND LAY CITIZENS TO UNDERSTAND AND COMMIT THEMSELVES TO, IF THEY ARE GOING TO BECOME SKILLED IN DEFUSING AGGRESSION.

*IT IS MY INTENTION IN MY WINOLOGY TRAININGS AND IN THIS BOOK, TO ENCOURAGE CITIZENS WHO WORK WITH ANTISOCIAL PEOPLE AS WELL AS LAW ENFORCEMENT PERSONNEL TO ADOPT THESE DE-ESCALATION TECHNIQUES SO THEY CAN **TRICK THE SNS!***

BUT FOR NOW, ALLOW ME TO PRESENT ONE MORE PLUG FOR THE CLUSTER OF SKILLS, TACTICS, STRATEGIES, AND PRINCIPLES THAT ARE THE CORE OF DE-ESCALATION.

MAYBE THE MOST POWERFUL FEAT THAT DE-ESCALATION ACCOMPLISHES IS TO TRICK THE SNS. BY ADOPTING THESE PRINCIPLES, YOU ARE ABOUT TO CREATE A HABIT OF MIND THAT, IN TIME, WILL CREATE FOR YOU A "STILL CENTER," MUCH LIKE THE CALM, CLEAR, AND UNROILED SURFACE OF WATER WHERE YOU CAN SEE CLEAR TO THE BOTTOM. YOU MUST

ALLOW THAT STILL CENTER TO HELP YOU "TRICK" THE SNS SO THAT
YOUR THINKING BRAIN WILL ALWAYS HAVE YOUR BACK.

HARRY HAMMER, 2014

CHAPTER 2.
WINOLOGY – THE
UNNATURAL ACT!

"A STORY OUT OF KANSAS CITY WHERE DEPUTIES HIT A WELL-KNOWN
AND DANGEROUS CRACK HOUSE. GANGBANGERS WHO FILLED THAT HOUSE
SOMEHOW KNEW FIVE-OH WAS COMING AND SWORE THEY WOULD KILL
THEMSELVES A COP OR THREE. BUT WHEN THE DEPUTIES HIT THE HOUSE,
THEY SAW THAT, IN THE LEAD, WAS A DEPUTY WHO ALWAYS SHOWED
THEM **RESPECT.** SEVERAL OF THE BANGERS FLED AND SEVERAL WERE BUSTED.
LATER IN COURT, ONE OF THE BANGERS TESTIFIED THAT THEY DID NOT
SHOOT BECAUSE OF THAT DEPUTY WHOM THEY RESPECTED."

KANSAS CITY OFFICER DISCUSSING THE VALUE OF TACTICAL RESPECT AND ETHICAL
PRESENCE AT AN ADVANCED VERBAL JUDO SEMINAR IN JACKSONVILLE,
FLORIDA (MAY, 1998)

*TO BE EFFECTIVE AND SAFE, WE MUST ADOPT A DIFFERENT WAY OF
THINKING AND RESPONDING WHEN DEALING WITH OTHERS IN THE
PUBLIC. THIS NEW WAY OF THINKING IS NECESSARY IF WE ARE TO
TRICK THE SNS AND* KEEP OUR THINKING BRAIN WORKING FOR US,
EVEN UNDER DEBILITATING SURVIVAL STRESS.

*I HAVE ALREADY PROPOSED AND WILL DO IT AGAIN LATER IN THIS
OPUS, THAT BEFORE WE CAN EVER HOPE TO DEFUSE OTHERS –
ESPECIALLY AGGRESSIVE AND HOSTILE PEOPLE – WE MUST FIRST
DEFUSE OURSELVES. IN THIS CHAPTER, HOWEVER, I AM PROPOSING
THAT THE MESSAGE CONCERNING (FIRST) DEFUSING OURSELVES,
MUST GO A FEW CLICKS FURTHER.*

LIKELY, THEN, THE BEST PLACE TO START IS WHAT I CALL THE
UNNATURAL ACT.

EXAMINING "AN UNNATURAL ACT."

*I REPEAT, FOR CLARIFICATION, MY STATEMENT AT THE START OF
THIS BOOK. TO ME, THE WORDS THAT FORM THE TITLE OF THIS
BOOK – (AN) UNNATURAL ACT – ARE PROBABLY THE MOST
IMPORTANT TWO WORDS IN* SUCCESSFULLY UNDERSTANDING AND

EMPLOYING DE-ESCALATION ON AND OFF THE JOB. *IN COMING PAGES, WE WILL TALK ABOUT MANY OF THE AXIOMS AND PRINCIPLES CENTRAL TO DE-ESCALATION. RIGHT NEAR THE TOP OF THESE* TRUTHS *IS THIS:*

IN SURVIVAL STRESS SITUATIONS, ANY SUCCESSFUL PROCESS OF CALMING AGITATED PEOPLE IS BASICALLY AN ACT, ONE THAT YOU CONSTRUCT. AN ACT THAT WILL ACHIEVE YOUR PROFESSIONAL OBJECTIVE(S) IN THE SAFEST AND MOST EFFECTIVE WAY POSSIBLE. THIS IS KEY TO DEFUSING CASCADING AGGRESSION AND VIOLENCE BECAUSE, UNDER SNS ACTIVATION WHEN THE RESTING HEART RATE SPIKES TO 220 BPM AND ABOVE, UNLESS EXPERT TRAINING IS AVAILABLE TEACHING SKILLS IN TRICKING THE SNS, *YOU WILL BE FORCED TO ACT WITHOUT THE BENEFIT OF YOUR INTELLIGENT BRAIN (AVAILABLE UNDER PNS). RESPONDING WHILE UNDER THE* LIZARD, OR PRIMITIVE BRAIN *CAUSES US TO REACT PERSONALLY, EMOTIONALLY – THE NATURAL ACT!*

SOME MIGHT ARGUE THAT USING CALMING TACTICS DOES NOT REQUIRE AN UNNATURAL ACT. *THAT THERE ARE THOSE AMONG US WHO POSSESS* THE GIFT. *"THE GIFT" IS A NATURAL ABILITY TO CALM OTHERS AND TO INSPIRE TRUST AND CONFIDENCE SIMPLY BY HOW THEY PRESENT THEMSELVES, THEIR DEMEANOR AND THE TONE AND RHYTHM OF THEIR VOICE. I KNOW PEOPLE LIKE THIS, COPS AND OTHERS WHO ARE NATURAL DE-ESCALATORS. YOU WILL READ THEIR STORIES IN UPCOMING EPISODES. THEY ARE RARE IN OUR PROFESSIONAL, BUT THEY DO EXIST. MOST OF US, INCLUDING MYSELF, DO NOT HAVE THAT GIFT.*

BUT HERE'S THE THING. EVEN FOR THOSE WITH THAT ABILITY, IN THE HEAT OF BATTLE, OR IN A SITUATION WHEN FACED WITH AN EMOTIONALLY DISTURBED OR HIGHLY AGGRESSIVE SUBJECT, EVEN THE "GIFTED ONES" MUST RESORT TO TACTICS AND STRATEGIES FEATURING A CONSTRUCTED METHOD OF DEFUSING AGGRESSION.

IT IS LARGELY AN ACT BECAUSE IN A GREAT MAJORITY OF SCENARIOS, THE AUTHORITY FIGURE MUST ACT IN SUCH A WAY AND IN SUCH A MANNER TO END THE "ATTACK(S)" IN THE QUICKEST, SAFEST AND MOST EFFECTIVE WAYS POSSIBLE WITHOUT RELYING ON HIS EGO.

*IT IS AN **ACT** BECAUSE THE TARGET OF VERBAL HOSTILITY MUST RESORT TO TACTICS THAT ARE OFTEN IN CONFLICT WITH WHAT HE IS THINKING OR FEELING AT THE TIME. HE MUST **DEMONSTRATE OR SHOW RESPECT** EVEN THOUGH HE MAY **FEEL** AND BELIEVE THE SUBJECT **MERITS LITTLE OR NO RESPECT** WHY? BECAUSE SHOWING RESPECT AND/OR EMPATHY IS RESPONSIBLE IN AN UNTOLD NUMBER OF SCENARIOS* FOR ASSUAGING EVEN THE MOST AGGRESSIVE AND ANGRY PEOPLE, *ACCORDING TO NUMEROUS STUDIES.*

*IT IS AN **ACT** BECAUSE THE OFFICER SHOULD, IF GENERATING VOLUNTARY COMPLIANCE AND/OR ESTABLISHING CALM IS THE GOAL OF THE INTERACTION, **SHOW** EMPATHY WHEN HE **FEELS ZERO EMPATHY.** MUST FORCE HIMSELF TO SLOW EVERYTHING DOWN, EVEN THOUGH HIS HEART IS POUNDING LIKE A JACKHAMMER AND HIS INSTINCT IS TO RUSH FORWARD AND TO BEGIN SHOUTING OUT COMMANDS. HE MUST TAKE THE TIME TO LISTEN TO NOT ONLY WHAT THE AGGRESSOR IS SAYING, BUT HOW HE IS SAYING IT, AND ALSO, WHAT HE IS NOT SAYING, EVEN THOUGH LISTENING IS THE FURTHEST THING FROM WHAT HIS NATURAL INSTINCTS ARE SCREAMING IN HIS EAR TO DO!*

*IT IS AN **ACT** BECAUSE IN A CONFRONTATIONAL SITUATION, THE OFFICER-TARGET MUST (AND I MEAN **MUST) DEMONSTRATE OR SHOW** THAT HE IS A **PROFESSIONAL ABLE TO DEPERSONALIZE, EVEN** WHEN HE **FEELS** VERBALLY ATTACKED, BELITTLED, EMBARRASSED, FEARFUL, OR OF COURSE, ANGRY.*

HERE IS SOMETHING TO THINK ABOUT. IT IS WHY I BELIEVE THAT DE-ESCALATION OR TACTICAL COMMUNICATIONS (TACT COM) IS AN ACT THAT, WHEN PERFORMED WELL, CAN SHORT CIRCUIT MANY ACTS OF VERBAL AND PHYSICAL AGGRESSION DESIGNED TO INFLUENCE THE OFFICER TO GIVE UP CONTROL OF AN INTERACTION, AND CONCOMITANTLY, HIS PROFESSIONALISM:

IN THE POPULAR MOVIE, ROADHOUSE, *PATRICK SWAYZE PLAYED A ROUGH-HEWN COOLER (DALTON). IN AN EARLY SCENE, DALTON, WHO HAS JUST BEEN HIRED TO MANAGE A CREW OF BOUNCERS AT WHAT HE CALLED A SLAUGHTERHOUSE - A BAR, WHICH UP UNTIL THAT DAY HAD BEEN PLAGUED BY BAR FIGHTS, STABBINGS, YOU*

NAME IT, ADDRESSES HIS NEW CREW. HE TELLS THEM THAT NO RESPECTABLE PERSON WILL PATRONIZE A SLAUGHTERHOUSE, SUCH AS THIS (THE DOUBLE DEUCE). AMONG OTHER THINGS, DALTON DELIVERS HIS PHILOSOPHY OF BOUNCING, AND IN GENERAL, KEEPING AN ENVIRONMENT RIFE WITH VIOLENT PEOPLE INFLUENCED BY ALCOHOL AND TESTOSTERONE CALM AND VIOLENCE FREE:

"NUMBER ONE, EXPECT THE UNEXPECTED," HE SUGGESTED, "AND TWO, DON'T TAKE IT PERSONALLY....."

"OH, YEAH," ONE OF HIS BOUNCERS PIPED UP. "BEING CALLED A COCKSUCKER OR A MOTHERFUCKER AIN'T PERSONAL?"

TO WHICH DALTON REPLIED, "NO. IT'S JUST A JOB. SECONDLY, AND MOST IMPORTANTLY, ALL THOSE PROFANE WORDS (COCKSUCKER, MOTHERFUCKER, ASSHOLE, ETC.) ARE JUST TWO NOUNS STRUNG TOGETHER TO <u>ELICIT A PRESCRIBED RESPONSE</u>."

FOR A SIMPLE SHIT-KICKER FLICK, ROADHOUSE'S PHILOSOPHY IS TIMELESS AND BEYOND WISE. IT ADVOCATES UNIVERSAL PRINCIPLES OF ESTABLISHING AND MAINTAINING CALM IN ANY SCENARIO, EVEN ONE AS CHAOTIC AND DANGEROUS AS THAT IN THE FICTIONAL DOUBLE DEUCE. THE AMATEUR, OR UNSKILLED OFFICER WILL ALMOST ALWAYS REACT WITH PERSONAL ANGER WHEN TRIGGERED BY PROFANITY, INTIMIDATION, OR FOR THAT MATTER, ANY WORDS THAT REFLECT DISRESPECT TOWARD THE OFFICER AND/OR HIS BADGE.

PUTTING IT IN MY TERMS, UNSKILLED OR POORLY TRAINED OFFICERS ENDANGER THEMSELVES AND OTHERS BY ALLOWING THEMSELVES TO BE TRIGGERED BY THE WORDS AND ACTIONS OF A BELLIGERENT PERSON AND PLUNGED INTO SNS ACTIVATION.

THE "PRESCRIBED RESPONSE" THAT DALTON WAS TALKING ABOUT IS OFTEN THE OBJECTIVE OF ANY VERBAL ATTACK. THE BAD GUY WANTS THE OFFICER TO TAKE HIS WORDS PERSONALLY AND TO REACT WITH UNPROFESSIONAL WORDS AND ACTIONS. BY DOING SO, THE OFFICER IS EMPOWERING THE BAD GUY, DISEMPOWERING HIMSELF, AND REDUCING THE INTERACTION OR CONFRONTATION

TO TWO ADRENALIZED THUGS OR PUNKS THROWING HAYMAKERS ON A STREET CORNER! I MUST ASK, WHO THEN IS THE PEACE OFFICER CHARGED WITH THE RESPONSIBILITY OF PROTECTING SOCIETY, AND PROTECTING THE BAD GUY FROM HIMSELF? AND, WHO IS IN CONTROL OF THE INTERACTION AND WHO IS THE KEEPER OF THE PEACE? SURELY IT IS NOT THE UNSKILLED POLICE OFFICER!

OR, WHO IS <u>REALLY IN CHARGE</u> OF A SITUATION WHEN AN OFFICER IS TRIGGERED BY A THUG INTO ACTING RECKLESSLY, MAYBE VIOLENTLY? NOT THE AUTHORITY FIGURE, FOR CERTAIN. ON THE OTHER HAND, THE TRUE PROFESSIONAL UNDERSTANDS THE WORLD AROUND HIM, KNOWS HIS TRIGGERS, AND OF COURSE, "GETS" WHAT THE OTHER PERSON IS TRYING TO LURE HIM INTO DOING – LOSE HIS COOL. INSTEAD OF BECOMING A VICTIM OF THE INTERACTION, HE TAKES CONTROL OF IT.

AND, ALSO, HE MUST BE ABLE TO FIND OUT THE FACTS. MEANING ASKING ARTFUL QUESTIONS, USING PEACE PHRASES, SORTING THROUGH ALL THE INSIDE AND OUTSIDE "NOISES" TO DETERMINE WHAT THE AGGRESSOR WANTS AND NEEDS TO CREATE A SAFE PLACE. KNOWING WHAT YOU KNOW ABOUT THE PNS AND SNS CYCLE(S), YOU LIKELY CAN SEE HOW HARD THAT WOULD BE WHEN SNS EXCISES YOUR THINKING BRAIN.

YOUR BRAIN ON ADRENALIN

"THAT IS WHAT EVERY POLICE OFFICER SHOULD THINK. 'THE PEOPLE IN MY COMMUNITY ARE SAFER BECAUSE OF MY PRESENCE…"

I REMIND YOU THAT IN SCENARIOS WHERE YOU ARE BEING VERBALLY ATTACKED AND/OR ON THE VERGE OF WHAT YOU BELIEVE IS GOING TO BE A PHYSICAL ASSAULT, YOUR HEART RATE WILL SPIKE FROM A NORMAL RESTING RATE OF 60 TO 80 BPM TO SOMEWHERE IN THE MID-200'S IN A MATTER OF A FEW SECONDS. WHEN THAT RATE EXCEEDS 175 BPM, YOU WILL MOST LIKELY EXPERIENCE VISUAL, AUDITORY AND COGNITIVE DIFFICULTIES. AT 220, YOU MAY EXPERIENCE IRRATIONAL BEHAVIOR THAT, IF NOT CORRECTED, CAN LEAD TO ACTIONS THAT COULD CAUSE YOUR OR SOMEONE ELSE'S INJURY, MAYBE EVEN DEATH.

IRRATIONAL BEHAVIOR AND/OR TACTICAL MISSTEPS MAY INCLUDE INABILITY TO COMMUNICATE RATIONALLY AND LOGICALLY; INABILITY TO USE PERIPHERAL VISION; INABILITY TO HEAR; AND WHAT IS KNOWN AS A CATASTROPHIC REACTION(INCLUDING FREEZING IN PLACE, HYPERVIGILANCE. FEEDBACK LOOPS, WHICH IS THE CONTINUOUS REPETITION OF DISASTROUS ACTIONS UNTIL STOPPED BY INJURY OR DEATH – LIKE CONTINUING TO "FIRE" A GUN EVEN THOUGH IT IS EMPTY AND THE SORT.

COGNITIVE ISSUES CAN BEGIN AS EARLY AS 175-BEATS@MINUTE, WHICH IN A SURVIVAL STRESS SITUATION, CAN HAPPEN WITHIN 1 ½ SECONDS. COGNITIVE ISSUES AFFECT YOUR ABILITY TO THINK CLEARLY (THE NEOCORTEX OR THINKING BRAIN), TO MAKE NECESSARY QUICK DECISIONS AND TO COMMUNICATE DECISIONS TO HIS STAFF/TEAM, AND IMPORTANTLY, COMMUNICATE TO THE BAD GUY AND WITNESSES ON THE SCENE THE MOST BASIC TACTICAL ISSUES, INCLUDING, BUT NOT LIMITED TO WHY YOU ARE INTERACTING WITH HIM OR HER IN THE FIRST PLACE, WHAT HE AND/OR OTHERS ON THE SCENE MUST DO TO BE CONSIDERED COOPERATIVE, AND WHAT IS THE NEXT (SAFE) STEP IN THE INTERACTION.

WHICH IS MY POINT. EVEN THOSE WITH A NATURAL GIFT FOR DEFUSING , MUST CREATE AND DISPLAY A CONTRIVED OR ARTIFICIAL

ACT TO DE-ESCALATE UNDER SURVIVAL STRESS WHEN HIS NEOCORTEX IS EVAPORATED BY SURVIVAL STRESS.

***A** TRUTH WHICH **I** BELIEVE IS AXIOMATIC IN DEFUSING AGGRESSIVE AND HOSTILE PEOPLE IS THAT YOU WILL BE "PERFORMING AN ACT" CREATED OF <u>UNNATURAL OR</u> CONTRIVED SKILLS AND TACTICS. **THEY** MUST NOT BE IN ACCORDANCE WITH YOUR NATURAL EMOTIONS DURING A CRISIS SCENARIO.*

*SO, HOPEFULLY, THE PREMISE IS SET ABOUT THE TACTICAL MINDSET AND PHILOSOPHY NECESSARY TO SUCCESSFULLY DE-ESCALATE ANYBODY, ANYTIME, ANYWHERE. **NOW,** HOW DO WE GO ABOUT THE TACTICS THAT ARE THE FOUNDATION OF THIS FORMIDABLE SKILL SET?*

*INTRODUCING THE NEXT CHAPTER AND **THE SKILL SET.***

A TALE FROM THE STREETS

ON DE-ESCALATING PSYCHOTIC FOLKS

By Monica Cassari, MD, 2008

One thing I think you need to know when you are confronted by extremely violent, emotionally disturbed or mentally ill people: they usually don't "just snap" like a rubber band that has been too taut for too long. No, it is generally a progression of behavior leading down a pathway toward violence.

We need to be able recognize these signs of danger that sometimes can be as clear as an apparition waving blood red flags in our faces.

It is always worth assuming that the situation – no matter how grim – can be defused. I think the secret is learning how to CONNECT. Once that connection is made with that other human being, it is possible to create trust and to calm the other person. Even a violent person.

It's all about learning, listening, and being kind to ourselves and others.

From having a knife held to my throat by two psychotics on two separate occasions, I speak from experience when I

SAY PSYCHOTICS AND THOSE COMMITTED TO BRUTAL VIOLENCE CAN BE COMMUNICATED WITH. CAN BE CALMED.

I SAW THEIR FEAR AND I DID NOT RESPOND WITH FEAR. LIKE I SAID, I HAVE EXPERIENCED AND SURVIVED TWO PSYCHOTIC MEN ON TWO SEPARATE OCCASIONS HOLDING ME AND FORCING SHARP EDGED WEAPONS AGAINST MY NECK. THE SECOND GUY WHO HELD ME AT KNIFE POINT WAS SOMEONE OUT OF HIS MIND ON LSD. WE WERE ON THE STREET AT ABOUT 3 A.M. I WAS WALKING HOME FROM WORK AND HE LEAPED OUT AT ME, YELLING, "I'M A CRAZY MOTHERFUCKING INDIAN ON ACID, BITCH. YOU BETTER WATCH OUT!"

LIKE I SAID A MINUTE AGO, I SAW HIS FEAR AND I DID NOT RESPOND WITH FEAR. INSTEAD, I CALMLY STARTED ASKING HIM QUESTIONS. "WHEN DID YOU TAKE THE ACID?" "DO YOU KNOW THAT YOU ARE SCARING ME?" "DO YOU REALLY WANT TO HURT ME?"

HE CAME DOWN QUICKLY. HE BACKED OFF AND APOLOGIZED. HE WENT HIS WAY AND I WENT HOME.

I WOULD LIKE TO POINT OUT A FEW THINGS THAT WE CAN LEARN FROM DR. CASSARI WHEN IT COMES TO DEFUSING DANGEROUS PEOPLE. OR, FOR THAT MATTER, DEFUSING ANYONE YOU MAY CONFRONT.

MAYBE IT'S JUST ME. MAYBE YOU WOULD HAVE REPLICATED HER RESPONSE, AND JUST AS SHE DID, BE LUCKY ENOUGH TO WALK HOME WHILE HER PSYCHOTIC ATTACKER "WENT HIS WAY." I DOUBT THAT I COULD HAVE BEEN THAT COOL, EVEN THOUGH I HAVE BEEN KNOWN TO DEFUSE SOME ROUGH INDIVIDUALS IN MY DAY.

NEVERTHELESS, HERE ARE A FEW TACTICS THAT SHE EMPLOYED THAT SAVED HER LIFE IN BOTH SITUATIONS. THE FIRST EPISODE WAS SIMILAR TO THE LAST, WITH A PSYCHOTIC MADMAN TAKING HER HOSTAGE IN HER OFFICE, GRINDING A KNIFE AGAINST HER THROAT AND COMMANDING AN INVISIBLE THIRD PERSON TO "BACK OFF OR I WILL KILL THIS BITCH!"

61

- *FIRST, "I SAW THEIR FEAR AND I DID NOT RESPOND WITH FEAR." THIS IS A DIRECT QUOTE FROM DR. CASSARI. I TAKE HER AT HER WORD. "FEAR" IS CONTAGIOUS. BUT, SO IS CONFIDENCE. I CAN ONLY ASSUME THAT, BY HER SHOWING NO FEAR, SHE TOOK HER ASSAILANTS BY SURPRISE. SURPRISE WEAKENS ANGER AND AGGRESSION. REMEMBER THAT. WE CAN SAY THE SAME THING ABOUT CONFIDENCE.*

- *"I CALMLY STARTED ASKING HIM QUESTIONS." WHAT I THINK WE ARE SEEING HERE IS THAT (A) SHE SURPRISED THE ASSAILANT, WHICH SLOWED HIM IN HIS TRACKS. (B) SHE MADE HIM* "CATCH CALM." (C) SHE ASKED HIM QUESTIONS. IN A PURSUANT CHAPTER, I WILL GO INTO THE IMPORTANCE OF ASKING QUESTIONS. WELL FORMULATED AND CONCERNED QUESTIONS CAN CAUSE WHAT I CALL "AN INTELLECTUAL DELAY (WHAT I OFTEN CALL A "FIREBREAK"), WHICH CAN SLOW THE AGGRESSION!

- *SHE SLOWED HER BREATHING AND IN DOING SO, SLOWED THE MANIAC'S. THE BEST PRACTICE IN THESE SITUATIONS IS TACTICAL OR CYCLE BREATHING . TACTICAL BREATHING IS INSTRUMENTAL IN ALLOWING OFFICERS TO KEEP THEIR COOL IN STRESSFUL SCENARIOS BY HOUSING THEIR BREATHING IN THEIR ABDOMINAL REGION, THEREBY PROVIDING DEEP AND SLOW SURVIVAL-TYPE RESPIRATION. ACCOMPANYING* SURVIVAL RESPIRATION *IS ALMOST ALWAYS THE WARRIOR'S MANTRA OF* "I KNOW THIS IS A BAD SITUATION, BUT I AM READY FOR IT AND I WILL WIN, NO MATTER *WHAT* THE SITUATION OR THE BAD GUY THROWS AT ME ("WINOLOGY")."

SURVIVAL RESPIRATION OFTEN RESULTS IN THE BAD GUY ALSO SLOWING HIS RESPIRATION. EMPIRICAL RESEARCH SHOWS THAT THIS TRANSITION FROM SHALLOW AND QUICK RESPIRATION TO SLOW AND MEASURED BREATHING OFTEN PROMOTES CALMING.

- FINALLY, DR. CASSARI ADHERED TO A WELL-KNOWN DE-ESCALATION PRINCIPLE, WHICH IS, " *WHEN A PERSON IS UPSET AND YOU ARE EMPATHIZING OR ASKING QUESTIONS,*

YOU CAN ALWAYS USE THE SUBJECT'S WORDS TO FIND A SOLUTION TO THE PROBLEM."

CHAPTER 3. THE ART OF DEFUSING AGGRESSIVE & HOSTILE PEOPLE

ATTITUDE IS EVERYTHING!

"YOU KNOW I BELIEVE THE REASON WE LOST THE VIETNAM WAR WAS BECAUSE YOU SIMPLY CANNOT WIN A WAR AND INFLUENCE THE VILLAGERS WITH A **GOOK MENTALITY**. IT IS THE SAME HERE (IN AMERICA) TRYING TO KEEP THE PEACE..."

GAVIN DEBECKER

IN A LATER CHAPTER, WE WILL DISCUSS AND ILLUSTRATE SOME OF THE (STRESS) REDUCTIVE TECHNIQUES AND STRATEGIES YOU CAN USE TO DE--ESCALATE BELLIGERENT PEOPLE AND DEFUSE OVER-ADRENALIZED AND DANGEROUS ENVIRONMENTS. ALL OF WHICH ARE TIME-PROVEN TO KEEP YOU SAFE IN ALMOST EVERY SITUATION. STRATEGIES LIKE PEACE AND JUMP PHRASES DESIGNED TO ABSORB STRESS AND EMOTIONAL OVERLOAD. TACTICS LIKE DISTRACTION TECHNIQUES, THE FIVE-STEP HARD STYLE AND OTHERS. ALL OF WHICH WILL MAXIMIZE YOUR CHANCES OF GENERATING VOLUNTARY COMPLIANCE, WHICH SHOULD BE THE GOAL OF ALL LAW ENFORCEMENT AND CRIMINAL JUSTICE PROFESSIONALS.

*BUT THOSE ARE **TECHNIQUES, TACTICS, AND STRATEGIES**. ALL OF WHICH CAN BE IMMEASURABLY IMPORTANT IN MOVING A POTENTIALLY VIOLENT INDIVIDUAL PAST THAT EGREGIOUS*

*MINDSET AND INTO A COMPLIANCE MENTALITY. THE
TECHNIQUES AND TACTICS, I ASSURE YOU, WILL ALSO BE
EFFECTIVE WHEN TRYING TO DEAL WITH SIMPLE VERBAL
AND/OR PHYSICAL RESISTANCE.*

*IT HAS LONG BEEN MY CONTENTION, HOWEVER, THAT
UNDERSTANDING AND ADOPTING TIME-PROVEN* **PRINCIPLES** *IS
WHAT IS CRUCIAL FOR BEING ABLE TO SUCCESSFULLY
INTERVENE ON DISRUPTIVE, AGGRESSIVE AND EVEN VIOLENT
BEHAVIOR.*

PRINCIPLE NUMBER 1. *"ATTITUDE IS EVERYTHING."*

*BELIEVE ME WHEN I SUGGEST THAT THE FEELINGS AND
THOUGHTS (ATTITUDE) YOU BRING WITH YOU INTO AN
INTERACTION – EVEN THOUGH UNSPOKEN – ARE ACCURATELY*
HEARD AND FELT BY WHOMEVER IT IS YOU ARE DEALING WITH.
MAYBE HEARD AND FELT SUBLIMINALLY, BUT NEVERTHELESS
HEARD AND FELT. *IT CAN BE REFLECTED IN YOUR* **TONE,** *AND
YOUR BODY LANGUAGE.*

*THE ATTITUDE, OR MENTALITY, YOU CARRY WITH YOU INTO
ANY INTERACTION, NO MATTER HOW NUANCED, IS FELT AND
HEARD LOUD AND CLEAR BY ANYONE WITH WHOM YOU ARE
DEALING. A*TTITUDE IS *EVERYTHING THAT CONTRIBUTES TO A
MINDSET BROUGHT INTO ANY INTERACTION OR CONTACT.
POLICE, CORRECTIONS, SECURITY, PROBATION, AND PAROLE
OFFICERS (AS WELL AS EDUCATIONAL AND HEALTH CARE
PROFESSIONALS) CANNOT AFFORD – RELATIVE TO THEIR SAFETY
AND ABILITY TO EFFECTIVELY DEAL WITH THE PUBLIC – TO
WANDER HAPHAZARDLY INTO SITUATIONS WITH CLIENTS,
PATIENTS, INMATES, PAROLEES, AND/OR CITIZENS WITH
WHATEVER RANDOM MINDSET FROM THEIR EVERYDAY LIFE.*

*NO. WE MUST CULTIVATE AND GENERATE THE APPROPRIATE
ATTITUDE GEARED FOR DEALING WITH WHATEVER*

INDIVIDUAL(S) AND ENVIRONMENTS WE FIND OURSELVES IN. IT CAN'T BE THE SAME NATURAL "WHITE ZONE – TOTAL TACTICAL UNAWARENESS – MINDSET THAT A REGULAR CITIZEN MIGHT ADOPT WHILE SITTING AT HOME EATING A SLICE OF PIZZA. THAT SAME CARELESS MINDSET THAT ALLOWS THEM TO BLINDLY ANSWER A KNOCK ON THEIR DOOR WITHOUT FIRST CHECKING WHOM THEY ARE OPENING THEIR DOOR FOR.

"HERE'S WHAT I THINK ABOUT CULTIVATING THE PROPER MINDSET. I SAY, FUCK YOUR REGULAR, DAY-TO-DAY MINDSET. I SAY, FLUSH THAT MINDSET DOWN THE PROVERBIAL TOILET BECAUSE IT IS SO MUCH CRAP. I SAY, OBLITERATE YOUR MINDSET AND COME IN NEUTRAL WITH ALL ASSUMPTIONS, PREJUDICES, FEARS, ANXIETIES, AND EVEN POSITIVE FEELINGS ABOUT THIS SUBJECT OR SUSPECT FLUSHED AWAY. AND, THAT, MY FELLOW OFFICERS, IS HOW YOU WILL GO HOME TO YOUR LOVED ONES TONIGHT AND TOMORROW NIGHT"

RETIRED PA. POLICE CHIEF WHO WISHES ANONYMITY, 2014, WHOM I ASKED FOR DE-ESCALATION TIPS AND "SECRETS" PRIOR TO A DE-ESCALATION SEMINAR.

NO, WE MUST DO WHATEVER IT TAKES TO SLOW OURSELVES DOWN AND TAKE INVENTORY OF WHAT WE THINK AND FEEL ABOUT THE PERSON OR PEOPLE WITH WHOM WE ARE ABOUT TO CONTACT. THEN, ONCE YOU DO THAT, ELIMINATE ANY FEELINGS, THOUGHTS, AND/OR PREJUDICES YOU MAY HARBOR ABOUT THAT PERSON THAT MAY DISTRACT YOU OR INFLUENCE HOW YOU TREAT THAT PERSON. ENTER THAT CONTACT WITH AN **OPEN, NIMBLE, AND FLEXIBLE MIND!**

"SHOSHIN – OR, CULTIVATING THE BEGINNER'S MIND."

"IN THE BEGINNER'S MIND, ANYTHING IS POSSIBLE. IN THE EXPERT'S MIND, THERE ARE ONLY A FEW (POSSIBILITIES)."

IN A RECENT ARTICLE FROM CALIBRE PRESS, NOVEMBER 28. 2016. SHAWN PERRON WROTE ABOUT THE POWERFUL BENEFITS OF OFFICERS AND OTHERS USING WHAT HE CALLED THE "BEGINNER'S MIND (BM)" DURING THEIR DAY-TO-DAY INTERACTIONS WITH THE PUBLIC. THIS ATTITUDE OR APPROACH STEMS FROM ANCIENT ZEN TEACHINGS SUGGESTING THAT WE MENTALLY AND EMOTIONALLY APPROACH DUTIES IN A PEACEFUL STATE (OF MIND). PERRON HAD STUDIED ZEN BUDDHIST PRACTITIONERS WHO TAUGHT FOLLOWERS TO "NEGOTIATE LIFE WITH AN ATTITUDE OF CURIOSITY, OPEN-MINDEDNESS, LIKE A CHILD OR A BEGINNER WOULD ADOPT, WITHOUT ANY PRECONCEIVED IDEAS OR THOUGHTS" ABOUT PEOPLE, THINGS, AND/OR SITUATIONS.

INTERESTINGLY, BM IS BEING TAUGHT TO MODERN SAMURAIS AND FENCING STUDENTS AND IS THOUGHT TO GREATLY IMPROVE REACTION AND RESPONSE TIMES TO ATTACKS AND AGGRESSION. BM RELATES BEAUTIFULLY TO WINOLOGY AND DE-ESCALATION IN THE CRUCIAL AREA OF COMMUNICATING AND CONNECTING WITH PEOPLE WITH WHOM WE INTERACT.

RELATIVE TO COMMUNICATIONS, MOST OFFICERS APPROACH PEOPLE MINDFUL OF THEIR PAST EXPERIENCES WITH THOSE PEOPLE OR BASED UPON THE TOTALITY OF WHAT HAS OCCURRED IN THE PAST. WHEN THEY APPROACH THOSE PEOPLE WITH WHOM THEY ARE FAMILIAR, THEREFORE, OFFICERS WILL ALMOST ALWAYS ADJUST THEIR DEMEANOR AND TACTICS. FOR INSTANCE, THOSE PEOPLE WHOM OFFICERS KNEW ONLY FROM

VIOLENT ENCOUNTERS OFTEN CAUSED "OFFICERS TO APPROACH HOT," THUS ESCALATING SITUATIONS UNNECESSARILY. HOWEVER, BY APPROACHING WITH A BEGINNER'S MIND – IN AN OPEN-MINDED BUT ALERT ATTITUDE, OFFICERS CAN BE SAFER AND MORE EFFECTIVE..."

PERRON ALSO POINTS OUT THAT OFFICERS ALSO TEND TO APPROACH INDIVIDUALS WITH WHOM THEY HAVE HAD PEACEFUL AND COOPERATIVE EXPERIENCES IN THE PAST WITH A SOFT AND UN-TACTICAL ATTITUDE, WHICH HAS CONTRIBUTED TO MANY DEATHS OR INJURIES OVER THE YEARS WHEN SO-CALLED "GOOD GUYS" SUDDENLY TURNED BAD.

THE "GOOD OLE' BOY TACTICAL ATTITUDE CAN GET YOU KILLED!

SEVERAL YEARS AGO, DANGEROUS DAN SOLLA, AN AWARD-WINNING PPCT INSTRUCTOR TRAINER, WAS THE LEAD PRESENTER AT AN ASLET TRAINING CONFERENCE IN MOBILE, ALABAMA. DURING A BREAK, DAN STRUCK UP A CONVERSATION WITH A MONTGOMERY, ALABAMA OFFICER, AND, BEING AWARE THAT AREA OF ALABAMA HAD AN UNUSUALLY HIGH RATE OF OFFICERS KILLED ON DUTY, ASKED THE OFFICER HIS OPINION ON WHY THIS WAS HAPPENING.

"SIMPLE, DAN, REALLY," THE OFFICER RESPONDED. "IT'S THE 'GOOD OLE BOY' ATTITUDE MANY OF OUR OFFICERS GO INTO ARRESTS AND TRANSPORTS WITH."

"GOOD OLE BOY?" SOLLA SAID IT LIKE A QUESTION, EVEN THOUGH HE ALREADY HAD GUESSED THE ANSWER."

"YEAH. HERE'S HOW IT GOES. OFFICER A ARRESTS A DRUNK FOR SOME MINOR STUFF. MAYBE A DUI. MAYBE A BAR FIGHT. OFFICER A STARTS HANDCUFFING THE ASSHOLE, BUT OFFICER B INTERJECTS WITH SOMETHING LIKE, "HOLD UP, JETHRO, I KNOW THIS GUY FROM WAY BACK. HE'S A GOOD OLE BOY. YOU DON'T HAVE TO HANDCUFF (AND SEARCH) HIM." THEN, OFFICER B TURNS TO THE SUBJECT AND SAYS, "YOU ARE GOOD OLE' BOY, AIN'T YOU?"

AND, OF COURSE, OFFICER A GOES AGAINST HIS COP INSTINCTS BECAUSE YOU JUST DON'T SEARCH AND HANDCUFF A GOOD OLE BOY, GETS BEHIND THE WHEEL, AND, MAYBE TWO MINUTES LATER, THE GOOD OLE' BOY LIBERATES HIMSELF A PISTOL FROM HIS BRITCHES AND SHOOTS BOTH OFFICER A AND OFFICER B!

*IN CONCLUSION, THIS NEW BEGINNER'S MIND APPROACH IS SIMILAR TO WHAT MY DE-ESCALATION SYSTEM HAS BEEN ADVOCATING IN THIS BOOK. AND THAT IS TO APPROACH EVERYBODY, IRRESPECTIVE OF PAST RELATIONS, SOCIAL STATUS, ECONOMIC CONDITION, RELIGION, CULTURE, OR RACE WITH AN OPEN, FLEXIBLE **BEGINNER'S MIND ATTITUDE.** AND, ACCORDING TO SHAWN PERRON, BEING OPEN TO ALL IDEAS, NO MATTER HOW DIFFERENT (FROM YOURS), IRRESPECTIVE OF CIRCUMSTANCES ONE MAY ENCOUNTER, "[WILL] CULTIVATE*

GREATER COMPASSION AND CONCERN FOR THOSE YOU MEET AND SERVE, [AND] WILL CREATE LASTING CONNECTIONS BETWEEN POLICE AND THEIR COMMUNITIES.

BUT EVEN MORE, THE BEGINNER'S MIND APPROACH, CAN ULTIMATELY MAKE OFFICERS SAFER.

*PERRON PREDICTS THAT "*THE OUTCOME CAN BE A RETURN TO SMILES ON OFFICERS' FACES. A SMILE IS THE MOST UNIVERSAL RECOGNIZED FACIAL EXPRESSION. A SMILE PEACEFULLY NEGOTIATES MANY OF THE BARRIERS YOU FACE, LIKE LANGUAGE, CULTURE, RACE, SOCIOECONOMIC DIFFERENCES..."

SIMILARLY, IN MY DE-ESCALATION SEMINARS, I ASK PARTICIPANTS TO CONSIDER THE PHILOSOPHY OR TACTIC OF SLOWING THEIR ACTIONS AND THOUGHT-PROCESS ENOUGH SO THEY CAN BE HONEST TO THEMSELVES ABOUT THESE ISSUES:

> *DO I HAVE ANY ASSUMPTIONS ABOUT THIS PERSON? IF SO, OBLITERATE THEM NOW.*

> *DO I HARBOR ANY PREJUDICES ABOUT THIS PERSON? IF SO, OBLITERATE THEM FOR THEY HAVE NO CONSTRUCTIVE VALUE TO YOU. THEY MAY JEOPARDIZE YOUR SAFETY.*

> *ESTABLISH AND MAINTAIN TACTICAL BREATHING AND SLOW EVERYTHING DOWN.*

> *CAN I "EXPECT HOSTILITY" AND ADOPT A MENTALITY AND ATTITUDE TO KEEP MY COOL AND REMAIN PROFESSIONAL?*

IT MUST BE AN ATTITUDE WHERE YOU ARE OBSERVING YOUR SURROUNDINGS - A YELLOW STATE OF MIND, WHERE AN OFFICER OR CITIZEN CAN DEVELOP AND MAINTAIN A RELAXED

BUT ALERT 360-DEGREE STATE-OF-AWARENESS - FOR ELEMENTS THAT COULD ENDANGER YOU OR OTHERS. BUT THIS IS A TACTICAL CONSIDERATION. TACTICS ARE IMPORTANT, OR COURSE, BUT THE ATTITUDE OF WHICH I AM SPEAKING CONCERNS HOW YOU APPROACH PEOPLE, HOW YOU THINK ABOUT HIM OR THEM, HOW YOU THINK ABOUT YOURSELF, AND OF COURSE, HOW YOUR ATTITUDE IS EXPRESSED IN THE WORDS YOU USE AND THE ACTIONS YOU TAKE.

PRINCIPLE NUMBER 2. "ATTITUDE IS NOTHING!" *THE SKILLED OR PROFESSIONAL OFFICER NOT ONLY UNDERSTANDS THAT HIS ATTITUDE COMING INTO A CONTACT IS IMPORTANT, BUT MAINTAINS A HEALTHY PERSPECTIVE ABOUT THE ATTITUDE OF THE SUBJECT. SPECIFICALLY, THE OFFICER WHO IS GOING TO BE ABLE TO COMMUNICATE EFFECTIVELY WITH A DIFFICULT PERSON UNDERSTANDS THAT THE SUBJECT'S ATTITUDE IS IRRELEVANT. TAKING THAT BELIEF ONE STEP FURTHER, IT IS NOT THE ATTITUDE THAT YOU PERCEIVE THAT IS IMPORTANT, IT IS ONLY HIS BEHAVIOR – WHAT HE DOES – THAT IS IMPORTANT!*

AS THE LEGENDARY WARRIOR AND PHILOSOPHER SUN TZU PROPOSED IN HIS SEMINAL WORK, THE ART OF WAR:

> *"LET YOUR ENEMY'S ATTITUDE FLOAT BY LIKE A BOAT ON A RIVER. MIND ONLY HIS BEHAVIOR."*

I AM AN OLD DOG. I AM FAMILIAR WITH THE AGES-OLD POLICE PRACTICE OF ATTITUDE ADJUSTMENTS. YOU MIGHT KNOW THEM WELL. IF YOU DO, YOU ARE FAMILIAR WITH THINGS LIKE WRITING ATTITUDE TICKETS AS WELL AS THE ALWAYS AMUSING SCREEN TESTS, WHERE A HANDCUFFED BUT UN-SEAT-BELTED SUSPECT WITH A "SHITTY ATTITUDE" IN THE BACK SEAT OF A CRUISER WAS UNCEREMONIOUSLY HURLED FACE-FIRST AGAINST

THE PROTECTIVE METAL SCREEN SEPARATING THE BACK SEAT FROM WHERE THE OFFICERS WERE IN THE FRONT.

*NICE. BUT ATTITUDE ADJUSTMENTS SUCH AS THESE OR OTHERS ARE ANTITHETICAL TO GOOD COMMUNITY RELATIONS, COMMUNITY POLICING, DE-ESCALATION, OR AS A MATTER OF FACT, **ADJUSTING ATTITUDES!** AS A PAROLE AGENT FOR TWO DECADES AND AN INSTRUCTOR TRAINER FOR ANOTHER TWO PLUS DECADES, I HAVE TALKED WITH HUNDREDS OF EX-OFFENDERS. BELIEVE ME, IF ANYTHING, WHAT WE (I?) KNOW IS THAT ATTITUDES HARDEN AND GEL. ONLY HATRED FOR POLICE IS ADJUSTED, THE RESULTS OF WHICH CAN ONLY BE DISASTROUS!*

THE D.E.F.U.S.E EQUATION

"BILLY JOE SMITH MIGHT BE A BIGOT, BUT
OFFICER BILLY JOE SMITH CANNOT BE."

CENTRAL WINOLOGY PRINCIPLE.

*PROBABLY THE BEST WAY I CAN CLARIFY THE ISSUE OF "ATTITUDE IS EVERYTHING" IS MY DEFUSE EQUATION, WHICH I HAVE BEEN USING IN MY ADVANCED DE-ESCALATION SEMINARS FOR SEVERAL DECADES. TO ME, THIS EQUATION SAYS JUST ABOUT EVERYTHING I CAN THINK OF WHEN I SPEAK ABOUT **PROFESSIONAL FACE,** OR THE PROFESSIONAL ATTITUDE WE NEED TO BRING WITH US, ESPECIALLY WHEN WE ARE TRYING TO MANAGE RESISTIVE, BELLIGERENT, OR EVEN VIOLENT BEHAVIOR.*

*A LITTLE ABOUT **PROFESSIONAL FACE** – OR **ATTITUDE.** ITS DESTRUCTIVE COUNTERPART IS **PERSONAL FACE.** BRINGING ONE'S PERSONAL FACE INTO ANY WORKPLACE INTERACTION IS*

*SYNONYMOUS WITH REACTING TO RESISTIVE OR AGGRESSIVE WORDS OR ACTIONS (BY THE PUBLIC, YOUR CLIENT, A SUSPECT) WITH YOUR **NATURAL EMOTIONS.***

*YOUR **NATURAL VOICE** IS ALMOST ALWAYS PROVOCATIVE. IT IS ALMOST ALWAYS DISASTROUS IN A TENSE CONFRONTATION, ESPECIALLY WITH AN AGGRESSIVE, HOSTILE, MENTALLY ILL, OR EMOTIONALLY DISTURBED PERSON!*

WHY? VERBAL JUDO SAYS "YOUR NATURAL VOICE MUST LIE." YOUR NATURAL VOICE REFLECTS YOUR TRUE FEELINGS. IF YOU ARE PREJUDICED AGAINST THE OTHER PERSON, IF YOU HAVE A GRUDGE AGAINST THE OTHER PERSON, IF THE OTHER PERSON REPRESENTS A GROUP THAT YOU FEAR, HATE, OR DON'T AGREE WITH, YOUR TRUE VOICE WILL ATTACK SOMETHING ABOUT THE OTHER PERSON, SOMETHING THAT VERY WELL COULD TRIGGER HIM INTO ESCALATING HIS VERBAL ATTACKS, WHICH IN TURN MAY ESCALATE YOU INTO DOUBLING DOWN ON YOUR VERBAL ATTACKS. EVEN IF NONE OF THOSE ISSUES ARE YOURS AND YOU COME INTO A CONTACT FREE OF PREJUDICES, HATRED, FEAR OF THE OTHER PERSON, OR HAVE HAD NO PREVIOUS CONTACTS WITH THAT PERSON, SOMETHING THAT OTHER PERSON WILL SAY OR DO ABOUT OR AGAINST YOU CAN TRIP A WIRE THAT COULD SET YOU OFF, THAT MIGHT CAUSE YOU TO GO OFF LIKE A FIRECRACKER.

*THIS IS A **VICIOUS, CONTINUOUS CYCLE OF VIOLENCE.** A CYCLE I KNOW AND HAVE EXPERIENCED TOO MANY TIMES. THIS VICIOUS CYCLE THAT CAN ONLY STOP WHEN SOMEONE EITHER GIVES UP, GETS HURT, OR WORSE.*

*REMEMBER THIS. **FACE IS ALWAYS A FIGHTING ISSUE** (*"FACE" MEANS THAT WHEN YOU VERBALLY ASSAULT SOMEONE, YOU HAVE MADE HIM LOSE "FACE"). ONCE THE BAD GUY, PATIENT, STUDENT, PAROLEE, LOSES FACE, YOU HAVE KNOCKED DOWN

THE FIRST **EGO DOMINO**. **MY** *EXPERIENCE PROVES THAT ONCE THAT FIRST DOMINO GOES, SOON, SO GO THE OTHERS.*

TRUST ME ON THIS, WHEN THOSE DIGNITY DOMINOS *BEGIN TO COLLAPSE, THEY FALL QUICK, AND IF YOU ARE CLOSE BY, WATCH THE HELL OUT!*

D.E.F.U.S.E – THE KEYS TO GENERATING VOLUNTARY COMPLIANCE (VC).

FROM 1990 TO 2000, OVER 855 OFFICERS HAVE BEEN KILLED. SEVEN HUNDRED TIMES
THAT NUMBER HAVE ENDED UP IN EMERGENCY ROOMS....98% OF
THESE INCIDENTS WERE PRECEDED BY MIND-TO-MOUTH DISHARMONY...THE MISUSE
OF WORDS..."

VERBAL JUDO, INC.

VOLUNTARY COMPLIANCE (VC), BY THE WAY, MEANS SEVERAL THINGS. FIRST, WE MUST **GENERATE** *VC. IMPORTANT TO KNOW BECAUSE IT IS A CRITICAL COMPONENT OF THE* **PROFESSIONAL ATTITUDE** *OF WHICH I HAVE SPOKEN. AN AMATEUR OR UNSKILLED OFFICER OR WORKER OFTEN* <u>EXPECTS</u> *THE SUBJECT TO COMPLY BECAUSE HE (THE AUTHORITY FIGURE) IS COMMANDING THE SUBJECT TO DO SOMETHING. LIKE ONE LOCAL POLICE OFFICER TOLD ME DURING A* DT INSTRUCTOR *SEMINAR IN 2016:*

"HARRY, I'M A NICE GUY AND A GOOD COP. SO, LONG AS THE PERSON I AM DEALING WITH TREATS ME WITH RESPECT, I TREAT HIM WITH RESPECT. QUID PRO FUCKING QUO. BUT THE MOMENT THE GUY GIVES ME CRAP OR OTHERWISE TREATS ME WITH NO RESPECT, I BECOME NOT SUCH A NICE GUY. RESPECT (FOR HIM) GOES OUT THE WINDOW."

Which is fine, save for the fact that, obviously, several citizens decided to treat him with a lack of respect on several occasions, resulting in that officer's suspension (twice) and at least one investigation for excessive force.

And another thing, if we calibrate our attitude and tactics based upon the subject's piss poor or outstanding attitude, who then is in control of the interaction?

In my opinion, we should __EXPECT__ THE CITIZEN OR SUSPECT TO RESIST OR CONDUCT HIMSELF LIKE AN ADRENALIN-JUNKY OR AN ASSHOLE. Make no mistake, the law of the land requires citizens to comply with all orders by law enforcement. But, on the street – in the real world, where you are likely to contact every possible type of person, from nice-cooperative to evil-homicidal – to safely and effectively manage resistive and/or aggressive actions by citizens, we need to understand and prepare ourselves __BEFORE__ an encounter for the probability of verbal as well as physical resistance.

The Supreme Court, as a matter of fact, has cited that belief in many of their rulings against police and others (parole officers) who have reacted with an arrest or (excessive) force because a citizen (perhaps a drunk stopped for DUI) who used profanity and a veiled threat against an officer (see the __Fighting Words Doctrine, Houston V Hill__).

"The plaintiff was acting in a drunken and aggressive manner, and it is true that his language was profane, but the fact is, Officer _____ was expected to act and respond as a **professional** charged with the protection

OF SOCIETY, INCLUDING THE PLAINTIFF. IT IS THE PROFESSIONAL WHO SHOULD UNDERSTAND THAT MR. _____ WAS ACTING IRRESPONSIBLY AND CONCOMITANTLY IT IS THE PROFESSIONAL WHO SHOULD BE ABLE TO PUT ASIDE SUCH INSULTS AND USE BETTER DISCRETION AND DISCIPLINE..."

SO, POINT MADE, I HOPE. THE SECOND COMPONENT OF THE GOAL OF GENERATING VC IS THE TERM VOLUNTARY COMPLIANCE ITSELF. VC GOES A FEW CLICKS FURTHER THAN EXPECTING A SUBJECT TO COOPERATE WITH THE OFFICER'S COMMANDS SIMPLY BECAUSE THAT IS WHAT GOOD CITIZENS ARE

REQUIRED BY LAW TO DO. WHICH, BY THE WAY, IS HOW MANY OF US THINK AND ACT. TRULY, THOUGH, IF THIS WERE TRUE, THERE WOULDN'T BE A NEED FOR POLICE OFFICERS, PROBATION AND PAROLE OFFICERS, SECURITY POLICE, AND OF COURSE, CORRECTION OFFICERS.

NOR WOULD THERE BE A NEED FOR THIS BOOK.

*NO. THE ONUS OR BURDEN OF **GENERATING** VC IS ON THE OFFICER OR AUTHORITY FIGURE. I LIKE THIS DEFINITION OF VOLUNTARY COMPLIANCE USED BY VERBAL JUDO: VOLUNTARY COMPLIANCE IS INFLUENCING THE CITIZEN OR AGGRESSOR TO DO WHAT YOU WANT AND NEED HIM TO DO WHILE MAKING HIM THINK IT WAS HIS IDEA IN THE FIRST PLACE.*

ERGO, IT IS AS GOOD A TIME AS ANY TO INTRODUCE MY DEFUSE EQUATION. THE PRINCIPLES I AM GOING TO INTRODUCE WILL TRAVEL A LONG WAY TOWARD DEFUSING AGGRESSIVE PEOPLE, OR MAYBE JUST AS IMPORTANTLY, INFLUENCE OTHERS WHO ARE SIMPLY GOING THROUGH A CRISIS IN THEIR LIVES TO COOPERATE OR AT LEAST KEEP THEM FROM BECOMING BELLIGERENT.

*IN OTHER WORDS, MY FORMULA IS THE DEFUSE EQUATION =
VOLUNTARY COMPLIANCE.*

THE DEFUSE EQUATION –
THE
CRUCIAL ELEMENT OF *PROFESSIONAL
PRESENCE

"ALL TOO OFTEN, TENSE ENCOUNTERS DEVELOP OVER NOTHING MORE
THAN A PERSON'S REFUSAL TO COMPLY WITH AN ORDER, WITHOUT
ANY ACTIVE AGGRESSION OR HOSTILE ACTIONS TOWARD THE OFFICER.
DOESN'T MATTER SOMETIMES. MINIMAL RESISTANCE IS PERCEIVED
AS A PERSONAL ATTACK..."

PHILADELPHIA P.D. CAPTAIN FRAN HEALEY

Don't Lose Your Cool.

*PROFESSIONAL OR COMMAND PRESENCE IS AN OFFICER'S ABILITY TO COMMAND RESPECT AND IMPLICITLY GENERATE (VOLUNTARY) COMPLIANCE BY HOW HE CONDUCTS HIMSELF DURING INTERACTIONS WITH THE PUBLIC. **PROFESSIONAL PRESENCE** REPRESENTS THE FIRST TWO CATEGORIES OF PPCT'S LEVELS OF CONTROL, WHICH ARE **OFFICER PRESENCE AND VERBAL DIRECTION.** IT IS IMPORTANT TO UNDERSTAND THAT THE FIRST TWO LEVELS OF CONTROL ACCOUNTS FOR ANYWHERE FROM 96 TO 97% OF ALL USE OF FORCE INTERACTIONS.*

LET'S DO THE MATH. IF ESTABLISHING COMMAND OR PROFESSIONAL PRESENCE CAN HELP US MANAGE 97 TO 98% OF ALL USE OF FORCE CONTACTS, AND THE PRINCIPLE OF KEEPING ONE'S COOL OR POISE UNDER PRESSURE IS CRITICAL TO THAT PRINCIPLE, THAT MAKES THE ABILITY TO KEEP ONE'S EMOTIONS ON THE DOWN-LOW IMPORTANT, DON'T YOU THINK?

*AND IT IS. IT IS AXIOMATIC TO THE MANAGEMENT OF AGGRESSIVE AND DISRUPTIVE BEHAVIOR THAT **BEFORE YOU CAN DEFUSE ANYONE ,ANYPLACE, YOU MUST FIRST DEFUSE YOURSELF.** EMOTIONS SUCH AS ANGER, RAGE, FEAR, DOUBT, OR EVEN DEFENSIVENESS ARE CONTAGIOUS DURING AN INTERACTION. EXPRESSING ANY OF THESE FEELINGS - VERBALLY OR NON-VERBALLY – CAN BE PROBLEMATIC. IT IS IMPORTANT THAT WE DON'T CAUSE A POTENTIALLY VIOLENT PERSON, OR EVEN A "NICE" PERSON, WHO IS GOING THROUGH SOME DIFFICULT ISSUES, TO BE AFFECTED BY ANY OF THOSE EMOTIONS.*

*EQUALLY CONTAGIOUS, HOWEVER, IS **CALM.** IF YOU CAN INTERACT WITH A PERSON WHILE **MIRRORING** CALM AND CONFIDENCE (BODY LANGUAGE, TACTICAL POSITIONING, AND*

THE WORDS YOU CHOOSE), THE PERSON WITH WHOM YOU ARE
DEALING CAN **CATCH CALM AS WELL AS CONFIDENCE IN YOU.**

ALL OF THIS IS TRUE AND ALL OF THIS IS GOING TO COMMAND
YOU RESPECT ON THE STREET. BUT NONE OF THIS IS WORTH A
SOGGY HOTDOG BUN IF YOU

FALL TO PIECES WHEN VERBALLY ATTACKED OR GO RAMBO ALL
OVER A CLIENT OR OFFENDER THE FIRST TIME HE SHOWS YOU
DISRESPECT. SO, HOW DO YOU STAY COOL UNDER THE
DEBILITATING EFFECTS OF SURVIVAL STRESS (SNS
ACTIVATION)?

INHALE CONFIDENCE. EXHALE DOUBT. IT IS CALLED CYCLE
OR TACTICAL BREATHING. LIKE MANY OTHERS IN LAW
ENFORCEMENT, I HAVE USED IT, ALONG WITH VISUAL IMAGING.
AND IT WORKS. FOR INSTANCE, WHEN I FEEL STRESSED –
MAYBE GOING INTO A HOSTILE ENVIRONMENT TO RETRIEVE A
BAD GUY, OR NOW THAT I AM RETIRED BUT GET A LITTLE
STRESSED BEFORE A CLASS IN FRONT OF A BIG CROWD – I FIND A
RELAXING SITE, CLOSE MY EYES, AND PERFORM THE FOLLOWING
DRILL. BY PRACTICING CYCLE BREATHING IN TIMES OF PEACE,
WHILE RELAXING, IT ALWAYS WORKS TO DROP MY HEART RATE
FROM MAYBE 200 BPM DOWN TO 140 OR EVEN LESS (OUR
MAXIMUM COMBAT HEART RATE IS BETWEEN 115 AND 145
BPM), WHICH PUTS ME IN THE IDEAL CONDITION TO DEAL
WITH WHATEVER MAY OCCUR CALMLY AND WITH CONFIDENCE.

I KNOW I HAVE USED THE TERM **MIRROR CALM (MC)** SEVERAL
TIMES AND WILL USE IT A FEW MORE AS YOU READ ON. THE
REASON: IT IS AN IMPORTANT TECHNIQUE. ONE THAT CAN PUT
YOU IN A STATE OF HARMONY BETWEEN YOUR BODY AND YOUR
MIND NECESSARY FOR DEALING WITH ALL THAT THE MEAN
STREETS WILL THROW AT YOU. TACTICAL OR CYCLE
BREATHING COMPLIMENTS MC BY HOUSING YOUR BREATHING
IN YOUR ABDOMINAL AREA SO THAT YOUR BREATHING WILL BE
SLOW AND DEEP. IMPORTANT BECAUSE, WHEN YOUR
BREATHING IS HOUSED IN YOUR CHEST AREA, WHAT RESULTS
WILL BE FAST AND SHALLOW BREATHING UNDER (SURVIVAL)
STRESS.

*THE CONTRAST IS STARK BECAUSE BREATHING FROM YOUR CHEST AREA IS CHARACTERISTIC OF **PANIC BREATHING**. AND PANIC BREATHING IS ALMOST ALWAYS ACCOMPANIED BY THOUGHTS SUCH AS:* "I AM IN DEEP SHIT HERE!" *WHICH, OF COURSE, ONLY MAKES MATTERS WORSE BY INCREASING RESPIRATION, DOUBLING YOUR HEART RATE, DULLING YOUR AUDITORY SENSES, AND MAKING ACCURATE VISION ALMOST IMPOSSIBLE. HOWEVER, WHEN AN OFFICER IS AWARE OF HIS BREATHING AND CAN ADD A FEW POSITIVE MENTAL MESSAGES HE CAN SLOW HIS BREATHING AND CAN TRULY **MIRROR CALM** BY ACHIEVING A* PSYCHIC SURVIVAL MENTALITY *WITH THOUGHTS LIKE:* "I SEE THE THREAT COMING (I SAW IT FORMULATING A MILE AWAY), AND I AM READY FOR IT."

TRY THIS CYCLE BREATHING DRILL.

INHALE SLOWLY THROUGH YOUR NOSE FOR A COUNT OF FOUR (ONE-ONE THOUSAND, TWO-ONE-THOUSAND, THREE ONE-THOUSAND, FOUR ONE-THOUSAND) AND THEN HOLD YOUR BREATH FOR A COUNT OF FOUR (ONE-THOUSAND). NOW, SLOWLY EXHALE THROUGH YOUR MOUTH FOR THE SAME COUNT. REPEAT THIS CYCLE UNTIL YOU FEEL A STATE OF CALMNESS. BY PERFORMING THIS DRILL MAYBE ONCE OR TWICE A WEEK IN A RELAXING ATMOSPHERE, YOU SHOULD BE ABLE TO LEARN HOW TO CONTROL YOUR BREATHING IN (SURVIVAL) STRESS SCENARIOS.

ONE OTHER SUGGESTION. ACTUALLY, TWO. MY FIRST IS CALLED VISUAL IMAGING OR AUTOGENICS. WHEN YOU CLOSE YOUR EYES WHILE PERFORMING CYCLE BREATHING, SEE YOURSELF ENCOUNTERING DANGER OR DISASTER IN WHATEVER FORM IT MIGHT MANIFEST, AND THEN TRY TO SEE YOURSELF SUCCESSFULLY OVERCOMING THAT THREAT. MY SECOND SUGGESTION IS THAT, WHEN YOU ARE PERFORMING THE BREATHING DRILL, YOU EITHER THINK OR SAY THESE WORDS UNTIL YOU BELIEVE THE WARRIOR'S MANTRA:

"INHALE CONFIDENCE. EXHALE DOUBT."

Other Factors That Can Help You Keep Your Cool Under Pressure.

"I am a believer in the beauty of the Double-Edged Sword. Meaning, the more you feel Fear, the Braver you must act. The more the other person makes You feel Hate, the more Kind and Respectful you Need to act. I am convinced that the more anti-social the person is, the more **professional you are** required to act..."

Harry "Hammer" Wigder, Treatment Trends, 2014/Allentown, Pa.

DEPERSONALIZE. *I am sure I could go on and on for chapters about not taking anything a bad guy throws at you personally. Depersonalizing is maybe one of the hardest acts a person can perform, especially under the debilitating effects of SNS. It requires the officer to resist the urge to react personally*

*or naturally. Why? Because being called a cocksucker, motherfucker, asshole, nigger, kike, spic or white trash is immeasurably **personal!** But, suffice it to say that this requires huge **Unnatural Powers,** or ability! As "Unnatural" as that act is, it is critical to not only maintaining your cool, but to establishing and maintaining your Professional Presence. Another powerful factor in this power equation is the ability and power to......*

DEPRECIATE THE VERBAL ICON,
which is an esoteric way of saying not to award any value to the words the person with whom you are dealing is saying to you about you, your badge, your department or agency, other people close to you. Even your family. An unskilled or untrained person or

OFFICER WILL PAY HIGH REGARD TO THE PROFANITY AND/OR DISRESPECTFUL WORDS LAUNCHED AT HIM. THAT HIGH REGARD FOR THE VERBAL ICON *WILL RESULT IN THAT UNSKILLED PERSON BASICALLY GIVING CREDENCE TO THE INSULT AND BUILDING GROUND THAT DID NOT PREVIOUSLY EXIST THAT WILL ALLOW THE BAD GUY TO NOT ONLY CONTINUE WITH THE DISRESPECTFUL WORDS BUT TO INCREASE THE INTENSITY AND DEPRAVITY OF HIS VERBAL ATTACKS! HOWEVER, THE SKILLED OR PROFESSIONAL OFFICER WILL DISREGARD, OR AWARD ZERO MERIT TO THOSE WORDS, BY DEFLECTING THOSE WORDS AND MAINTAINING HIS PROFESSIONAL IMAGE!*

BY DOING SO, THE PROFESSIONAL WILL ACCOMPLISH TWO POSITIVE ACTS: HE WILL EMPOWER HIMSELF AND TOTALLY DISEMPOWER THE BAD GUY!

*THE SKILLED OFFICER UNDERSTANDS THAT THE DISTURBED PERSON RANTING AND RAVING IN FRONT OF HIM UNDERSTANDS THAT HE HAS ZERO CONTROL OVER HIS LIFE AND IS DOING WHATEVER HE CAN TO IMPACT WHAT HAPPENS NEXT. IF HE CAN SOMEHOW CAUSE THE OFFICER TO GO UNHINGED, USING PROFANITY, THREATS, EVEN EXCESSIVE FORCE, WELL, HELL, DOG, SO MUCH THE BETTER **FOR THE BAD GUY, NOT THE OFFICER!***

SO, WHAT YOU MAY GET, AS AN EXAMPLE, IS:

"IF YOU DIDN'T HAVE THAT BADGE AND GUN, YOU'D BE SORRY YOU EVER TRIED TO WALTZ IN HERE AND START GIVING

TO WHICH AN OFFICER SKILLED IN TACTICAL COMMUNICATIONS AND KEEPING HIS COOL, TO DEPERSONALIZE, AND TO DEPRECIATE THE VERBAL ICON, MIGHT RESPOND:

"I HEAR THAT, MISTER ANDREWS, BUT THE FACT IS, I DO HAVE A BADGE AND I DO HAVE A GUN. I AM HOPING I WON'T HAVE TO USE EITHER, SIR. CAN YOU WORK WITH ME TODAY?"

OR MAYBE THE SUSPECT INVOKES THE OLD RELIABLE: "FUCK YOU, OFFICER!"

TO WHICH, OUR OFFICER WITH PROFESSIONAL PRESENCE MIGHT RESPOND.

"THAT IS NOT GOING TO HAPPEN TONIGHT, SIR. PLEASE MAKE A NOTE."

NOW, SERIOUSLY, YOU MAKE THE JUDGMENT. HOW IN CONTROL, COOL AND PROFESSIONAL DOES THAT OFFICER SOUND? THAT'S PROFESSIONAL FACE. IT IS ALSO COMMAND PRESENCE.

REDUCING AGGRESSION OFTEN MEANS UNDERSTANDING WHAT DALTON, THE COOLER IN ROADHOUSE, *IMPLORED HIS BOUNCERS TO COMPREHEND, THAT,* VERBAL HOSTILITY ALMOST ALWAYS COMES DOWN TO TWO NOUNS STUCK TOGETHER TO ELICIT A PRESCRIBED RESPONSE. NEVER TAKE IT PERSONALLY.

DEFLECT VERBAL ABUSE.

ANOTHER OUTSTANDING STRATEGY FOR KEEPING ONE'S COOL IS **THE ART OF DEFLECTION.** THIS TACTIC INVOLVES BOTH THE SKILLS OF DEPERSONALIZATION AND DEPRECIATING THE VERBAL ICON.

THE BAD GUY WILL OFTEN USE PROFANITY, INTIMIDATION, BELITTLEMENT, INSULTS, AND VEILED THREATS AS A MEANS OF "FOOT SWEEPING" AN OFFICER INTO OVERLOOKING EVIDENCE OR ONCOMING VIOLENCE, OR AS A MEANS OF CAUSING THE OFFICER TO CEDE HIS PROFESSIONALISM. HOWEVER, BY BEING ABLE TO DEFLECT – RATHER THAN ABSORB – VERBAL ABUSE, THE OFFICER CAN "STAY PROFESSIONAL" AND DISEMPOWER BOTH THE ATTACKER AND THE VERBAL ATTACK ITSELF. VERBAL JUDO CALLS

THE TECHNIQUE A *STRIP PHRASE* BECAUSE THE
TACTICS STRIPS THE ATTACK OF ALL POWER.

I CALL THESE JUMP PHRASES, BUT, WHATEVER TERM YOU LIKE,
IT INVOLVES *IGNORING OR JUMPING OVER THE VERBAL ABUSE,
MAYBE USING A PEACE PHRASE OR TWO, AND THEN USING
PROFESSIONAL LANGUAGE TO ACHIEVE YOUR **PROFESSIONAL
OBJECTIVE(S).*** FOR INSTANCE, A REAL EXAMPLE OF JUMPING
OVER THE PROVOCATIVE VERBAL ABUSE AND STAYING IN
CONTROL MIGHT BE:

*BAD GUY: "I WASN'T DOING NOTHIN' WRONG, YOU FAT FUCK (A
TRAFFIC STOP WHERE THE DRIVER SPED THROUGH A RED LIGHT
AND A STOP SIGN)!"*

*OFFICER: "SIR, I HEAR THAT, AND THANKS, I'VE BEEN THINKING
OF GOING ON A DIET, BUT STILL, I NEED TO SEE YOUR
REGISTRATION AND OPERATOR'S LICENSE."*

THE BEAUTY OF THE STRIP OR JUMP PHRASE IS ITS SIMPLICITY
AND EFFECTIVENESS IN SHUTTING DOWN ANY VERBAL ATTACK.
WE WILL DELVE INTO THIS TACTIC IN A PURSUANT CHAPTER,
BUT AS YOU CAN SEE, THE BAD GUY LAUNCHES A NASTY ATTACK
AGAINST THE OFFICER IN HOPES OF GETTING HIM UPSET. THE
OFFICER JUMPS OVER THE ABUSE BY USING A PEACE PHRASE ("I
HEAR THAT, SIR."), AND, INSTEAD OF GOING BALLISTIC ABOUT
THE INSULT, THANKS THE BAD GUY FOR POINTING OUT HE IS
FAT. THE OFFICER THEN USES THE SPRINGBOARD-WORD *"BUT,"*
AND EVERY WORD AFTER "BUT" IS PROFESSIONAL LANGUAGE
DESIGNED TO ACHIEVE THE OFFICER'S PROFESSIONAL
OBJECTIVE.

DEFUSE

EGO SUSPENSION. EGO IS WHAT I CALL A KEY
ESCALATION OR **WAR FACTOR.** ON THE ROAD TO ANY
PEACEFUL OR HARMONIOUS INTERACTION OR RELATIONSHIP
WITH ANOTHER PERSON, *THERE IS NO PLACE ON THAT ROAD
FOR EGO.* LET ME GO A STEP FURTHER. ONE OF THE KEY

POWER PRINCIPLES TOUTED BY VERBAL JUDO IS *"AS EGO RISES, AN OFFICER'S POWER AND SAFETY GOES DOWN!"*

I ESTIMATE, BASED UPON MY EXPERIENCE AS AN ADVANCED DE-ESCALATION AND VERBAL JUDO INSTRUCTOR, PLUS BOUQUET TIME ON THE STREETS AS AN AGENT (WORKING EVERY DAY WITH COPS AND CORRECTION OFFICERS), THAT AT LEAST 75 % OF *PROBLEMS MANY OF US EXPERIENCE DEALING WITH DIFFICULT AND BELLIGERENT PEOPLE COMES DOWN TO PROTECTING EGO.*

EGO, AT THE VERY LEAST, INTERFERES WITH OUR EFFECTIVE INTERACTIONS WITH COMMUNITY MEMBERS. AT ITS WORST, RELIANCE ON EGO CAN GET US KILLED. WE WILL TALK MORE ABOUT EGO AND ITS EFFECTS LATER, BUT FOR NOW, A NOTE ABOUT WHAT RELYING UPON EGO WILL OFTEN RESULT IN:

*EGO IS **TACTICALLY UNSAFE** BECAUSE IT CAUSES US TO TURN OUR FOCUS INWARD DURING TIMES OF SURVIVAL STRESS INSTEAD OF OUTWARD TO WHERE A THREAT MAY BE FORMULATING. FOR INSTANCE, AN OFFICER INVOLVED IN AN EXCHANGE OF VERBAL TAUNTS WITH A BAD GUY WILL BE LOOKING INSIDE TO COME UP WITH HIS NEXT PUTDOWN – WHAT VERBAL JUDO CALLS THE F-YOU-SHUFFLE - WHILE THE SUSPECT OR A CONFEDERATE IS CIRCLING AROUND TO THE SIDE (THE REAL OUTWARD THREAT) UNNOTICED (BASED UPON A REAL SCENARIO).*

EGO OFTEN CREATES A NEED TO DEFEND OURSELVES WHEN AN AGGRESSIVE PERSON LAUNCHES AN ACCUSATION TOWARD US. PERHAPS THE AGGRESSOR CHARGES YOU WITH STOPPING HIM ONLY BECAUSE HE IS BLACK OR A MUSLIM. ONE DESIRING TO PROTECT HIS EGO WILL DEFEND HIMSELF AND MAYBE EVEN COUNTERATTACK THE ACCUSER, WHILE THE SKILLED OFFICER WILL JUMP OVER EGO AND TOTALLY STRIP THE VERBAL ICON OF ANY POWER BY SAYING SOMETHING LIKE, "I HEAR THAT, SIR, BUT LET ME TELL YOU EXACTLY WHY I STOPPED YOU."

THE TRICK IS TO SEPARATE YOURSELF FROM YOUR EGO. THAT SIMPLE. INSTEAD, DEVELOP WHAT I CALL REASONABLE

TACTICAL INDIFFERENCE *WHERE YOU CAN EASILY AND UNEMOTIONALLY LET INSULTS, ACCUSATIONS AND OTHER ATTEMPTS TO ELICIT AN UNPROFESSIONAL RESPONSE FLY* ON BY YOU AS IF THEY WERE FECKLESS MOTES OF DUST IN THE AIR. IN THIS *WAY, THESE ATTEMPTS AT DISTRACTION DRIFT ON BY SO THAT YOU CAN FOCUS ON WHAT IS IMPORTANT. ON WHAT CONCERNS THE SAFETY OF YOURSELF AND OTHERS.*

EGO IS ALSO A HUGE FACTOR IN MANY COP-TRAGEDIES WHEN AN OFFICER FAILS TO CALL FOR BACKUP BECAUSE "I CAN HANDLE THESE BOZOS WITHOUT ANY HELP (BACK-UP)!"

A TRUE STORY FROM THE STREETS OF KANSAS CITY

EGO'LL GET YOU KILLED!

DR. THOMPSON *OFTEN TOLD THE STORY OF A KANSAS CITY POLICE OFFICER WHO RESPONDED TO A DISTURBANCE CALL FROM A LOCAL HONKEY-TONK AND ENCOUNTERED TWO MEN WHOM HE ASSUMED WERE JUST TWO DRUNK FARM BOYS. WHAT HE WAS IN FACT ENCOUNTERING WERE TWO VIOLENT BANK ROBBERS.*

THE OFFICER (THOMPSON FELT IT KINDER NOT TO DIVULGE THE OFFICER'S NAME) ENCOUNTERED THE TWO "FARM BOYS" IN THE BAR'S PARKING LOT AND ONE OF THE MEN GREETED THE OFFICER BY SHAKING A FIST IN THE AIR AND SHOUTING SOMETHING LIKE, "LISTEN, FAGGOT, YOU KNOW WHAT'S BEST FOR YOU, GET THE FUCK OUT OF OUR WAY!"

TO WHICH THE KC OFFICER REACTED WITH HIS OWN BLISTERING BATTERY OF PROFANITY AND THREATS. PREDICTABLY, THE LARGER OF THE PAIR REPLIED WITH MORE THREATS AND PROFANITY, AND AS THOMPSON TOLD IT, THAT OFFICER WAS NOW DEEP INTO DEFENDING HIS EGO, MEANING HIS ATTENTION WAS FOCUSED DEEP INSIDE HIMSELF (THE F-

YOU-SHUFFLE), WHICH RESULTED IN THE OFFICER NOT SEEING THE SMALLER OF THE TWO ROBBERS CIRCLING TO HIS (OFFICER'S) RIGHT UNTIL, WHEN THOMPSON – THEN AN OFFICER – PULLED UP ON THE SCENE – THE SMALLER BAD GUY WAS STANDING CLOSE TO THAT OFFICER, WHO SEEMED OBLIVIOUS TO ANYTHING OTHER THAN THE BIGGER BAD GUY WITH WHOM HE WAS ENGAGED IN A SHOUTING MATCH.

"WHEN I PULLED UP ON THE SCENE, HERE WAS THE OFFICER, TOTALLY ENGAGED IN A VERBAL TUSSLE WITH THIS BIG DUDE AND HERE WAS THE BIG GUY'S BUDDY STANDING RIGHT NEXT TO THE OFFICER – TOTALLY UNSEEN - AND BANG, THE LITTLE GUY POPS MY COP PAL WITH THE BUTT OF A SHOTGUN AND THE COP IS DOWN AND HERE THEY ARE, JUST ABOUT SET TO FINISH HIM OFF, WHEN I LIGHT THEM UP, RACK MY SHOTGUN AND ORDER THEM BOTH DOWN ON THEIR FACES..."

THOMPSON TALKED WITH THE OFFICER AFTER THE OFFICER RECOVERED. HE (THE OFFICER) ADMITTED THAT HE DIDN'T CALL FOR BACKUP BECAUSE HE FELT HE COULD HANDLE TWO DRUNK FARM BOYS BY HIMSELF. HE ALSO ADMITTED – SHEEPISHLY – THAT HE HAD FIGURED THE BIGGER OF THE TWO WAS THE ONLY MAN HE HAD TO WORRY ABOUT AND DISMISSED THE LITTLE GENT IN HIS MIND.

AND FINALLY, THE OFFICER ADMITTED THAT THE BIG GUY GOT HIM FURIOUS WITH HIS VERBAL TAUNTS THAT HE SORT OF LOST HIMSELF *IN THE ARGUMENT, CONSUMED BY THE DESIRE TO PUT* "THAT BIG ASSHOLE DOWN!"

DEFUSE

FIND OUT THE FACTS. DEFUSING AGGRESSIVE PEOPLE OFTEN REQUIRES INFORMATION. FACTS ABOUT THE INDIVIDUAL, INCLUDING SEEMINGLY TRIVIAL FACTS, LIKE HIS NAME. HIS PROBLEM OR ISSUE, AS HE SEES IT, AND WHAT IT IS THAT THE PERSON BELIEVES MIGHT RESOLVE HIS ISSUE(S).

EVEN THE MOST ROUTINE "STOPS" REQUIRES INFORMATION.

BUT EVEN BEYOND GATHERING INFORMATION, ASKING **ARTFUL QUESTIONS** SERVES A VARIETY OF PURPOSES, INCLUDING SHOWING THAT YOU ARE TRYING TO GET THINGS RIGHT, AND THAT YOU ARE GENUINELY CONCERNED ABOUT RESOLVING HIS PROBLEM. IMPORTANTLY, ASKING THE RIGHT QUESTIONS IN A TIMELY MANNER CAN OFTEN STOP A DISTURBED CITIZEN WHO IS IN THE MIDDLE OF AN ENRAGED DIATRIBE BETTER THAN A SOLID BRACHIAL STUN.

IN SOME OF MY DE-ESCALATION TRAININGS I ASSIGN ONE STUDENT TO PORTRAY AN EMOTIONALLY DISTURBED SUBJECT AND ASSIGN ANOTHER TO BE A COUNSELOR, PAROLE OFFICER, OR POLICE OFFICER (DEPENDING UPON THE AUDIENCE) WHO MUST DO OR SAY SOMETHING TO CALM THE DISTURBED PERSON. I TELL THE DISTURBED GUY OR GAL TO KEEP "RANTING AND RAVING" UNTIL THE OTHER PERSON SAYS OR DOES SOMETHING THAT HE OR SHE (THE BAD GUY) BELIEVES WOULD HAVE CAUSED HIM TO CALM DOWN.

WITHOUT FAIL, WHENEVER THE AUTHORITY FIGURE INTERJECTED WITH THE QUESTION, "SIR/MISS, COULD I ASK YOU A QUESTION?" THE BAD GUY STOPPED RANTING FOR A FEW SECONDS. IF THE "OFFICER" FAILED TO FOLLOW UP WITH A QUESTION, THE DISTURBED PERSON RESUMED HIS RANT WITH EVEN MORE INTENSITY.

BUT, IMPORTANTLY, IF THE AUTHORITY PERSON FOLLOWED UP WITH A GOOD QUESTION THAT WAS IN TANDEM WITH WHATEVER THE NUT CASE WAS RAVING ABOUT, HE (NUT CASE) STAYED CALM, ALMOST FORGETTING WHAT HE WAS RAVING ABOUT.

THE GREAT MAJORITY OF PEOPLE ARE NATURALLY CURIOUS REGARDING WHAT YOU ARE GOING TO ASK. ANOTHER THING. I WAS NEVER BIG ON PARAPHRASING EMOTIONS OR CONTENT, BUT EXPERT AFTER EXPERT – AS WELL AS MANY PEOPLE IN MY AUDIENCES – SWEAR THAT WHEN THEY PARAPHRASE, MOST

PEOPLE WILL PAUSE TO SEE IF YOU GOT WHAT THEY ARE SAYING
OR FEELING CORRECT.

VERBAL JUDO CALLS THE PARAPHRASE QUESTION **THE HOOK.**
MEANING THE KEY QUESTION OF, "SIR, LET ME SEE IF I
UNDERSTAND WHAT YOU WERE SAYING (OR, FEELING), OKAY?"
SOMEHOW CREATES THE NEED TO PAUSE TO SEE IF YOU GOT IT
RIGHT.

ONE OF MY FAVORITE HOOK-QUESTIONS WAS AND STILL IS,
"SIR, EXCUSE ME, BUT I WONDER IF I COULD ASK YOU A
QUESTION?" WHICH ALMOST ALWAYS CAUSED A NICE LITTLE
PAUSE, MAYBE BECAUSE, HERE I WAS, A PAROLE OFFICER AND
THEY MY SUBORDINATE (PROBATIONER OR PAROLEE) ASKING
THEM FOR PERMISSION TO ASK A QUESTION. POWERFUL STUFF,
THIS. WHY? MAYBE BECAUSE IT IS THE LAST THING THEY
EXPECT IN A CONFRONTATION. INSTEAD OF GETTING
DEFENSIVE OR THREATENING THEM WITH JAIL, HERE I AM
DEFERRING TO THEM. SURPRISE AND EMPATHY KILLS ANGER!

NEVER UNDERESTIMATE THE POWER OF **SURPRISE** IN A CRISIS.
SURPRISE OR INVOKING THE UNEXPECTED ACTS LIKE A MENTAL
STUN, WHICH IS DEFINED AS STIMULATION OF OVERWHELMING
SENSORY INPUT THAT IS SUDDEN, INTENSE AND UNEXPECTED.

ANOTHER TECHNIQUE THAT INVARIABLY WORKED TO BRING A
"RANTING" PERSON TO EITHER SLOW DOWN HIS RAGE, OR
OFTEN, STOP RANTING

COMPLETELY, WAS **SILENCE.** IN THE SAME EXERCISE, WHEN THE
PERSON PORTRAYING THE OFFICER OR COUNSELOR APPEARED
INTERESTED IN WHAT THE SUBJECT WAS SAYING, BUT SAID
NOTHING FOR OVER 20-SECONDS, THE "DISTURBED PERSON"
WOULD PAUSE, ALMOST AS IF TO ASK, "HEY, AREN'T YOU GOING
TO SAY ANYTHING?"

THAT PAUSE CREATES WHAT I CALL A *FIREBREAK,* WHICH
INVARIABLY THROWS WATER ON THE FLAMES OF ANGER.

DEFUSE

UNDERSTAND FEELINGS. *EMPATHY, EXPERTS*
AGREE, ABSORBS TENSION. REASON ENOUGH TO BE CERTAIN TO
BE AS EMPATHIC AS POSSIBLE DURING ALL CONFRONTATIONAL
INTERACTIONS. AND THE THING IS, YOU REALLY, ONCE AGAIN,
DO NOT HAVE TO UNDERSTAND THE OTHER PERSON'S FEELINGS
(BECAUSE EMPATHY, LIKE MANY OF OUR TECHNIQUES, IS A
CONSTRUCTED ACT, AFTER ALL). WHAT IS IMPORTANT IS TO BE
SURE TO SHOW THE SUBJECT THAT YOU DO UNDERSTAND THAT
HE IS ANGRY, HURT, DEPRESSED, FEARFUL, ET AL., *AS WELL AS*
WHY HE IS FEELING THAT WAY.

WHICH, BY THE WAY, REQUIRES THE OFFICER TO ACTIVELY
AND REFLEXIVELY LISTEN TO WHAT THE SUBJECT IS SAYING
AND HOW HE IS SAYING IT. REMEMBER, YOU NEED TO GET
THINGS RIGHT. YOU NEED TO FIND OUT THE FACTS!

AS IN: "SIR, I UNDERSTAND THAT YOU ARE UPSET. UNDER THE
SAME CIRCUMSTANCES, I MIGHT FEEL THE SAME WAY, BUT THE
FACT IS I HAVE NO CHOICE BUT TO---"

OR, AS IN: "JOHN, I CAN HEAR ANGER AND HURT IN YOUR VOICE.
I CAN SEE IT IN YOUR EYES, HELP ME HELP YOU." *THIS*
QUESTION, OR I-STATEMENT, HELPED CALM AN EMOTIONALLY
DISTURBED INMATE WHO HAD MINUTES EARLIER BEEN
INFURIATED BY A MALE NURSE WHO HAD SHOUTED AT THE
INMATE WHO WAS EATING BARS OF SOAP AND TRYING TO CLIMB
A WALL – "JOHN, WHAT THE FUCK IS YOUR PROBLEM?" – A
POORLY USED YOU-STATEMENT!

DEFUSE

*S*LOW EVERYTHING DOWN. TO GENERATE CALM IN A*
SCENARIO WHERE THERE IS BELLIGERENCE AND CHAOS, YOU
MUST FIRST GENERATE CALM WITHIN YOURSELF. NOT A SIMPLE
AND EASY TASK, FOR SURE. STILL, IT MUST BE ACCOMPLISHED.

YOU ARE THE PEACE OFFICER, MEANING, MORE LIKELY THAN NOT, YOU ARE *THE ONLY PERSON OR ENTITY* CAPABLE OF RESTORING ORDER. IF YOU ARE IN A STATE OF DISORDER, THAT BECOMES AN IMPOSSIBILITY!

"SLOWING EVERYTHING DOWN, THEREFORE, IS AN ESSENTIAL PRINCIPLE OF NOT ONLY DEFUSING YOURSELF, BUT IN "MIRRORING CALM" TO THE DISTURBED PERSON OR PEOPLE ON THE SCENE. I CALL THIS ACTION THE RULE OF MINUS-ONE. MEANING, YOU SHOULD ALWAYS SEEK TO THINK, ACT, MOVE, AND SPEAK AT LEAST ONE DEGREE SLOWER AND SOFTER THAN WHAT YOU EXPERIENCE ON THE SCENE. I REPEAT BECAUSE THIS IS AN IMPORTANT POINT: STRIVE TO EXEMPLIFY *THE FIVE S'S: SLOW, SLOW, SLOWER, SOFT AND SINCERE!* WHY? WHEN YOU SLOW THINGS DOWN, SEVERAL PRINCIPLES TAKE OVER:

YOU NATURALLY THINK BETTER WHEN YOU SLOW THINGS DOWN! MY EXPERIENCE AND RESEARCH SHOWS THAT MOST TACTICAL MISTAKES OFFICERS MAKE CAN BE TRACED BACK TO RUSHING. IN FACT, MOST MISTAKES *YOU* MAKE IN LIFE HAPPEN WHEN YOU RUSH. SIMPLE.

WHEN YOU RUSH, YOU ACTIVATE THE SYMPATHETIC NERVOUS SYSTEM (SNS)), WHICH RESULTS IN YOUR MIND AND BODY BEING FLOODED WITH STRESS HORMONES –EPINEPHRINE, NOR EPINEPHRINE, AND CORTISOL. SNS ACTIVATION IS NOT CONDUCIVE TO CALM. MATTER OF FACT, SNS ACTIVATION IS ONLY CONDUCIVE TO SPIKING YOUR STRESS AROUSAL, FEAR AND AGGRESSION TRIGGERS. SO, SNS ACTIVATIONS ENCAPSULATES FIGHT OR FLIGHT. THE FURTHEST THING FROM CALM!

WORSE, WHEN YOU SPEED UP YOUR SPEECH PATTERNS (WAR-FACTORS, SUCH AS VELOCITY, TONE, ETC.) AND YOUR BODY LANGUAGE (MORE WAR-FACTORS LIKE QUICK, JERKY MOVEMENTS, THE GORILLA-WALK AND TENSE FACIAL FEATURES), YOU WILL *TRIGGER* SNS ACTIVATION IN THE SUSPECT, SUBJECT, PATIENT, INMATE. HE OR SHE PERCEIVES SPEED AND SPEED OFTEN WILL

*TRANSLATE SPEED TO AGGRESSION. BY DRIVING SNS INTO THE BAD GUY, YOU MAKE HIM TWO TO THREE TIMES STRONGER AND FASTER! IN SHORT, WHEN YOU MOVE QUICKLY OR WITH SPEED DURING AN INTERACTION, YOU ARE PERCEIVED BY PEOPLE AS A **THREAT!***

SLOW EVERYTHING DOWN – OR THE MINUS-ONE PRINCIPLE, MEANS THAT YOU NEED TO BE CONSCIOUS OF HOW YOU MOVE AND HOW YOU SPEAK. IT IS ESSENTIAL THAT YOU KNOW HOW TO APPEAR SLOW, CALM AND SELF-ASSURED ON THE SCENE. I ALWAYS ADVOCATE THAT OFFICERS AND CIVILIANS STOP, LOOK AND LISTEN BEFORE ENTERING A POTENTIALLY DANGEROUS SCENE AND ADJUST OR MODERATE YOUR TACTICS BASED UPON WHAT YOU LEARN WHEN YOU ARE LOOKING AND LISTENING.

*BE A **TACTICAL CHAMELEON**. MEANING, ALWAYS BE WILLING AND ABLE TO CHANGE IN TUNE WITH THE NATURE OF THE OTHER PERSON, PERSONS OR ENVIRONMENT.*

DEFUSE

EMPOWER YOURSELF. DISEMPOWER THE BAD GUY. IN A PURSUANT CHAPTER, WE WILL DISCUSS HOW TO DEFLECT VERBAL ABUSE. WHEN WE DEFLECT VERBAL HOSTILITY WITH JUMP PHRASES, WHAT WE WILL DO REFLECTS THE THEME OF THIS ENTIRE BOOK: TO EMPOWER THE OFFICER (AUTHORITY) BY ASSURING THAT HIS PROFESSIONALISM WILL BE NOT ONLY MAINTAINED BUT ENHANCED.

MANY OF THE UNNATURAL ACTS I ADVOCATE IN THIS BOOK WILL HAVE THE EFFECT OF GIVING THE SENSE TO THE SUBJECT THAT HE IS BEING HEARD AND BEING RESPECTED. VALIDATED. THIS RESULTS IN THE SUBJECT FEELING EMPOWERED. HOWEVER, WHEN IT COMES DOWN TO A BAD GUY VERBALLY ASSAULTING AN OFFICER, I ADVOCATE STRIPPING THAT ABUSE OF ALL POWER AND TO EMPOWER HIMSELF WHILE WEAKENING THE BAD GUY AND HIS VERBAL AGGRESSION.

DEFUSE

DON'T LOSE YOUR COOL/DEPERSONALIZE DEPRECIATE THE VERBAL ICON & DEFLECT/EGO SUSPENSION/ EMPATHIZE/FIND OUT THE FACTS/UNDERSTAND FEELINGS/SLOW EVERYTHING DOWN AND EMPOWER YOURSELF WHILE DISEMPOWERING THE AGGRESSOR!

CHAPTER 4.
DEFANGING THE
BEAST

IT IS IMPORTANT THAT WE UNDERSTAND SEVERAL IMPORTANT ISSUES WHEN IT COMES TO DEALING WITH DIFFICULT AND VIOLENT PEOPLE. ONE IS THAT DIFFICULT, ANTISOCIAL, BELLIGERENT AND HARD-CORE VIOLENT PEOPLE ARE NOT ONLY OUT THERE, THEY ARE ALL OVER THE FRIGGING PLACE! NOT ONLY THAT, THERE ARE LITERALLY THOUSANDS (MILLIONS?) OF SEVERELY MENTALLY AND EMOTIONALLY DISTURBED PEOPLE WHO HAVE BEEN RELEASED UNTREATED FROM MENTAL INSTITUTIONS FORCED TO CLOSE THANKS TO GOVERNMENTAL, POLITICAL AND ECONOMIC FACTORS.

MEANING THAT THE CONTEMPORARY POLICE OFFICER MUST BE PREPARED TO EFFECTIVELY DEAL WITH AND MANAGE AN ENTIRE CONTINUUM OF POTENTIALLY VIOLENT PEOPLE, RANGING FROM DIFFICULT PEOPLE ALL THE WAY TO THE HARD CORE DEADLY CRIMINAL.

TO CLARIFY, A DIFFICULT PERSON IS SOMEONE LIKE ME, OR IF YOU WORK IN THE CRIMINAL JUSTICE SYSTEM, VERY LIKELY YOU. DIFFICULT PEOPLE ARE NOT BAD PEOPLE. THEY ARE OFTEN STRONG-MINDED PEOPLE WHO ARE CONSIDERED DIFFICULT BECAUSE THEY WILL NOT DO WHAT THEY ARE ORDERED OR TOLD TO DO, AT LEAST THE FIRST TIME THEY ARE COMMANDED TO DO

SOMETHING. DIFFICULT PEOPLE ARE STRONG-MINDED, AND YOU CAN FIND THEM ANYWHERE YOU LOOK IN OUR PROFESSION (LAW ENFORCEMENT, CORRECTIONS, ETC.).

IN MANY ASPECTS, DE-ESCALATION TECHNIQUES TRAINING IS PERFECTLY DESIGNED FOR DEALING WITH THE MILLIONS OF DIFFICULT PEOPLE OFFICERS MAY CONTACT DAILY. IN THIS CHAPTER, WE EXAMINE SOME TIME PROVEN AGGRESSION MANAGEMENT TECHNIQUES THAT YOU MIGHT CONSIDERING USING WHEN DEALING WITH THE DIFFICULT PERSON. THESE PRINCIPLES AND TACTICS, I ASSURE YOU, WILL ALSO WORK EFFECTIVELY FOR THE MENTALLY AND EMOTIONALLY DISTURBED AS WELL AS MANY OF THE ANTISOCIAL AND CRIMINAL TYPES ROAMING OUR STREETS.

IN A SENSE, IT MAY BE POSSIBLE THAT DIFFICULT PEOPLE – PEOPLE WHO ARE WIRED IN A WAY THAT MAKES IT NATURALLY PROBLEMATIC FOR THEM TO BE COMPLIANT WHEN AN OFFICER COMMANDS THEM TO DO SOMETHING, AND WHEN ASKED "WHY?" RESPONDS WITH THE TRADITIONAL HARD-ASSED ANSWER, "BECAUSE I TOLD YOU SO, THAT'S WHY" – MAY CREATE MORE OF A PROBLEM THAN THE TRUE BAD GUYS FOR OFFICERS WHO EXPECT THEIR ORDERS TO BE COMPLIED WITH **RIGHT NOW!** IN THE 120 OR SO POLICE ENCOUNTERS I STUDIED, MAYBE 20 OR MORE STARTED WITH AN OFFICER GIVING AN ORDER AND THE SUBJECT EITHER QUESTIONING THE RECTITUDE OF THE STOP, OR SIMPLY JUST HESITATING IN COMPLYING WITH THE ORDER.

IN SEVERAL OF THOSE CONTACTS, WHICH I WILL DETAIL IN PURSUANT CHAPTERS, THE SUBJECTS WERE RESPECTABLE CITIZENS CAUGHT IN DIFFICULT CIRCUMSTANCES, WHO QUESTIONED AN OFFICER'S RIGHT TO INTERVENE, AND IN ONE CASE, HESITATED IN OBEYING AN OFFICER'S ORDERS – WHICH I THOUGHT WERE RUDE AND DISRESPECTFUL – TO SIT HERSELF BACK IN HER CAR.

IN THIS CHAPTER, AS WELL AS A FEW OF THE PURSUANT CHAPTERS, WE WILL DISCUSS HOW TO MANAGE ALL CONTACTS, FROM THE DIFFICULT PERSON, LIKE YOU AND ME, TO THE HARD- CORE CRIMINAL, OR BEAST.

LET'S BEGIN WITH ONE OF THE SIGNATURE CALMING TECHNIQUES OF VERBAL JUDO, INC., PERHAPS THE LEADING (DE-ESCALATION) TRAINING SYSTEMS IN THE WORLD TODAY.

VERBAL JUDO'S FIVE-STEP HARD STYLE WORKS 98 TO 99% OF THE TIME.

WHEN OFFICERS ALLOW THEMSELVES TO BE ENRAGED, OR TRIGGERED BY WORDS AND EVENTS, THEY BECOME TOO ANGRY AND DISTRACTED TO EVEN REMEMBER THE SKILLS THAT, IF USED, COULD RESOLVE THE SITUATION...
PUBLIC AGENCY TRAINING COUNCIL, 2014

BEING A FORMER ADVANCED VERBAL JUDO INSTRUCTOR, I HAVE TAUGHT THIS PROCESS HUNDREDS OF TIMES, AND BEING A PA. STATE PAROLE OFFICER, I EMPLOYED THE HARD-STYLE A FEW TIMES IN REAL SITUATIONS. THIS SYSTEM IS DESIGNED TO BE USED WHEN DEALING WITH DIFFICULT PEOPLE AS WELL AS AGGRESSIVE AND/OR VIOLENT PEOPLE. IT HAS NEVER FAILED TO WORK, IN MY CASE, AT LEAST.

AN IMPORTANT REASON TO CONSIDER USING THIS INTERVENTION TECHNIQUE IS THAT THE FIVE STEP HARD STYLE WILL BENEFIT OFFICERS BY BUYING THEM VALUABLE ASSESSMENT TIME. THERE IS MORE, OF COURSE, BUT BUYING TIME TO ASSESS THE PERSON OR PEOPLE WITH WHOM YOU ARE DEALING COULD BE THE DIFFERENCE BETWEEN A PEACEFUL AND PRODUCTIVE INTERACTION AND SHEER TERROR. I HAVE FOUND THAT THE FIVE-STEP WILL ALSO HELP OFFICERS LOOK GOOD AND SOUND GOOD IN COURT, WHICH WILL GO A LONG WAY TOWARD ENHANCING THE OFFICERS' PROFESSIONAL IMAGE.

A BRIEF NOTE HERE: THIS AND MANY OF THE OTHER DE-ESCALATION STRATEGIES I WILL BE DISCUSSING WILL WORK IN NOT

ONLY YOUR PROFESSIONAL ENDEAVORS, BUT CAN BE EFFECTIVE WHEN DEALING WITH OTHERS IN YOUR PERSONAL LIFE. THESE STRATEGIES REPRESENT A CLUSTER OF STRESS-REDUCTION TACTICS THAT CAN HELP ENHANCE YOUR ABILITY TO STAY CENTERED AS WELL AS HELPING YOU ACHIEVE THE MASTERY OF LANGUAGE THAT ENHANCES INTERPERSONAL COMMUNICATIONS.

THE 5-STEP

STEP ONE – ASK INSTEAD OF COMMAND. EARLIER I HAD ADMITTED THAT I AM A DIFFICULT PERSON. FACT IS, LIKE MOST DP'S -EVEN THE TOTALLY COOPERATIVE AMONG US - I JUST CANNOT MUSTER UP THE HUMILITY TO DO ANYTHING WHEN I AM **ORDERED OR TOLD TO DO IT!** HOWEVER, LIKE OVER 97% OF (DIFFICULT) PEOPLE, I WILL DO DAMN NEAR ANYTHING I AM <u>ASKED</u> TO DO.

VERBAL JUDO PROPOSES THAT 97 TO 98% OF ALL PEOPLE, WHEN **ASKED (NOT COMMANDED)** TO DO SOMETHING, WILL COOPERATE ALMOST RIGHT AWAY.

THE TRUTH IS, IT IS ALMOST IMPOSSIBLE WHEN YOU **COMMAND, TELL, OR DEMAND** SOMEONE TO DO SOMETHING WITHOUT THE OTHER PERSON HEARING A PARENTHETICAL "ASSHOLE!" AT THE END OF THAT DIRECT ORDER OR COMMAND.

IN ASKING, IT IS NOT WHAT WE SAY (OR ASK), BUT *HOW* WE ASK. USING A SINCERE AND CONCERNED TONE IS CRUCIAL. IT IS NOTEWORTHY THAT USING GOOD (UNNATURAL) LANGUAGE, WHICH SHOWS AN OFFICER'S CONCERN AND RESPECT IS CRUCIAL FOR REDUCING CIVILIAN COMPLAINTS.

STEP TWO -SET THE CONTEXT. EXPLAIN WHY.
DIFFICULT OR BELLIGERENT PEOPLE WILL ORDINARILY NOT COOPERATE IF **TOLD** TO DO SOMETHING, ESPECIALLY WHEN THAT PERSON ASKS "WHY?" AND IS TOLD "BECAUSE I TOLD YOU SO!" BECAUSE I TOLD YOU TO IS OFTEN WHAT A PARENT TELLS A CHILD WHO ASKS "WHY?" DEFIANTLY. THE TRICK HERE IS TO RESPOND PROFESSIONALLY TO ANY DEFIANCE AND SET THE CONTEXT FOR

*THE REQUEST TO DO SOMETHING (HAVE A SEAT, SIGN THE PAPER, EXIT THE VEHICLE, ETC.). AS A MATTER OF FACT, WE SHOULD **EXPECT** SOME RESISTANCE OR EVEN DEFIANCE TO AN ORDER, BASED UPON THE TYPE OF PEOPLE WE OFTEN DEAL WITH. THE BEST TACT HERE (TO DE-ESCALATE) IS TO EXPLAIN WHY THE SUBJECT IS BEING ASKED TO DO SOMETHING.*

"SIR, I UNDERSTAND YOU ARE UPSET, BUT SINCE THERE IS AN OPEN CONTAINER IN YOUR CAR, I HAVE NO CHOICE BUT TO ASK YOU TO EXIT YOUR VEHICLE. WORK WITH ME TODAY, SIR."

RESEARCH TELLS US THAT OVER 98% OF ALL PEOPLE WILL COOPERATE AT THIS POINT. OFTEN, THE LAST THING A COMMITTED ANTISOCIAL PERSON EXPECTS FROM AN OFFICER IS FOR THAT OFFICER TO ASK HIM TO DO SOMETHING, AND TO NICELY EXPLAIN THE REASON FOR THE REQUEST.

*WHY IS THIS A DE-ESCALATION FACTOR? BECAUSE THIS TACTIC CAUSES **SURPRISE** AND SURPRISE (THE UNEXPECTED) MESSES WITH THE BAD GUY'S MIND, WEAKENING IT BY CHANGING HIS "CHANNEL." NOT ONLY THAT, ASKING AND EXPLAINING WHY YOU ARE ASKING SOMEONE TO DO SOMETHING IS BEING NICE. BEING NICE ROCKS! IT IS BEING HUMAN AND NOT BEING A POWER-JOCKEY JERK! BEING HUMAN ALSO CONNECTS. GIVE IT A TRY.*

STEP THREE – GIVE GOOD ALTERNATIVES (TO RESISTANCE). *CHANCES ARE, IF YOU HAVE GONE TO STEP THREE, YOU ARE DEALING WITH A HARD- CORE ANTISOCIAL PERSON. NO PROBLEM. REMEMBER, WE HAVE DEVELOPED **TACTICAL INDIFFERENCE**. WE WOULD LIKE TO RESOLVE THIS ISSUE QUICKLY AND NICELY, BUT EITHER WAY, YOU WILL ACCOMPLISH YOUR TACTICAL OBJECTIVES. THE TRICK HERE IS TO PRESENT VIABLE OPTIONS TO FURTHER RESISTANCE. "SIR, YOU HAVE SOME GOOD OPTIONS HERE. YOU CAN EXIT YOUR CAR AND I CAN WRITE YOU THE CITATION AND YOU WILL BE ON YOUR WAY IN ABOUT FIVE MINUTES. FAILING THAT, I WILL HAVE NO CHOICE BUT TO REMOVE YOU FROM YOUR VEHICLE AND YOUR CAR WILL BE IMPOUNDED. TELL ME SIR, DO YOU REALLY NEED THAT TYPE OF PROBLEM TONIGHT?"*

EVERYBODY, ESPECIALLY BONA FIDE BAD GUYS, DESIRE TO HAVE SOME SAY IN SITUATIONS SUCH AS INTERACTIONS WITH LAW ENFORCEMENT AND CIVILIAN AUTHORITY. YOU PROBABLY ARE AWARE THAT MANY OF THE MOST DIFFICULT AND AGGRESSIVE PEOPLE ARE CONTROL FREAKS. ESPECIALLY THE ONES WHO WILL GIVE YOU THE MOST TROUBLE. MEANING, ISSUING COMMANDS WITH NO MARGIN FOR A BAD GUY'S INPUT CAUSES SNS ACTIVATION WHERE THE BODY AND MIND ARE FLOODED WITH STRESS HORMONES. THE TRICK TO DE-ESCALATE OR DEFUSE SOMEONE THEN, IS TO PRESENT HIM WITH ALTERNATIVES TO RESISTANCE OR VIOLENCE. ALLOW HIM TO COMMIT SOME OF HIS THOUGHTS AWAY FROM VIOLENCE TO WHAT IT IS HE WISHES TO DO TO AVOID CONFLICT.

STEP FOUR – CONFIRM. WHAT THIS STAGE DOES IS CONFIRM THAT THE SUBJECT DOES NOT INTEND TO COOPERATE. BY THIS TIME IN THE FIVE-STEP PROCESS, 98 TO 99- PERCENT OF DIFFICULT OR AGGRESSIVE PEOPLE HAVE AGREED TO DO WHAT YOU HAVE ASKED. IN ALMOST ALL SCENARIOS WITH THIS TYPE OF PERSON, YOU ARE GOING TO END UP HANDCUFFING HIM OR MAYBE HAVING TO USE SIGNIFICANT FORCE. THEREFORE, I SUGGEST YOU USE THIS STEP TO ESTABLISH THAT, DESPITE EVERYTHING, HE IS NOT GOING TO WORK WITH YOU. YOU ARE ASKING THE CONFIRMATION QUESTION (A) FOR THE RECORD, (B), AS A TRIGGER POINT TO INSTIGATE YOUR TEAM INTO ACTION, (C) TO GIVE THE PERCEPTION TO WITNESSES, FAMILY, FRIENDS AND POTENTIAL CONFEDERATES THAT YOU ARE SHOWING PROFESSIONAL RESPECT FOR THE PERSON AND ARE BEING CONSIDERATE. A FIFTH REASON FOR THE CONFIRMATION QUESTION IS THAT, IN SOME CASES, THE RESISTANT PERSON MAY DECIDE TO COOPERATE UPON BEING ASKED THE FOLLOWING PEACE PHRASE QUESTION:

"SIR, IS THERE ANYTHING I CAN SAY OR DO TO GET YOU TO GO ALONG WITH THE PROGRAM TONIGHT? I REALLY HOPE THERE IS."

OTHER CONFIRMATION-TYPE QUESTIONS THAT HAVE A CALMING EFFECT AND GIVE THE RESISTOR AN OPPORTUNITY TO THINK TWICE ABOUT BEING DEFIANT MIGHT INCLUDE:

"SIR, ARE YOU SAYING THAT YOU WILL NOT COOPERATE, EVEN IF THAT MEANS YOU WILL BE ARRESTED?"

"MISTER ALBERT, LET ME ASK YOU THIS: EVEN IF YOU DO NOT AGREE WITH IT, YOU DO UNDERSTAND THAT THE LAW REQUIRES YOU TO COOPERATE? SO, SIR, WILL YOU COOPERATE WITH ME NOW?"

"SIR, YOU DO UNDERSTAND THAT, IF YOU COOPERATE, YOU WILL NOT BE HURT? "

STEP FIVE – TAKE ACTION. *WORDS DON'T ALWAYS WORK. IN MAYBE ONE PERCENT OF THE SCENARIOS, NO MATTER HOW CLEVER THE TACTICS, THE SUBJECT REFUSES TO "GO ALONG WITH THE PROGRAM." IF REFUSAL TO COOPERATE OR THE FIRST SIGNS OF RESISTANCE OCCURS, THIS IS THE TIME FOR YOU AND YOUR TEAM TO TAKE WHATEVER ACTION IS REQUIRED. IF YOU GET TO STEP-FOUR ,AND YOU ASK THE CONFIRMATION QUESTION, AS SOON AS THE BAD GUY INDICATES HE WILL NOT COOPERATE, YOUR TEAM SHOULD MOVE IN IMMEDIATELY AND TAKE CONTROL OF THE SUBJECT (WHICH IS WHAT I MEAN BY THE TERM TRIGGER POINT)!*

OFFICER: "SIR, IS THERE ANYTHING WE CAN SAY OR DO TO GET YOU TO GO COOPERATE WITH US TODAY? I REALLY HOPE SO."

BAD GUY: GRABS HIS CROTCH. "THIS IS YOUR COOPERATION, DICKHEAD..."

ARREST TEAM: WITHOUT ANY ADDITIONAL WORDS OR COMMANDS, QUICKLY MOVES IN AND TAKES CONTROL OF THE SUBJECT BEFORE THE SUBJECT CAN UTTER "DICKHEAD."

BUT, YOU NEVER KNOW. ON SEVERAL OCCASIONS WHEN I HAD TO USE A CONFIRMATION QUESTION, THE SUBJECT SIGHED, SHRUGGED HIS SHOULDERS AND GAVE IT UP. THIS CONFIRMATION STATEMENT HAS WORKED TO INFLUENCE THAT ONE-PERCENTER TO GO ALONG WITH "THE PROGRAM," AND WE WERE GOOD TO GO. HOWEVER, IF THE RESISTOR KEEPS ON RESISTING, ANOTHER PROFOUND VALUE OF THIS FIVE-STEP PROCESS WORKS WONDERS: YOU HAVE ESTABLISHED PRECLUSION, OR JUSTIFICATION FOR THE USE OF FORCE AND/OR THE

ARREST. YOU CAN CONVINCE THE COURTS AND/OR YOUR ADMINISTRATION THAT YOU DID EVERYTHING POSSIBLE TO EARN THE BAD GUY'S COOPERATION. **HE CHOSE** *TO RESIST DESPITE BEING ASKED, BESIDES HAVING THE REASON FOR THE* REQUEST *EXPLAINED AND DESPITE BEING GIVEN VIABLE OPTIONS. YOU HAVE DONE* DUE *DILIGENCE TO PRECLUDE THE TO USE PHYSICAL FORCE.*

IF YOU HAVE AN ARREST TEAM OR A PARTNER WITH YOU, BY GOING THROUGH THIS PROCESS IN AN ORDERLY AND CALM FASHION, YOUR TEAM KNOWS **YOU ARE IN CONTROL OF YOURSELF AND THE SITUATION.** *THIS WILL GIVE YOUR TEAM CONFIDENCE.*

IF YOU HAVE – AND IF YOU HAVEN'T, I WOULD SUGGEST DOING IT FROM NOW ON – DISCUSSED THIS TACTIC WITH YOUR PARTNER AND/OR TEAM, YOU HAVE ESTABLISHED A **TRIGGER POINT** *– MEANING, A POINT AFTER WHICH YOU AND YOUR PARTNERS WILL TAKE PREVIOUSLY PLANNED ACTION. IN THIS CASE, WHEN YOU ASK THE CONFIRMATION QUESTION, YOUR TEAM KNOWS THAT, IF THE SUBJECT DOESN'T AGREE TO COOPERATE, THEY WILL GO INTO ACTION AND HANDCUFF THE SUBJECT, OR WHATEVER OTHER ACTION IS REQUIRED BY THE SITUATION.*

IN THE TITLE STATEMENT ABOVE (VERBAL JUDO'S FIVE STEP HARD STYLE – WORKS **98 TO 99 %** *OF THE TIME – I AM USING VERBAL JUDO'S ESTIMATE FROM MY NOTES AND FROM THEIR HANDOUTS. BUT MY ESTIMATE, FROM MY EXPERIENCE AND FROM MY WAY OF THINKING, IS THAT THE* **FIVE STEP WORKS 100%** *OF THE TIME. EVEN IF THE SUBJECT ELECTS TO RESIST, OR NOT TO COOPERATE ANYTIME DURING THE FIVE STEP, YOU CAN DEMONSTRATE IN COURT AND/OR IN YOUR USE OF FORCE REPORT THAT WHATEVER FORCE YOU WERE REQUIRED TO USE WAS JUSTIFIED. AFTER ALL, VERBAL JUDO AND/OR ADVANCED DE-ESCALATION IS A* **THREAT MANAGEMENT SYSTEM. IT IS TACTICAL, AND AS A TACTICAL PROCESS, THE FIVE STEP ACCOMPLISHES ITS MISSION – SAFELY, PROFESSIONALLY, AND EFFECTIVELY ACHIEVING YOUR PROFESSIONAL OBJECTIVE(S).***

MY ADVANCED DE-ESCALATION TECHNIQUES WORK 100% OF THE TIME BECAUSE SIMPLY MAKING THE EFFORT TO CONNECT *WITH THE SUBJECT – EMPATHIZING, SHOWING RESPECT, LISTENING, GIVING*

*OPTIONS, ETC. – CREATES THE PERCEPTION AND THE REALITY OF COMMAND OR PROFESSIONAL PRESENCE, THE HALLMARK OF THE TRUE PROFESSIONAL PEACE WARRIOR. BY GOING THROUGH THIS PROCESS, CULMINATING WITH THIS CONFIRMATION QUESTION, YOU WILL BE PERCEIVED AS BEING **PROFESSIONAL.** AND PROFESSIONAL TRANSLATES TO "PROFESSIONAL, OR COMMAND, PRESENCE!"*

CHAPTER 5.

ON DEFUSING THE MENTALLY ILL

"TWENTY-FIVE TO FIFTY PERCENT OF THE PEOPLE WE
KILL HAVE A MENTAL ILLNESS."
TREATMENT ADVOCACY CENTER, CALIBRE PRESS, NOVEMBER 21, 2016

"IT IS IMPOSSIBLE TO REASON WITH A BLOKE WHEN HE IS BRAIN
DAMAGED -UNDER THE INFLUENCE OF ANGER, RAGE, FEAR, ET AL. OUR FIRST
TASK MUST BE TO SLOW THE PERSON DOWN AND TO CONCENTRATE
UPON CALMING HIM IN SOME WAY. THEN AND ONLY THEN, CAN WE BEGIN
TO REASON WITH HIM..."

CHRIS "BRAVEHEART" WALKER, DIRECTOR, OPTIONS-8, SYDNEY, AUSTRALIA

"HE WHO OVERCOMES ONLY BY FORCE
OVERCOMES BUT HALF HIS FOE..."

SIR JOHN MILTON, CIRCA 1670, ENGLISH POET, POLEMIST, MAN OF
LETTERS, CIVIL SERVANT TO THE QUEEN.

DEALING WITH THE MENTALLY ILL AND EMOTIONALLY DISTURBED IS A REAL PROBLEM FOR LAW ENFORCEMENT AND CORRECTIONAL INSTITUTIONS. THE JOURNAL OF MENTAL HEALTH NURSING *RECENTLY (SEPTEMBER, 2016) SUGGESTED THAT "INCIDENTS OF AGGRESSION AND VIOLENCE IN OUR HEALTH CARE SETTING HAS INCREASED MARKEDLY AROUND THE WORLD IN RECENT YEARS." IT STANDS TO REASON THEN, IF OUR HEALTH CARE SETTINGS ARE EXPERIENCING INCREASED INCIDENTS OF VIOLENCE, OUR CORRECTIONS, POLICE AND OTHERS ON OUR STREETS WILL EXPERIENCE THE SAME.*

POLICE ADMINISTRATIONS HAVE BEEN STRUGGLING WITH THE ISSUE OF HOW TO MANAGE THE TIDAL WAVE OF MENTALLY DISTURBED PEOPLE IN CRISIS. THE TREATMENT ADVOCACY CENTER *REPORTED RECENTLY THAT "*MORE THAN ONE-HALF OF EVERYONE WITH A SERIOUS MENTAL ILLNESS IN THIS COUNTRY RECEIVES NO TREATMENT. NONE."

THE TREATMENT ADVOCACY CENTER *ALSO REPORTED THAT PARENTS WHO SAY THEY ARE AFRAID TO CALL POLICE BECAUSE OF FEARS THAT RESPONDING OFFICERS WILL KILL THEIR CHILD, ARE FORCED TO RELY ON POLICE BECAUSE OF THE DEPLORABLE LACK OF MENTAL HEALTH RESOURCES IN THEIR COMMUNITIES.*

THE REASON THIS TREND HAS SPILLED OVER INTO OUR STREETS IS A RESULT OF DEINSTITUTIONALIZATION, *A TERM GIVEN TO THE PRACTICE STARTED SEVERAL DECADES AGO OF RELEASING THE MOST SEVERELY MENTALLY ILL PATIENTS FROM PUBLIC PSYCHIATRIC FACILITIES ONTO THE STREETS AND THEN CLOSING THOSE INSTITUTIONS.*

IN MY AREA, FOR INSTANCE, THE ALLENTOWN STATE HOSPITAL CLOSED IN 2010. MANY OF THE PATIENTS RELEASED – BETWEEN 50 AND 60% - WERE DIAGNOSED WITH SCHIZOPHRENIA. MANY OF THE OTHERS – 10 TO 15% - WERE CONSIDERED MANIC-DEPRESSIVE AND/OR SEVERELY DEPRESSED. THIS CREATED A MENTAL-ILLNESS CRISIS FOR BOTH OUR POLICE AND CORRECTIONAL OFFICERS TO DEAL WITH BECAUSE THESE UNFORTUNATE PEOPLE WERE RELEASED WITHOUT ENSURING THAT THEY COULD RECEIVE PROPER MEDICATION AND REHABILITATION SERVICES. THIS CREATED A

SECOND CRISIS WHEN THOSE WHO HAD BEEN SO CARELESSLY RELEASED WERE NOWHERE NEAR CAPABLE OF LIVING SUCCESSFULLY IN THEIR COMMUNITIES.

LAW ENFORCEMENT OFFICERS WHO ARE READING THIS PROBABLY KNOW THAT PEOPLE WHO SUFFER FROM PARANOID SCHIZOPHRENIA ARE MORE LIKELY TO BE ARRESTED FOR ASSAULT BECAUSE THEY OFTEN MISTAKENLY BELIEVE SOMEONE IS FOLLOWING THEM OR IS TRYING TO HARM THEM AND WILL LASH OUT.

NO OTHER HUMAN-SERVICE WORKER CONFRONTS THE VARIETY OR VOLATILITY OF PROBLEMS AT THE HEART OF EVERYDAY POLICE WORK. YET THE TRAINING IN EVEN THE MOST SOPHISTICATED POLICE DEPARTMENTS IS A FRACTION OF THAT REQUIRED OF A SOCIAL WORKER, TEACHER, HEALTH CARE WORKER, OR A PROBATION/PAROLE OFFICER. THIS FACT CREATES A SEVERE PROBLEM WHEN AN OFFICER COMES FACE-TO-FACE WITH A SEVERELY MENTALLY ILL OR EMOTIONALLY DISTURBED PERSON IN CRISIS.

THE PROFESSIONAL OFFICER AND THE MENTALLY ILL

"I THINK YOU HAVE TO SOMETIMES FIGURE OUT THE CODE TO WHATEVER PARTICULAR REALITY THEY MAY BE LIVING IN AT THE MOMENT. LIKE, MAYBE HE WHISPERS TO YOU CONSPIRATORIALLY THAT HE DOESN'T HAVE TIME TO ANSWER YOUR QUESTIONS RIGHT THEN BECAUSE HIS LONG-AWAITED ROCKET SHIP IS ABOUT TO LAND IN 'YONDER FIELD' TO PICK HIM UP AND FLY HIM AWAY. SO, YOU PUT YOURSELF INTO THAT REALITY AND SAY, 'AWESOME, MR. FOSTER. MINE WAS SUPPOSED TO PICK ME UP LAST YEAR BUT I'M STILL WAITING...' AND, MR. FOSTER SMILES AND THERE'S A TEAR IN HIS EYE AS HE WANDERS DOWN THE HALL, AND I AM HOPING HE FEELS HEARD AND VALIDATED..."

MS. TRACY MEDLLIN, NURSE,
GRACEDALE HOSPITAL, NAZARETH, PA.

NOT TERRIBLY LONG AGO, I BELIEVED THAT BY ADHERING TO THE UNIVERSAL PRINCIPLES OF DE-ESCALATING HOSTILE PEOPLE, YOU COULD ALSO CALM THE SEVERELY MENTALLY ILL AND THE

EMOTIONALLY DISTURBED. TO A CERTAIN EXTENT, I WAS CORRECT, BUT THE MORE I STUDY THE ISSUES SURROUNDING HOW LAW ENFORCEMENT AND OTHERS DEAL WITH THESE PEOPLE, THE MORE I CONCLUDE THAT WE NEED A DIFFERENT GAME PLAN FOR HOW WE MANAGE THEM. ESPECIALLY WHEN OFFICERS RUN SMACK INTO DISTURBED PEOPLE IN CRISIS ACTING IN BIZARRE WAYS. FOR INSTANCE, THERE'S THIS RECENT NEWS REPORT...

POLICE OFFICER FATALLY SHOOTS 'EMOTIONALLY DISTURBED' WOMAN

MARK BERMAN WASHINGTON POST

AUTHORITIES IN NEW YORK WERE SHARPLY CRITICAL WEDNESDAY (OCTOBER 19. 2016) OF A POLICE SERGEANT, RESPONDING TO A CALL ABOUT AN "EMOTIONALLY DISTURBED PERSON" ON TUESDAY NIGHT, WHO OFFICIALS SAID FATALLY SHOT A 66-YEAR-OLD WOMAN WIELDING A BASEBALL BAT. *POLICE SAID THEY WERE INVESTIGATING THE SHOOTING, WHICH OCCURRED IN THE BRONX APARTMENT OF DEBORAH DANNER, A WOMAN WHO AUTHORITIES SAID WAS KNOWN TO OFFICERS AFTER PREVIOUS CALLS REGARDING HER MENTAL ILLNESS.* IN BLUNT PUBLIC STATEMENTS WEDNESDAY. OFFICIALS SAID SGT. HUGH BERRY DID NOT FOLLOW HIS TRAINING AND SAID THEY WERE SEEKING TO DETERMINE IF HE FIRED HIS GUN RATHER THAN HIS TASER.

"THE SHOOTING OF DEBORAH DANNER IS TRAGIC AND IT IS UNACCEPTABLE," NEW YORK MAYOR BILL DE BLASIO SAID DURING A NEWS CONFERENCE WEDNESDAY. "IT SHOULD NEVER HAVE HAPPENED. IT'S AS SIMPLE AS THAT. IT SHOULD NEVER HAVE HAPPENED."

NEW YORK POLICE COMMISSIONER JAMES O'NEILL SAID EARLIER WEDNESDAY THAT "WE FAILED." AND HE WANTED TO KNOW WHY. O'NEILL SAID THAT WHILE THE DEPARTMENT HAS PROTOCOLS GOVERNING SUCH CALLS, "IT LOOKS LIKE SOME OF THOSE PROCEDURES WEREN'T FOLLOWED." HE PLEDGED THAT POLICE AND PROSECUTORS WOULD "FIGURE OUT WHAT WENT WRONG."

POLICE IN NEW YORK HAVE RESPONDED TO MORE THAN 128,000 CALLS REGARDING PEOPLE SUFFERING EMOTIONAL DISTURBANCES. SAID DE BLASIO.

IT IS EASY TO BE A MONDAY MORNING QUARTERBACK IN SCENARIOS SUCH AS THIS ONE. BUT IT IS TRUE THAT DESPITE PROTOCOLS, PROCEDURES, AND TRAINING MANY POLICE DEPARTMENTS ARE PROVIDING, WHEN IT COMES RIGHT DOWN TO BALLS-TO-THE-WALL SCENARIOS INVOLVING SEVERELY MENTALLY ILL PEOPLE INTERSECTING WITH POLICE, IT IS JUST NOT ENOUGH!

LET ME BE CLEAR ABOUT THIS. POLICE WHO OVERREACT TO THE ACTIONS, WORDS AND THREATS OF MENTALLY AND EMOTIONALLY DISTURBED PEOPLE ARE NOT EVIL. WITHOUT A DOUBT, THE GREAT MAJORITY OF THEM WERE AND ARE TRYING TO DO THE RIGHT THING. BUT IT IS CLEAR TO NOT ONLY ME, BUT MENTAL HEALTH EXPERTS AND POLICE ADMINISTRATORS, THAT IMPROVEMENTS MUST BE MADE IN HOW WE ARE TRAINING OUR OFFICERS TO REACT TO WORDS AND ACTIONS THEY SIMPLY DO NOT UNDERSTAND.

OR PERHAPS, IMPROVEMENTS NEED TO BE MADE ON HOW OUR POLICE ARE TRANSITIONING FROM THE TRAINING BAY TO THE STREETS.

I THINK ONE OF THE KEY CONTRIBUTORS TO THIS LAW ENFORCEMENT CRISIS IS THE FACT THAT, BECAUSE OF THE INFLUENCES THE EDP OR MENTALLY DISTURBED PERSON IS UNDER – DELUSIONS, HALLUCINATIONS, COMMAND VOICES, FEAR, ET AL. – THE PERSON CANNOT PROPERLY COMMUNICATE WITH POLICE ON THE SCENE. IN MANY CASES, THE SUBJECT MAY APPEAR TO BE UNCOOPERATIVE OR THREATENING, WHEN, IN FACT, HE IS UNABLE TO UNDERSTAND THE OFFICER'S QUESTIONS, REQUESTS, AND/OR ORDERS.

THE THING IS, DESPITE MANY DEPARTMENTS DELIVERING TRAINING ON DE-ESCALATING AND/OR TACTICALLY MANAGING THE EDP (EMOTIONALLY DISTURBED PERSON) OR THE SEVERELY MENTALLY ILL, POLICE OFFICERS ALL OVER THE UNITED STATES ARE OFTEN MAKING THE CRISIS WORSE. MAYBE IT IS OUT OF FEAR – WHICH IS

UNDERSTANDABLE, OR MAYBE IN A REFLEXIVE EFFORT TO CONTROL A SITUATION AND ENFORCE COMPLIANCE. HARD TO SAY WHICH, BUT THE FACT IS, TOO MANY OF OUR MENTALLY DISTURBED PEOPLE ARE BEING SHOT AND KILLED BECAUSE THEY ARE CONFUSED, DISORIENTED AND ACTING STRANGELY.

HERE'S ANOTHER RECENT NEWS REPORT THAT IS RIGHT ON TIME.

FROM THE NEW YORK TIMES
APRIL 1, 2014, TITLED
POLICE CONFRONT RISING NUMBER OF MENTALLY ILL SUSPECTS.

JAMES BOYD, A HOMELESS MAN, CAMPING IN THE SANDIA FOOTHILLS, COULD HEAR THE COMMANDS OF THE POLICE OFFICERS WHO WERE TRYING TO MOVE HIM OUT.

THE PROBLEM WAS, THAT BOYD, 38, HAD A HISTORY OF MENTAL ILLNESS, SO HE WAS LIVING IN A FAR DIFFERENT REALITY. ONE IN WHICH HE WAS A FEDERAL AGENT AND DEFINITELY NOT SOMEONE TO BE BOSSED AROUND.

"DON'T ATTEMPT TO GIVE ME, THE DEPARTMENT OF DEFENSE, ANOTHER DIRECTIVE," HE TOLD THE OFFICERS. A SHORT WHILE LATER, THE POLICE SHOT AND KILLED HIM, SAYING BOYD HAD PULLED OUT TWO KNIVES AND THREATENED THEIR LIVES.

ENSUING PUBLIC PROTESTS AND MEDIA COVERAGE AND AN FBI INVESTIGATION INTO THE POLICE SHOOTING, FOCUSED NATIONAL ATTENTION ON THE GROWING NUMBER OF PEOPLE SUFFERING FROM SEVERE MENTAL ILLNESS, WHO, IN THE ABSENCE OF ADEQUATE MENTAL HEALTH SERVICES, ARE COMING IN CONTACT WITH THE CRIMINAL JUSTICE SYSTEM, SOMETIMES WITH DEADLY CONSEQUENCES.

EXPERTS IN LOCAL, STATE AND FEDERAL GOVERNMENT CLAIM THAT THE PROBLEM HAS WORSENED IN RECENT YEARS BECAUSE LOCAL, STATE AND FEDERAL GOVERNMENTS HAVE CUT MENTAL HEALTH SERVICES FOR FINANCIAL REASONS. WORSE, THIS PROBLEM IS

TRENDING TO GET EVEN WORSE IF LAW ENFORCEMENT AND THE CRIMINAL JUSTICE SYSTEM DOESN'T ACT PROPHYLACTICALLY SOONER THAN LATER.

THE TRUTH IS, POLICE ARE BECOMING THE "FIRST LINE OF CONTACT" FOR SEVERELY TROUBLED PEOPLE! NOT THAT BEING A LAW ENFORCEMENT ENTITY AS WELL AS A SOCIAL WORKING ENTITY WAS EVER THEIR MISSION. STILL, THAT IS EXACTLY WHAT HAS HAPPENED, AND PREDICTABLY, THEY ARE NOT READY FOR THE CHANGE. TRUTH BE KNOWN, WHO THE HELL WOULD BE?

DR. E. FULLER TORREY, A PSYCHOTHERAPIST AND FOUNDER OF THE TREATMENT ADVOCACY CENTER, STATES THAT, IN SAN DIEGO, "CALLS FOR DEALING WITH AND RESPONDING TO THE SEVERELY MENTALLY DISTURBED HAVE DOUBLED FROM 2009 TO 2011." TORREY ADDED THAT IN MEDFORD, OREGON, POLICE IN 2011 REPORTED "AN ALARMING SPIKE IN THE NUMBER OF MENTALLY ILL PEOPLE WHOM POLICE CONTACT ON A DAILY BASIS."

A REPORT BY THE NATIONAL SHERIFF'S ASSOCIATION AND THE TREATMENT ADVOCACY CENTER (2015) ESTIMATED THAT "HALF OF THE NUMBER OF PEOPLE KILLED BY POLICE HAVE MENTAL ILLNESS PROBLEMS..."

IN ALBUQUERQUE, NEW MEXICO, DESPITE SCORES OF PROTOCOLS, PROCEDURES AND TRAINING, SINCE 2010, IT IS ESTIMATED THAT OVER 75% OF THOSE SHOT IN 2010 AND 2011 SUFFERED FROM MENTAL ILLNESS!

INVESTIGATIVE REPORTER KIMBERLY KINDY, IN HER REPORT EVALUATING THE ROLE THAT EMOTIONAL CRISIS PLAYS IN POLICE FATALITIES RELATED A STORY THAT SHE INTIMATED "STILL LINGERS WITH ME TO THIS DAY (JULY, 2014)."

THE LAVALL HALL STORY

THERE ARE SO MANY STORIES; ONE IN PARTICULAR, THOUGH, IS LAVALL HALL'S STORY. LAVALL, WAS A SCHIZOPHRENIC YOUNG MAN. HIS MOTHER HAD CALLED POLICE, "BECAUSE HE WAS OUTSIDE IN THE FREEZING COLD IN HIS UNDERWEAR SWINGING A BROOMSTICK. I JUST

WANTED HIM TO BE TAKEN SOMEWHERE SO HE COULD GET SOME HELP..."

WITHIN MINUTES OF THE ARRIVAL OF POLICE, LAVALL HALL WAS GUNNED DOWN.

CASE AFTER CASE AFTER CASE, IT IS THE SAME THING. IT'S HEARTBREAKING. FAMILIES AND MOTHERS WHO CALL FOR HELP, AND THE EMOTIONALLY DISTURBED PERSON ENDS UP DEAD.

BUT WHAT IS ALSO HEARTBREAKING IS, I THINK, THE DAMAGE TO THE POLICE OFFICERS WHO SHOOT THE EDP. THEIR LIVES ARE CHANGED FOREVER, WHEN YOU TAKE THE LIFE OF SOMEONE LIKE THIS.

SO, HOW CAN WE SAFELY DE-ESCALATE THE SEVERELY MENTALLY ILL?

"SADLY, WHAT POLICE ARE TRADITIONALLY TRAINED TO DO IS THE VERY OPPOSITE OF WHAT THEY SHOULD DO. THESE TACTICS JUST PLAIN DO NOT WORK WITH PEOPLE GOING THROUGH A MENTAL CRISIS..."

EDD/WORKING WITH THE MENTALLY DISTURBED/WEEKEND EDITION. JULY 14, 2015.

THE PRINCIPLES AND TACTICS I RECOMMEND COME FROM DECADES OF STUDY AND EXPERIENCE IN THE CRIMINAL JUSTICE FIELD, MY OWN EXPERIENCE AS A PO SUPERVISING ANTISOCIAL AND MENTALLY DISTURBED PEOPLE, PLUS NINE YEARS AS A LEHIGH COUNTY CRISIS INTERVENTION COUNSELOR, AND MANY INTERVIEWS AND INTERACTIONS WITH LOCAL, STATE, AND FEDERAL LAW ENFORCEMENT PERSONNEL. YET, IN NO WAY, AM I STATING THAT WHAT I SUGGEST AND ADVOCATE IS THE "END ALL AND BE ALL" OF TECHNIQUES TO DEFUSE THE SEVERELY MENTALLY ILL. AFTER ALL, THESE ARE HIGHLY VOLATILE AND UNPREDICTABLE PEOPLE. SOMETIMES WHAT I DID WORKED. SOMETIMES, NO DICE. THE IMPORTANT THING, I THINK, IS THAT I ALWAYS DID MY BEST

TO SHOW PATIENCE, RESTRAINT, AND SELF-CONTROL. EVEN IF WHAT I TRIED WASN'T EXACTLY THE "SILVER BULLET," JUST BY TRYING TO BECALM, IN SOME WAY IT HELPED– EVEN IF IT WAS ON AN UNCONSCIOUS LEVEL - I CONNECTED.

I ALSO MAKE THIS POINT. I AM NOT DEGRADING THE EFFORTS OF LAW ENFORCEMENT AND HOW THEY DEAL WITH THE MENTALLY DISTURBED. CAN YOU BLAME AN OFFICER FOR BEING IN FEAR FOR HIS LIFE, THE LIVES OF OTHERS IN THE AREA, WHEN A PERSON PULLS AN EDGED WEAPON AND ADVANCES TO AN UNSAFE DISTANCE? I THINK NOT. THE SAD THING IS, POLICE ARE ALSO VICTIMS BECAUSE THE SYSTEM IS BROKEN. YES, THE MENTAL HEALTH SYSTEM IS BROKEN AND OUR POLICE ARE SHOVED INTO THE FOREFRONT, AND IN THE END, WHEN THEY INTERACT WITH THE SEVERELY MENTALLY ILL, THEY ARE LEFT HOLDING THE PROVERBIAL BAG. THE VICTIMS OF PUBLIC OUTRAGE, THE BEARER OF GUILT OVER ALLEGED EXCESSIVE FORCE AND THE ONES FACING THE ONUS OF SEARING LITIGATION BY THE FAMILIES OF THE DEAD..

ANY RATIONAL PERSON READING WHAT I HAVE RELATED SO FAR MUST CONCEDE THAT WHAT LAW ENFORCEMENT AND THE MENTAL HEALTH COMMUNITIES HAVE DONE SO FAR IS AN ABJECT FAILURE.

DR. ROBERT MARINELLI, A RETIRED CALIFORNIA POLICE DETECTIVE, WHO NOW TRAINS THE USE-OF-FORCE, SUGGESTS THAT OFFICERS WHO ARE DISPATCHED TO A "DISTURBANCE," OR "AGITATED AND ERRATIC PERSON" CALL MUST UNDERSTAND THEY MAY BE FACING A PERSON WHO HAS SEVERE EMOTIONAL AND/OR MENTAL PROBLEMS. ONCE THEY UNDERSTAND THAT REALITY, THEY "MUST STOP THEMSELVES AND THEIR PARTNERS FROM RUSHING IN AND DOING PHENOMENALLY STUPID THINGS."

DR. MARINELLI'S 5-STEP PROGRAM FOR SAFELY & EFFECTIVELY HANDLING THE SEVERELY MENTALLY ILL.

1). Officers must know how their brains and bodies will **react to survival stress.**

2). Officers must be taught to **assess the subject(s) <u>before</u>** closing distance. Before and/or as he moves in, the officer(s) must do a mental inventory and analysis, including:

- ✓ *What is he saying? Is he saying anything?*
- ✓ *What about his appearance? Is he dirty or disheveled? Is his clothing weather appropriate? Is he naked, or nearly naked?*
- ✓ *How is he acting? How is he responding to my questions or requests?*
- ✓ *Are there indications of possible hypothermia from a drug reaction?*
- ✓ *The* **goal of the contact-assessment** is to determine if the officer(s) can handle the subject in order to take him into custody, or to take him to treatment. The officer will have to **execute six things:**
  1) Approach. 2) Communicate. 3). Lay on hands. 4). Arrest and Control. 5). Search and 6). Transport.
- ✓ **If the officer(s) cannot accomplish those six things, he will need to call in "help," like a Crisis Intervention Team, or back-up.**

3). **In this step, the officer(s) must give him or themselves <u>Time and Distance</u>** so they can keep the subject under surveillance and acquire additional resources. In this step, the officer has assessed the subject and the environment and reasonably understands that, if he penetrates, chances are he will get hurt or killed, or the disturbed subject will get hurt or killed!

Dr. Marinelli notes that **"Time and Distance Compression never favors the officer(s). If you can avoid it, do not get closer to them (the severely mentally ill or emotionally disturbed person)."**

(4). Officers must throw away any Macho-Beliefs that they must always have to triumph over the other person!

(5). Be especially cautious about foot chases with an EDP or mentally disturbed person. "Remember, when you catch them, they catch you, too. When that happens, you'd better be on better drugs or be a better fighter (than the EDP), or you are going to get hurt!"

I DO KNOW THIS. THERE ARE COMMON CHARACTERISTICS OF AN EDP (EMOTIONALLY DISTURBED PERSON) AND A SEVERELY MENTALLY DISTURBED PERSON. FOR INSTANCE, THE WAY THEY RESPOND – OR FAIL TO RESPOND – TO VERBAL DIRECTIONS OR QUESTIONS; MAYBE THE INAPPROPRIATE WAY THEY DRESS, MAYBE EVEN THEIR BODY MOVEMENT, WHICH IS AFFECTED BY SOME INANE CHEMICAL IMBALANCE. OR, WHAT ABOUT THE NATURE OF THE DISPATCH? "DISTURBED PERSON?" THESE ARE ALL CLUES. BETTER YET, THEY ARE RED FLAGS.

I HAVE BEEN THROUGH THESE TYPE OF CALLS AS A STATE P.O. AND I HAVE EXAMINED SCORES OF CASE STUDIES. I SPECULATE THAT, IN AT LEAST 25% OF THESE FATAL ENCOUNTERS, ADHERING TO THE FOLLOWING STRATEGIES FOR DEFUSING THE MENTALLY ILL, AND USING RESTRAINT AND COMMON SENSE COULD HAVE CREATED A MUCH HAPPIER ENDING.

SO, HOW DO WE SAFELY DEFUSE THE SEVERELY MENTALLY ILL?

ALONG WITH DR. MARINELLI'S FIVE-STEP OUTLINED ABOVE, HERE ARE A FEW OF MY STANDARD TACTICS FOR MANAGING AND DEFUSING THE MENTALLY ILL AND/OR THE EMOTIONALLY DISTURBED.

SLOW EVERYTHING DOWN. *BY NOW,* YOU MAY HAVE WEARIED OF MY SUGGESTION OF SLOWING THINGS DOWN, BUT ESPECIALLY WITH THE *EDP* OR THE MENTALLY ILL, SPEED OF MOVEMENT AND SPEECH CAN AND USUALLY WILL ELICIT FEAR AND ESCALATE DANGEROUS EMOTIONS. **SPEED** OFTEN **TRIGGERS SNS ACTIVATION.** ADDITIONALLY, SPEED, SINCE IT MAY TRIGGER SNS, SHORT CIRCUITS THE NEO CORTEX – OUR INTELLIGENT BRAIN, CREATING ERRORS IN THINKING AND BUMBLING ACTIONS ON THE OFFICER'S PART.

ASSESS. SLOWING EVERYTHING WILL RESULT IN TIME FOR ASSESSING THE ENVIRONMENT, THE OTHER PERSON, YOUR OWN **GUT INSTINCTS.** YOUR GUT INSTINCTS ARE 250-MILLION YEARS OF EVOLUTION WHISPERING IN YOUR EAR INEXORABLE TRUTHS, LIKE "SLOW IT DOWN. THERE'S DANGER AHEAD!"

CHECK OUT BODY LANGUAGE AND VERBAL CONTENT. IF YOU **STOP, LOOK, AND LISTEN,** YOU SHOULD BE ABLE TO ASSESS WHAT TYPE OF PERSON YOU ARE DEALING WITH.

TALK TO YOURSELF, THINK, AND ENGAGE YOUR INTELLIGENT BRAIN (NEO CORTEX)! *MAKE YOURSELF AND OTHERS ON YOUR TEAM AWARE OF THE COMPLEXITIES AND VAGARIES OF DEALING WITH THE MENTALLY ILL AND/OR EMOTIONALLY DISTURBED PERSON YOU KNOW YOU ARE ABOUT TO ENCOUNTER. IN ALMOST EVERY CASE I STUDIED, LAW ENFORCEMENT WAS AWARE OF THE CITIZEN'S MENTAL ISSUES **BEFORE** THEY APPROACHED. THE GOAL IS ALWAYS TO GO HOME IN ONE PIECE, I UNDERSTAND, BUT STILL, WHAT I AM TALKING ABOUT HERE IS YOUR **TACTICAL OR PROFESSIONAL OBJECTIVE IN THIS CONTACT!** YOU NEED TO GET THIS PERSON TO A PLACE WHERE HE CAN GET THE HELP HE NEEDS.*

OFFICERS, THEREFORE, MUST TAKE STEPS TO MINIMIZE THE CHANCES THAT SNS ACTIVATION WILL DISTORT THEIR MOTOR ACTIONS, THEIR THOUGHTS AND THEIR EMOTIONS BY COMMANDING THEMSELVES TO BE PATIENT, BE SLOW AND TO LISTEN TO WHAT IS GOING ON. IN OTHER WORDS, OFFICERS CAN AND SHOULD TAKE STEPS BEFORE AND DURING AN INTERACTION WITH AN EDP OR MENTALLY DISTURBED PERSON TO "TRICK THEIR SNS."

QUIET HANDS AND EYES. *AVOID MAKING DIRECT EYE CONTACT AND KEEP YOUR HANDS LOW AND QUIET. UNLESS THE SUBJECT BECOMES VIOLENT, AVOID TOUCHING HIM. IF YOU MUST TOUCH THE PERSON, ADVISE HIM AHEAD OF TIME, OR IF CIRCUMSTANCES PERMIT, ASK PERMISSION.*

AVOID TRAPPING. *AS CHRIS HERTIG, A SECURITY EXPERT FROM YORK, PA., RECENTLY TOLD ME,* "PROXEMICS ARE ULTRA-IMPORTANT WHEN DEALING WITH AGGRESSIVE PEOPLE. TRIPLE THAT WHEN WE ARE TALKING EDP'S AND/OR THE MENTALLY DISTURBED..." *MR. HERTIG WAS TALKING ABOUT HOW WE POSITION OUR BODY IN RELATIONSHIP TO THE SUBJECT, ETC. SIMPLY PUT, AVOID CLOSING DISTANCE WITHIN FOUR-FEET, AVOID BLOCKING EXITS, AND OF COURSE, REASSURE THE SUBJECT THAT YOUR MISSION IS TO HELP HIM!*

TRY TO SOLICIT HIS ASSURANCE HE IS NOT GOING TO HURT YOU. IN INSTANCES WHEN YOU ARE REQUIRED TO ESCORT, MOVE, HANDCUFF, OR PERFORM SOME OTHER TYPE OF HANDS-ON "FORCE," IT IS WISE TO TELL HIM WHAT YOU ARE ABOUT TO DO (AND, IF SAFE TO DO SO, WHY). ADVISE HIM THAT YOU HAVE NO INTENTION OF HURTING HIM IN ANY WAY. AT THAT POINT, YOU MIGHT ASK, "ARE YOU OKAY WITH THAT, SIR (OR, "I HOPE YOU ARE OK WITH THAT)?" ANOTHER PRUDENT PRECAUTION WOULD BE TO SAY, "SIR, I AM GOING TO HANDCUFF YOU. I HAVE NO INTENTION OF HURTING YOU.

I HOPE YOU HAVE NO INTENTION OF HURTING ME. WHAT ABOUT IT?" MAKE SURE THE SUBJECT GIVES YOU A RESPONSE BEFORE LAYING ON HANDS!

AVOID "BOXING-IN" VEHICLES AND PEOPLE. REDUCE THE ESCALATING "INFLUENCES!

A YEAR OR SO AGO, MEMBERS OF THE EASTON POLICE BOXED IN A MOTORIST WHO HAD LED THEM ON A LENGTHY CHASE. THE MOTORIST, WHO SUFFERED FROM DOCUMENTED MENTAL ISSUES, WAS TRAPPED BY POLICE BETWEEN A CRUISER AND A UTILITY POLE. THE SUBJECT BEGAN RAMMING HIS VEHICLE CONTINUOUSLY AGAINST THE CRUISER AND THE POLE. FINALLY, EVEN THOUGH THE MOTORIST WAS TRAPPED AND THEORETICALLY HAD NOWHERE TO GO, AN OFFICER FATALLY SHOT THE SUBJECT. AFTER THE SHOOTING, THE MOTORIST WAS FOUND WITH A KNIFE IMBEDDED DEEP IN HIS NECK, A SELF-INFLICTED WOUND.

I AM NOT ARGUING THAT POLICE SHOULD HAVE REDUCED THE NOISE CREATED BY THE VARIOUS SIRENS AND THE INFLUENCE OF THE SCORES OF PULSATING EMERGENCY LIGHTS FLASHING FROM ALL DIRECTIONS. HOWEVER, I THINK IT IS WORTH MENTIONING THE NUMBER OF ESCALATING INFLUENCES PRESENT AT THIS

DEADLY SCENE. I AM CONVINCED THAT THIS IS A
SITUATION WHERE OFFICERS ENGAGING THEIR
NEO CORTEX AND USING PATIENCE AND EGO-
REDUCTION TECHNIQUES WOULD HAVE SAVED
THIS MOTORIST'S LIFE. THE DRIVER, WHO, BY
THE WAY, WAS MENTALLY DISTURBED AS WELL AS
SUICIDAL, WAS TRAPPED BETWEEN A UTILITY
POLE AND A POLICE CRUISER. HE WAS ARMED
ONLY WITH A KNIFE, WHICH HE COULD NOT USE
AGAINST POLICE SINCE HE WAS TRAPPED INSIDE
HIS VEHICLE, AND AS FAR AS I KNOW, HE WAS NOT
EVEN ATTEMPTING TO DISENGAGE FROM HIS
VEHICLE TO ATTACK POLICE. WHO, BY THE WAY,
SURROUNDED HIS VEHICLE GEARED UP WITH ALL
SORTS OF DEADLY WEAPONS.

TRUE, HE WAS RAMMING THE POLICE VEHICLE,
BUT I HAVE SUSPICIONS THAT HE WAS NOT
TRYING TO ESCAPE THE SCENE (I ADMIT, THAT
WAS A POSSIBILITY). INSTEAD, I THINK HE WAS
ATTEMPTING TO IMPEL OFFICERS TO SHOOT AND
KILL HIM (SUICIDE-BY-COP) AND ONE OF THE
OFFICERS OBLIGED HIM. I BELIEVE THE FACT
THAT HE HAD IMBEDDED A KNIFE DEEP IN HIS
NECK AT THE SAME TIME THE OFFICER SHOT HIM
CONSOLIDATES MY THEORY.

I WOULD BE REMISS IF I DIDN'T NOTE THAT THE
OFFICER(S) AND THE DEPARTMENT WERE
INVESTIGATED BY CITY, STATE, AND FEDERAL

AUTHORITIES AND THEIR ACTIONS WERE FOUND TO BE JUSTIFIED. MY OPINION IS MY OPINION.

I ASK YOU TO CONSIDER THIS SCENARIO AGAINST THE BACKDROP OF WHAT I HAVE WRITTEN ABOUT THE CRISIS WITH DEALING WITH EMOTIONALLY DISTURBED PEOPLE. IS IT POSSIBLE THAT WAITING OUT THE SITUATION AND MAYBE SHUTTING DOWN ALL THE ESCALATORS ON THE SCENE MIGHT HAVE LED TO A BETTER END? SURE, THE DISTURBED MOTORIST MAY HAVE STILL DRIVEN THE KNIFE INTO HIS NECK. WHO KNOWS? BUT DO WE HAVE TO BE THE JUDGE, JURY AND EXECUTIONER?

GIVE YOURSELF SOME POSITIVE SELF MESSAGES. *IT IS IMPERATIVE THAT, PRIOR TO ANY CONTACT, ESPECIALLY ONE RIFE WITH POTENTIAL DANGER, THAT YOU TAKE A SECOND OR TWO AND INPUT SOME POSITIVE, TACTICAL THOUGHTS INTO YOUR COMPUTER-LIKE BRAIN. FOR INSTANCE,* "THIS GUY LOOKS OUT OF HIS MIND. I'D BETTER TAKE A FEW MINUTES, SLOW THINGS DOWN, MAKE SURE HE KNOWS I AM HERE TO HELP...." OR, "I EXPECT THIS GUY TO SAY SOME WEIRD THINGS AND I EXPECT HIM TO TEST MY PATIENCE, BUT I CAN BREATHE DEEP, GET MY SHIT TOGETHER, AND HANDLE THIS PERSON PROFESSIONALLY..."

OR, AS IN THE CASE OF THE TRAPPED MOTORIST: "OKAY, EVERYBODY'S EMOTIONS ARE HIGH; WE'VE JUST BEEN ON A HIGH-SPEED CHASE, TAKE A DEEP BREATH AND GET MY THOUGHTS STRAIGHT. HE'S OUT OF HIS MIND AND SMASHING OUR CRUISER, BUT NO ONE'S IN DEADLY DANGER HERE. NOT YET, ANYWAYS..."

ESTABLISH AND MAINTAIN A SAFE & OBLIQUE BODY POSITION. *MORE KEY PROXEMICS. WHEN ESTABLISHING AN "INTERVIEW" POSITION WITH AN EDP OR A MENTALLY ILL SUBJECT, ALLOW HIM AT LEAST 4 TO 6 FEET OF SPACE WHENEVER POSSIBLE, AND MORE IMPORTANTLY, AVOID ESTABLISHING A FACE-TO-FACE INTERVIEW POSITION. THIS MIGHT INTENSIFY EMOTIONS. INSTEAD BLADE YOUR BODY SLIGHTLY SO THAT YOUR "CENTER-LINE-BODY-PARTS" ARE AT AN OBLIQUE ANGLE. STUDIES (MOAB), PLUS MY OWN EXPERIENCE, SHOWS THAT THIS BODY POSITIONING TACTIC REDUCES TENSION IN MOST SUBJECTS. IT IS IMPERATIVE, I BELIEVE, THAT OFFICERS ALWAYS CONSIDER THEIR PROXEMICS, WHETHER THEY ARE APPROACHING ON FOOT OR IN THEIR VEHICLE(S).*

NEAREST WEAPON NEAREST TARGET (NWNT). *I FIRST HEARD THIS PROXEMICS SUGGESTION FROM TONY BLAUER, THE FOUNDER OF THE S.P.E.A.R SYSTEM. NWNT IS A TACTIC*

ANYONE CAN USE TO MAXIMIZE HIS SAFETY WHEN INTERVIEWING AND/OR DEALING WITH OTHER PEOPLE. NWNT PROPOSES THAT AN OFFICER – TO MAXIMIZE HIS SAFETY – SHOULD PLACE HIS HANDS IN A LOCATION (NEAREST TARGET) CORRESPONDENT TO WHERE THE SUBJECT HAS HIS HANDS (HIS NEAREST WEAPON). I ADVOCATE THIS PROXEMICS TACTIC DURING MY USE OF FORCE, WORKPLACE VIOLENCE, AND OF COURSE, DE-ESCALATION CLASSES. THIS POSITIONING WILL GIVE AN OFFICER A TACTICAL EDGE WHEN A PERSON TRIES TO STRIKE THE OFFICER. AN ANCILLARY BENEFIT OF NWNT IS THAT, IN MANY CASES, THE SUBJECT SENSES THAT THE OFFICER IS CONFIDENT AND READY FOR ANYTHING THE SUBJECT MIGHT THROW HIS (THE OFFICER'S) WAY, WHICH IN SOME CASES, PREVENTS THE BAD GUY FROM LAUNCHING AN ATTACK.

ESTABLISH & MAINTAIN SAFE & NON-THREATENING "INTERVIEW" POSITIONS.

BESIDES NWNT, I ALSO ADVOCATE USING BODY LANGUAGE THAT IS NON-THREATENING BUT THAT ALSO OFFERS AN OFFICER THE ABILITY TO RESPOND QUICKLY AND EFFECTIVELY TO A SPONTANEOUS ATTACK. THE JACK BENNY STANCE IS MODELED AFTER THE FAMOUS COMEDIAN WHO USUALLY KEPT HIS LEFT (SUPPORT) HAND ON HIS LEFT CHEEK WHILE FOLDING HIS RIGHT ARM ACROSS HIS ABDOMEN

AND HIS RIGHT HAND UNDER HIS ELBOW. IT IS A RELAXED AND NON-OFFENSIVE POSITION THAT PROVIDES OFFICERS THE ABILITY TO BLOCK INCOMING STRIKES AND TO QUICKLY COUNTERSTRIKE. ANOTHER STANCE IS **THE FATHER MURPHY,** WHICH AGAIN, IS A NON-COMBATIVE STANCE WITH THE OFFICERS LEANING FORWARD IN A "CONCERNED AND ATTENTIVE (LISTENING)" POSE WITH THE PALM OF HIS STRONG HAND FACING DOWN AND ON TOP OF HIS SUPPORT HAND. THIS IS CALLED THE FATHER MURPHY BECAUSE THIS STANCE LOOKS LIKE WHAT A PRIEST MIGHT ASSUME WHEN SPEAKING OR COUNSELING A MEMBER OF HIS CONGREGATION.

SPEAK SLOWLY, SPEAK SOFTLY AND SPEAK AS SINCERELY AS POSSIBLE. BE AS SOOTHING AND REASSURING AS POSSIBLE. NOT ONLY SHOULD YOUR WORDS BE REASSURING AND NON-THREATENING, BUT MAYBE EVEN MORE IMPORTANTLY, THE TONE AND PACE OF YOUR VOICE NEEDS TO BE JUST AS REASSURING AND NON-THREATENING. NO MATTER HOW SOPHISTICATED AND WELL-INTENDED YOUR WORDS AND DE-ESCALATION TECHNIQUES, IT ALL GOES TO HELL IF YOUR *TONE* BETRAYS ANGER, DISDAIN, OR DISRESPECT!

ALWAYS SHOW RESPECT!

ALWAYS REMEMBER: EMPATHY NEVER FAILS! *COMMUNICATE TO THE EDP OR MENTALLY DISTURBED PERSON THAT YOU UNDERSTAND WHAT HE IS FEELING, EVEN IF YOU DON'T REALLY UNDERSTAND EXACTLY WHAT IT IS THAT IS DISTURBING HIM. "DAVID, I KNOW YOU ARE UPSET. LET ME ASSURE YOU, SIR, THAT I AM HERE TO HELP YOU..."*

BEGIN THE INTERACTION HUMANELY. INTRODUCE YOURSELF! *BE FRIENDLY. ACT LIKE A HUMAN BEING. INTRODUCE YOURSELF. ASK HIS NAME. TELL HIM WHY YOU ARE HERE. TRY TO FIND OUT WHAT HIS PROBLEM IS, ETC. I REFERENCE THE TACTICAL-TEN CAR STOP, WHICH HAS HELPED COPS CUT OUT THE BULLSHIT, LIKE MOTORISTS' COMPLAINTS, EXCUSES, VERBAL INSULTS, RESISTANCE, ETC. DURING CAR STOPS. YOU MIGHT ALSO EXAMINE "THE BUD SHULL" STORY LATER IN THIS BOOK, WHERE SGT. SHULL DEFUSES A MENTALLY ILL AND SUICIDAL PATIENT BY STARTING OFF WITH A GREAT INTRODUCTION.*

CONSIDER THIS, IF YOU WILL: WE SHOULD ALWAYS WALK INTO SITUATIONS LIKE A GENTLEMAN. IF YOU WALK IN LIKE A BULLY, A HARD ASS, OR AN ASSHOLE, THERE IS NO WAY YOU CAN BACK DOWN. IF YOU IMMEDIATELY PULL

YOUR BATON, TASER, OR GUN, WELL, HELL, IT IS IMPOSSIBLE TO GO FROM THAT TO TALK. OR...

ALWAYS ORDER YOUR TACTICS FROM LOW TO HIGH. NEVER HIGH TO LOW!

ASK QUESTIONS, LISTEN REFLEXIVELY, FIND OUT THE FACTS AND GET THINGS RIGHT! *"MR. DOLAN (USE HIS NAME AS OFTEN AS REASONABLE TO HUMANIZE THE INTERACTION), "I WONDER IF YOU COULD DO ME A FAVOR? TELL ME IF I AM UNDERSTANDING WHAT YOUR PROBLEM IS. I HEAR YOU SAYING THAT THE REASON YOU ARE UPSET IS...."*

ASK HIM TO DO YOU A SOLID (A FAVOR). BY PARAPHRASING, YOU ARE USING "INTELLECTUAL DELAY." YOU ARE GIVING YOURSELF TIME TO ASSESS, PLUS, YOU ARE INTERJECTING A "FIRE BREAK" INTO THE CRISIS. TIME FOR HIM TO CALM. *ME, I HAVE ALWAYS BEEN IMPRESSED WITH THE SIMPLE POWER OF ASKING ANYONE TO DO ME A FAVOR. THEIR EARS PERK UP AND THEY SIT UP AND NOTICE. UP UNTIL RECENTLY, I THOUGHT THAT WAS JUST MY OWN IDEA, BUT RECENTLY, MY RESEARCH SHOWS THAT EXPERTS AGREE. AS OFTEN AS YOU CAN, INTERJECT TACTICAL SILENCE, OR INTELLECTUAL DELAY INTO THE MIX.*

BE HONEST WITH THE PERSON. IF HE SENSES DECEPTION, HE WILL WITHDRAW OR BECOME VIOLENT!

LATER, WHEN I TALK ABOUT "WHEN IN DOUBT, TELL HIM A STORY," THE FACT IS, YOUR STORY SHOULD **CROSS HIS EXPERIENCE WITH YOURS,** *WHICH IS ESPECIALLY EFFECTIVE WITH THE DISTURBED, WHICH IS WHAT I BELIEVE NURSE MEDELLIN WAS* SUGGESTING.

IN ONE CASE WHEN A MENTALLY DISTURBED SUBJECT TOLD AN OFFICER THAT HE WAS HEARING VOICES COMMANDING HIM TO DO TERRIBLE THINGS AND ASKED IF HE (THE OFFICER) COULD HEAR THE VOICES, THE OFFICER WISELY RESPONDED, "JOHN, I HAVE TO BE HONEST. I CAN'T HEAR THE VOICES, BUT I BELIEVE YOU WHEN YOU SAY YOU CAN HEAR THEM."

MANY EXPERTS SUGGEST THAT WE BE BRIEF WITH OUR RESPONSES. CHRISTOPHER HERTIG, AN EXPERT FROM YORK, PA., SUGGESTS THAT "THE LEAST SAID THE BETTER. THERE ARE TIMES WHEN SAYING NOTHING IS PREFERABLE. "

WHEN YOU DO ASK QUESTIONS, TRY TO AVOID CLOSE-ENDED QUESTIONS. ASK OPEN-ENDED QUESTIONS, LIKE, "PETE, CAN YOU TELL ME WHAT'S BOTHERING YOU TODAY?"

USE THE PERSON'S FIRST NAME AS OFTEN AS POSSIBLE. I KNOW I'VE SAID THIS BEFORE, BUT IT IS THAT IMPORTANT. USING HIS FIRST NAME LETS THE PERSON KNOW YOU ARE LISTENING. USING HIS FIRST NAME WHILE YOU ARE EMPATHIZING WITH WHATEVER IT IS HE IS GOING THROUGH IS DOUBLY EFFECTIVE. MORE THAN SIMPLY ASSURING HIM THAT YOU ARE LISTENING, THOUGH, THE FACT IS, THE DISTURBED SUBJECT INTERPRETS LISTENING AND PARAPHRASING AS COMPASSION AND CONSIDERATION, BOTH OF WHICH MAKES YOU MUCH LESS THREATENING IN HIS EYES!

REFLECT BACK. REFLECT WHAT YOU ARE SEEING AND HEARING! IT IS IMPORTANT TO <u>***PARAPHRASE,***</u> ***OR REPEAT BACK TO THE TROUBLED OR DISTURBED PERSON. THIS ALSO SHOWS YOU ARE LISTENING, WHICH MAKES THE EDP FEELS "HEARD," VALIDATED.***

"OKAY, PETE, YOU ARE HEARING A WOMAN. SHE IS CRYING AND SAYING AWFUL THINGS TO YOU AND NO MATTER WHAT YOU DO, YOU CAN'T MAKE HER GO AWAY...."

SHOW EMPATHY WITH YOUR BODY LANGUAGE AND TONE. PEOPLE IN CRISIS WILL RESPOND TO YOU ON AN UNCONSCIOUS LEVEL! *AS I DISCUSSED EARLIER, GETTING YOUR FACIAL EXPRESSION ("LISTENING FACE") AND BODY LANGUAGE "RIGHT" MAY TAKE SOME PRACTICE, ESPECIALLY IF YOU HAVE DONE SOME SELF-EVALUATION AND BELIEVE THAT YOUR BODY LANGUAGE AND FACIAL EXPRESSION MIGHT BE A PROBLEM IN SCENARIOS LIKE THIS. BUT FAILING THIS, WHEN YOU FIND YOURSELF IN SCENARIOS WITH DISTURBED PEOPLE, DO SOME SELF-TALK AND CONVINCE YOURSELF THAT WHAT THIS PERSON SAYS AND DOES IS CRITICALLY IMPORTANT AND THAT YOU ARE GOING TO DO YOUR BEST TO "ATTEND HIM." MAINTAINING YOUR DISTANCE, LIMITED EYE CONTACT, AND A CONFIDENT AND "AT EASE ATTITUDE" WILL ALWAYS BE HELPFUL IN CONNECTING WITH THE PERSON.*

AS FAR AS YOUR VERBAL TECHNIQUES, I SUGGEST PERUSING THE MANY DE-ESCALATION PRINCIPLES, TECHNIQUES AND STRATEGIES I HAVE DETAILED IN THIS BOOK. PICK OUT SOME THAT WORK WELL FOR YOU AND MAKE YOURSELF A DE-ESCALATION EXPERT IN THOSE AREA(S).

*ESPECIALLY IMPORTANT, THOUGH, IN THESE TYPE OF UNIQUE SCENARIOS, **FOCUS ON CALMING, MORE THAN THE CONTENT OF HIS STATEMENTS; USE SOFT, SLOW AND***

SINCERE WORDS AND TONES; NEVER INTERRUPT; NEVER GET DEFENSIVE (HE MAY ACCUSE YOU OF WEIRD THINGS); ALWAYS BE HONEST (I KNOW, ALREADY SAID); DO NOT ATTEMPT TO PERSUADE HIM OR ARGUE WITH HIM (LIKE PROFESSOR HERTIG SUGGESTED – THE LEAST SAID, THE BETTER); AND, WHENEVER POSSIBLE, USE I-STATEMENTS INSTEAD OF YOU-STATEMENTS.

AND NEVER BE AFRAID TO USE REASONABLE PERIODS OF SILENCE TO CREATE WHAT I CALL A "FIREBREAK," OR INTELLECTUAL DELAY.

AGAIN. BE HONEST WITH WHAT YOU ARE GOING TO DO AND EXPLAIN PROCEDURES BEFORE YOU TAKE ANY OF THE STEPS.

WATCH FOR VERBAL AND NON-VERBAL SIGNS OF CALM. THIS SHOULD BE AN IDEAL TIME TO PRESENT HIM WITH OPTIONS OR ALTERNATIVES.

"PETE, YOU HAVE A COUPLE GOOD OPTIONS HERE. MAYBE IT'S A GOOD TIME TO HAVE A SEAT, TAKE YOURSELF A DEEP BREATH, SO YOU CAN TELL ME WHAT IT IS YOU WANT. THE ONLY THING I CAN'T DO IS LEAVE YOU HERE. OTHER THAN THAT, IT IS UP TO YOU..."

ALLOW TIME FOR THE PERSON TO DECIDE.

IF THERE ARE RELATIVES, FRIENDS AND OTHERS ON THE SCENE, GATHER IMPORTANT INFORMATION AND FACTS THAT MAY HELP YOU RESOLVE THE ISSUE(S)!

WHENEVER PRACTICABLE, SUMMON ASSISTANCE FROM MENTAL HEALTH RESOURCES.

USE BONA FIDE DE-ESCALATION TECHNIQUES TO CALM THE EDP. REMEMBER: EMPATHY ALWAYS WORKS; PEACE PHRASES ABSORB TENSION. LISTEN REFLEXIVELY AND MIRROR CALM!

USE I-STATEMENTS INSTEAD OF ACCUSATORY YOU-STATEMENTS. "I CAN SEE THAT YOU ARE UPSET. I CAN HEAR IT IN YOUR VOICE, HANK. PLEASE TELL ME HOW I CAN HELP YOU?" IS TONS BETTER THAN A YOU-STATEMENT, LIKE: "WHAT THE HELL DO YOU THINK YOU ARE DOING, HANK. JUST STOP IT!" MORE ON I-STATEMENTS IN A LATER CHAPTER.

FORECAST WHAT YOU INTEND TO DO TO AND/OR WITH AN EDP OR MENTALLY ILL SUBJECT. TELL HIM WHAT YOU ARE ABOUT TO DO AND WHY _BEFORE_ YOU DO IT.

TELL THE SUBJECT BEFOREHAND, WHENEVER PRACTICABLE OR SAFE, WHEN YOU ARE ABOUT TO TOUCH HIM.

CONSIDER REDUCING OR ELIMINATING ANY "INFLUENCES" THAT MIGHT ESCALATE HIS EMOTIONS. FOR INSTANCE:

AVOID THESE TRIGGERS WHEN DEALING WITH THE EDP AND/OR THE SEVERELY MENTALLY ILL:

➢ WHENEVER PRACTICABLE OR SAFE, TURN OFF RED AND BLUE EMERGENCY LIGHTS. BRIGHT LIGHTS, ESPECIALLY THOSE THAT PULSATE CAN TRIGGER A PSYCHOTIC EPISODE OR ELEVATE TENSIONS.

➢ WHEN POSSIBLE, TURN OFF SIRENS. LOUD NOISES ELEVATE TENSIONS. LOUD NOISES, ESPECIALLY SIRENS, OFTEN COMPETE WITH OR ESCALATE DANGEROUS EMOTIONS, LIKE FEAR, RAGE, CONFUSION. LOUD NOISES HAVE BEEN KNOWN TO ELEVATE COMMAND VOICES!

➢ DISPERSE CROWDS AND/OR REMOVE ANY UNNECESSARY PEOPLE FROM THE SCENE (UNLESS HE/SHE OR THEY ARE PART OF THE EDP'S SUPPORT SYSTEM).

- *NEVER TRAP OR BOX-IN A MENTALLY DISTURBED OR EMOTIONALLY DISTURBED PERSON (EDP).*
- *NEVER ARGUE WITH AN EDP OR SEVERELY MENTALLY ILL PERSON.*
- *AVOID GETTING DEFENSIVE AT ALL COSTS!*
- *KEEP VERBAL CONTENT "SOFT, SLOW, SINCERE, AND SAFE." MEANING AVOID ALL TRIGGER WORDS, LIKE PRISON, INSTITUTION, DEATH, GUN, INSANITY, ETC.*
- *THE PERSON WILL OFTEN TRY INSULTS, PROFANITY, THREATS, INTIMIDATION, AND ACCUSATIONS. AVOID REACTING AGGRESSIVELY OR DEFENSIVELY. ALWAYS BE PATIENT AND TAKE YOUR TIME!*
- *ACCEPT ACCUSATIONS, EVEN FALSE AND BASELESS ACCUSATIONS, WITH PATIENCE AND UNDERSTAND- ING. RESPOND WITH PEACE AND/OR STRIP PHRASES, SUCH AS:*
- *"I HEAR THAT, JOHN..."*
- *"YOU'RE PROBABLY RIGHT, PETE..."*
- *"I UNDERSTAND, HELEN..."*

➤ "YOU'RE PROBABLY RIGHT, JEANNE. WHAT WOULD YOU SUGGEST WE DO?"

❖ THE APPEARANCE OF A FIREARM BRANDISHED DIRECTLY AT AN EDP CAN PROVOKE AGGRESSION, EVEN VIOLENCE. BE AWARE THAT AN OFFICER ASSUMING A TYPICAL STANCE WITH FEET SPREAD, FIRMLY PLANTED, DOMINANT SHOULDER BACK, AND HAND RESTING ON GRIP OF HIS HOLSTERED GUN DOES NOT SCREAM OUT TO A MENTALLY ILL PERSON EXPERIENCING A CRISIS, "WE ARE HERE TO HELP YOU!"

NO SURPRISES. SURPRISE ESCALATES THE MENTALLY ILL! TELL THE SUBJECT WHAT YOU ARE ABOUT TO DO BEFORE YOU DO IT (FORECAST).

FORECASTING COMFORTS ALL PEOPLE IN CRISIS. ESPECIALLY AN EDP OR A MENTALLY ILL PERSON   !

ALWAYS FOLLOW-THROUGH ON WHAT YOU PROMISE – OR FORECAST - THE PERSON YOU ARE GOING TO DO!

LEARN TO BE PATIENT WHEN DEALING WITH THE MENTALLY DISTURBED OR EDP. EXPECT TO HAVE TO REPEAT DIRECTIONS OR REQUESTS. EXPECT TO HAVE TO ANSWER QUESTIONS OVER AND OVER.

ANOTHER MENTALLY ILL PERSON INTERSECTS WITH POLICE!

WHITE PLAINS, N.Y.

DEADLY POLICE RESPONSE TO MEDICAL ALERT FOCUS OF TRIAL

TOM HAYS, ASSOCIATED PRESS
NEWS STORY

WHEN KENNETH CHAMBERLAIN SR.'S MEDICAL ALERT PENDANT ACCIDENTALLY WENT OFF FIVE YEARS AGO, THE 68-YEAR-OLD TOLD POLICE WHO SHOWED UP HE WAS FINE, BARRED THEM FROM ENTERING HIS APARTMENT AND REPEATEDLY ASKED THEM TO GO AWAY.

THEY DIDN'T. THAT SET OFF A TENSE, 90-MINUTE STANDOFF THAT ENDED WITH THE **MENTALLY ILL,** FORMER MARINE, SHOT DEAD.

WHAT LIVED ON WAS A DISPUTE OVER WHETHER THE BLACK VICTIM WAS AN ARMED THREAT WHEN A WHITE OFFICER FIRED HIS GUN -THE QUESTION CENTRAL TO A FEDERAL CIVIL CASE SET TO GO ON TRIAL THIS WEEK. OPENING STATEMENTS ARE SCHEDULED FOR WEDNESDAY (NOVEMBER 9, 2016).

THE DEADLY 2011 ENCOUNTER AT CHAMBERLAIN'S APARTMENT IN SUBURBAN WHITE PLAINS – MUCH OF IT CAPTURED ON AUDIOTAPE – WAS A PRECURSOR TO THE NATIONAL **DEBATE OVER THE USE OF FORCE BY POLICE IN COMMUNITIES OF COLOR AND THE RESPONSE TO CALLS** INVOLVING EMOTIONALLY DISTURBED PEOPLE.

IN COURT PAPERS, THE DEFENSE HAS INSISTED THE SHOOTING WAS JUSTIFIED, SAYING ANTHONY CARELLI, THE POLICE OFFICER WHO SHOT CHAMBERLAIN, "USED DEADLY FORCE ONLY AS A LAST RESORT."

133

A TALE FROM THE STREETS
THE BUD SHULL STORY

SGT. E.B. "BUD" SHULL, PICTURED ABOVE ON THE LEFT, IS A 30-YEAR VETERAN OF THE WILSON BOROUGH PD (EASTON, PA.). BUD IS AN OUTSTANDING PPCT DEFENSIVE TACTICS; SPONTANEOUS KNIFE DEFENSE; GROUND AVOIDANCE & GROUND ESCAPES AND DISRUPTIVE STUDENT MANAGEMENT INSTRUCTOR. BUD AND I HAVE HAD NUMEROUS INTELLECTUAL DISCUSSIONS CONCERNING THE DE-ESCALATION OF AGGRESSIVE AND HOSTILE PEOPLE.

IN SGT. SHULL'S OWN WORDS

THIS WAS ONLY A FEW MONTHS AGO (JULY, 2016). I WAS CALLED TO THE EMERGENCY AREA OF EASTON HOSPITAL. THE DISPATCHER IDENTIFIED THE PROBLEM AS A PATIENT-OUT-OF-CONTROL. I ARRIVED WITH THREE OTHER OFFICERS AND WAS MET BY A MALE NURSE, A FEMALE PSYCHIATRIC NURSE, A PHYSICIAN AND TWO OF THE HOSPITAL'S SECURITY STAFF.

THE MALE NURSE, LOOKING ANGRY, MAYBE FRIGHTENED, MAYBE A COMBINATION OF BOTH, INTERCEPTED ME A FEW YARDS INSIDE THE ER. "SARGE," HE SAID IN A RAGGED VOICE, "YOU'RE GOING TO HAVE TO TAZE THIS CRAZY SONOFABITCH!"

"OKAY", I RESPONDED, WITHOUT MOVING A MUSCLE TOWARD MY TASER, OR ANY OTHER OF MY WEAPONS, FOR THAT MATTER. "MAYBE BEFORE I DO ANYTHING, I COULD GATHER SOME OF THE SALIENT FACTS HERE, IF YOU DON'T MIND, THAT IS."

IT WAS TOUGH FINDING OUT THE FACTS SINCE EVERYONE WAS EXCITED BECAUSE THE PATIENT HAD CAUSED SUCH A DISTURBANCE, THROWING SOME HOSPITAL STAFF AROUND, YELLING EPITHETS AND THREATS, HURLING EQUIPMENT AND FURNITURE AROUND THE ER. AFTER CALM PREVAILED, HOWEVER, I LEARNED THAT THE "OUT-OF-CONTROL PATIENT" HAD BEEN HOSPITALIZED ON AN INVOLUNTARY COMMITMENT - BASED UPON A 302 PETITION INITIATED BY HIS FAMILY, WHO WERE FRIGHTENED AND CONCERNED ABOUT HIS BIZARRE BEHAVIOR AND SUICIDAL IDEATION. THE PHYSICIAN AND THE PSYCHIATRIC NURSE INTIMATED THAT THEY CONCURRED THAT THE PATIENT HAD SOME EXTREME EMOTIONAL AND MENTAL ISSUES AND, IF HE WASN'T SEDATED AND HOBBLED, HE CONSTITUTED A DANGER TO ANYONE AND EVERYONE WITH WHOM HE CAME IN CONTACT, INCLUDING HIMSELF.

IN THE HOUR OR SO BEFORE MY ARRIVAL, THE PATIENT HAD BEEN EXTREMELY VIOLENT, HAD REFUSED A SEDATIVE, INSISTED ON LEAVING THE HOSPITAL – WHICH WAS ILLEGAL BASED ON THE 302-PETITION COMMITTING HIM TO THE HOSPITAL. AND, OH YES, HE CONTINUALLY INSISTED – "ONE WAY OR THE OTHER – " HE WAS GOING TO KILL HIMSELF...

" "LIKE I SAID, SARGE," INTERJECTED THE MALE NURSE. " YOU'RE GOING TO HAVE TO TAZE THE CRAZY BASTARD!"

"YOU'RE PROBABLY RIGHT, SIR," I REPLIED TO THE NURSE. ALTHOUGH, TRUTHFULLY, MAKING THE PATIENT 'RIDE THE LIGHTNING' – ALWAYS A POSSIBILITY – WAS NOT YET AMONG MY TOP TACTICAL CHOICES. NOT YET, ANYWAY. NOT UNTIL I HAD A CHANCE TO SIT DOWN AND CHAT WITH THE PATIENT FOR A FEW MINUTES. I NEEDED TO FIND OUT THE FACTS, AT LEAST FROM HIS POINT OF VIEW.

I TURNED FROM THE MALE NURSE AND LOOKED AT THE PHYSICIAN AND THE PSYCHIATRIC NURSE. "I WONDER IF YOU WOULD HAVE ANY OBJECTIONS TO ME

TALKING WITH YOUR PATIENT BY MYSELF? MY OFFICERS WILL BE RIGHT OUTSIDE IN CASE ANYTHING HAPPENS."

"REALLY?" SAID THE DOCTOR, USING A TONE THAT IMPLIED I WAS BAT-SHIT CRAZY.
* * * * *
THE PATIENT WAS HORACE COOPER (NOT HIS REAL NAME). I KNEW THAT BECAUSE, EARLIER, WHEN I GATHERED FACTS FROM THE ER STAFF, THE FIRST PIECE OF INFORMATION I ASKED FOR WAS HIS NAME. I FELT, MAYBE, JUST MAYBE, IF I COULD USE HIS FIRST OR LAST NAME,
Along WITH GIVING HIM MINE, IT COULD HELP MAKE THE COMING INTERACTION PERSONAL, OR HUMANIZED.

I RECOGNIZED HIM IMMEDIATELY. COOPER HAD BEEN A STAR BASKETBALL PLAYER FOR EASTON HIGH 10 OR SO YEARS BACK. HE WAS ABOUT 6'8", A MUSCULAR BLACK MAN, AND THE FIRST THING HE DID WAS LOOK UP AT ME FROM WHERE HE WAS SPRAWLED ON THE DECK AND SAY SOMETHING LIKE, "GOOD, A COP WITH A GUN. TELL YOU WHAT, DOG, ONE WAY OR THE OTHER, YOU'RE GOING TO HAVE TO SHOOT ME DEAD!"

THE THING WAS, HORACE COOPER SPOKE IN SUCH A WAY THAT VIOLENCE – IN THE FORM OF SUICIDE – SEEMED INEVITABLE. BUT TO ME, HIS BODY LANGUAGE WAS TELLING ME HE WAS NOT AGITATED. THERE WAS LITTLE TENSION IN HIS FACE AND TORSO AND HE WAS NOT PACING. JUST SITTING, YOGA STYLE. HIS ARMS CROSSED LOOSELY ON HIS CHEST. I DECIDED TO GO WITH WHAT HIS BODY LANGUAGE WAS TELLING ME, NOT HIS WORDS.

"I HEAR YOU, MR. COOPER," I SAID. "THE LAST THING I WANT IS FOR YOU TO HURT YOURSELF. MAYBE, IF YOU DON'T MIND, WE COULD JUST CHAT FOR A MOMENT ABOUT WHAT YOU SEE AS THE PROBLEM HERE. TRY TO SEE IF THERE IS ANYTHING WE CAN DO TO GET YOU SOME HELP. HOW'S THAT SOUND?"

COOPER TURNED HIS HEAD DOWN, SAYING NOTHING.

"OK, HOW ABOUT THIS. FIRST THINGS, FIRST. MAYBE WE COULD SET SOME GROUND RULES? RULE NUMBER ONE. I DON'T WANT TO GET HURT HERE. AND FOR SURE, WHATEVER HAPPENS, I DON'T WANT YOU TO GET HURT. RULE TWO. I AM HERE TO HELP YOU. I AM HOPING YOU CAN HELP ME HELP YOU."

COOP STOOD AND MOVED TO A NEARBY STOOL. ONE OF THOSE STOOLS THAT CAN MOVE YOU AROUND IN A CIRCLE. HE SAID NOTHING. JUST CROSSED HIS BIG ARMS ON HIS CHEST AND LOOKED DOWN.

I PULLED A NEARBY STOOL CLOSE TO COOPER AND SAT. "MR. COOPER, I COULD REALLY USE SOME HELP HERE. CAN YOU HELP ME HELP YOU?"

COOPER SAID NOTHING BUT GAVE ME A BEGRUDGING NOD OF HIS HEAD. GOOD, I THOUGHT. THE FIRST STEP IN BUILDING HORACE COOPER A COMPLIANCE MENTALITY.

"FIRST OF ALL, I AM WONDERING IF I COULD POSSIBLY CALL YOU HORACE INSTEAD OF MR. COOPER? MY NAME IS BUD. BUD SHULL, BY THE WAY. YOU CAN CALL ME BUD, IF YOU WISH."

I REACHED OUT A FRIENDLY HAND AND HE STUDIED IT FOR A SECOND BEFORE TAKING IT AND GIVING IT A SHAKE.

"YEAH. SURE CHIEF. YOU CAN CALL ME HORACE. HOW'D YOU KNOW MY NAME?"

"WELL HECK, HORACE." I RESPONDED WITH MY BEST SMILE. "I MUST HAVE SEEN YOU PLAY LIGHTS OUT A DOZEN OR SO TIMES BACK IN THE DAY. ONCE OR TWICE, MAYBE THREE TIMES ON SECURITY, THE OTHERS AS A BIG FAN. YOU WERE SOMETHING ELSE. AND, BY THE WAY, IT'S NOT "CHIEF," IT'S BUD."

HE SMILED A TIGHT, HUMORLESS SMILE. "WELL, HELL, BUD, NOW THAT WE ARE PRACTICALLY PALS, MAYBE YOU CAN DO ME A SOLID AND HELP ME GET THE FUCK OUT OF HERE?"

I FIGURED I HAD GIVEN HORACE A FEW MINUTES OF WHAT I CALLED SITUATIONAL OR TACTICAL DELAY BETWEEN WHEN HE BASICALLY ASKED ME TO SHOOT HIM DOWN LIKE A DOG AND THIS MOMENT WHEN HE SEEMED TO HAVE RELAXED A BIT. NOT MUCH. BUT A BIT.

"HORACE, I TRULY WISH THAT I COULD, BUT..."

HORACE SHOOK HIS HEAD VIOLENTLY AND SPAT OUT THESE WORDS. "WHAT I THOUGHT. JUST LIKE ALL THE OTHER ASSHOLES HERE, WHO..."

I HELD OUT A HAND TO STOP HIM. "HORACE, PLEASE. LET ME FINISH. I SAY WHAT I HAVE TO SAY, THEN YOU GET YOUR SAY. THAT IS RULE NUMBER THREE. IT IS THE WAY THESE THINGS WORK. OKAY?"

I EXPLAINED THAT I HAD NO CHOICE. NEITHER DID HE. LEAVING HERE WAS ILLEGAL, BASED UP THE 302 HIS FAMILY HAD SIGNED.

HORACE POPPED OFF THE STOOL AND STARTED PACING. I CONTINUED SITTING, BUT I WAS PREPARED TO CUE MY RADIO AND SIGNAL MY BACK-UP TO POUR IN HERE.

"I CAN'T STAY HERE, BUD. I GOT ME PEOPLE COMING IN HERE TO VISIT THIS WEEKEND (THIS WAS A THURSDAY). SO ONE WAY OR THE OTHER, I GOTTA LEAVE, WITH OR WITHOUT YOUR HELP..."

I SMILED AND POINTED AT HIS STOOL AND SAID, "HORACE, PLEASE." AND HE SAT.

"MY TURN AGAIN," I SAID. "I AM ASKING THAT YOU LISTEN TO WHAT I SAY NEXT. WHY? BECAUSE THIS IS IMPORTANT. HOW AND WHEN YOU GET OUT OF HERE, WHICH IS WHAT YOU REALLY WANT, IS UP TO YOU. IT DEPENDS ON WHAT YOU DO AND HOW YOU DO IT IN THE NEXT FEW MINUTES. YOU MAY GET OUT OF HERE IN FIVE DAYS, 30-DAYS, MAYBE EVEN A YEAR, BASED UPON HOW YOU RESPOND IN THE NEXT MINUTE OR SO.

"THOSE PEOPLE ON THE OTHER SIDE OF THIS ROOM – THE DOCTOR THE NURSES – THEY WANT TO HELP YOU, BUT THEY CAN'T DO THAT UNTIL YOU ALLOW YOURSELF TO GET SEDATED, IF THAT IS STILL REQUIRED, I DON'T KNOW, AND EVALUATED. YOU CANNOT LEAVE AND I CANNOT ALLOW YOU TO LEAVE, BUT YOU CAN CONTROL HOW LONG YOU STAY.

"AND ONE MORE THING, HORACE. LOOKING AT YOU, I BELIEVE YOU INTIMIDATE THOSE PEOPLE OUT THERE. THEY'RE AFRAID OF WHAT YOU WILL DO, IF THEY TRY TO TREAT YOU. THAT IS WHY I AM HERE NOW.

"BUT HERE'S THE THING, OUTSIDE THAT DOOR," I PAUSED TO POINT AT A SLIDING GLASS DOOR COVERED WITH A GREEN CURTAIN. "ARE THREE OFFICERS CHOMPING AT THE BIT TO POUR IN HERE AND PUT YOU IN CUFFS. BELIEVE ME, THEY WILL NOT BE INTIMIDATED BY YOU. I DON'T THINK YOU NEED THAT KIND OF PROBLEM HERE TODAY. I SURE DON'T WANT THAT TO HAPPEN, EITHER.

"SO, MY FRIEND, YOU HAVE SOME GOOD OPTIONS HERE. YOU CAN WORK WITH ME NOW AND YOU AND I CAN WORK SOMETHING OUT TO HELP YOU, OR I WILL HAVE NO CHOICE BUT TO USE FORCE. IT IS TOTALLY UP TO YOU, HORACE. OKAY. YOUR TURN." I SAID SOFTLY, POINTING AT HIM.

HORACE LOOKED DOWN AND SHOOK HIS HEAD. "I DON'T KNOW, BUD." HE SHOOK HIS HEAD AND WRUNG HIS BIG HANDS ON HIS LAP. "FUCK ME. I JUST DON'T KNOW."

DESPITE HIS WORDS, I SENSED THAT HORACE WAS RESIGNED TO HIS FATE. HE SEEMED COMPLETELY CALM AND HIS BREATHING HAD GONE FROM FAST TO SLOW. I ALSO SENSED THAT IT WAS TIME TO MAKE THE SALE.

"SO, I AM ASKING YOU ONCE AGAIN TO HELP ME HELP YOU. I AM ASKING YOU TO VOLUNTARILY GET YOURSELF IN THAT GURNEY OVER THERE AND ALLOW THE STAFF TO DO WHAT THEY HAVE TO DO. BELIEVE ME, HORACE, IT WILL BE GOOD FOR YOU, GOOD FOR ME, GOOD FOR EVERYBODY. WHAT DO YOU SAY?"

HORACE LOOKED UP AND STUDIED THE GREEN CURTAIN BLOCKING HIS VIEW OF MY THREE OFFICERS SUPPOSEDLY HUDDLED BEHIND THE SLIDING GLASS DOOR. I COULD TELL HE WAS WEIGHING HIS OPTIONS.

"HORACE, LET ME ASK YOU THIS. IS THERE ANYTHING I CAN DO OR SAY TO GET YOU TO GO ALONG WITH THE PROGRAM TONIGHT? I REALLY HOPE THERE IS."

"MAYBE YOU CAN GET THEM TO FIRE THAT BIG REDNECK NURSE? HE TREATED ME LIKE A THUG, BUD."

"TRUST ME," I RESPONDED. "YOU GET INTO THAT GURNEY, AND I WILL GET YOU A DIFFERENT NURSE WITH A WHOLE DIFFERENT ATTITUDE, HORACE."

LESS THAN A MINUTE LATER, HORACE COOPER PUT HIMSELF IN THE GURNEY. MAYBE IT WAS MY PROMISE TO BRING IN A DIFFERENT NURSE, THIS ONE A VETERAN BLACK NURSE, WHO TREATED HIM WITH EXCEPTIONAL KINDNESS. MAYBE IT WAS MY AGREEMENT TO HANG AROUND FOR AN EXTRA HALF-HOUR TO MAKE SURE EVERYTHING WENT WELL AND THAT THE PROPER HOSPITAL STAFF WERE AWARE AND HAD CONFIRMED THAT. IN THE END, HE WAS COOPERATIVE AND CALM THROUGHOUT THE ENTIRE PROCEDURE.

ABOUT TWO MONTHS LATER, I WAS INFORMED BY A CONTACT AT THE HOSPITAL THAT HORACE WAS DISCHARGED FROM THE PSYCH WARD IN LESS THAN TWO WEEKS. I HAVEN'T HEARD FROM HIM SINCE.

DO YOU WANT TO KNOW WHAT I THINK ABOUT DEALING WITH THE MENTALLY ILL AND/OR THE EMOTIONALLY DISTURBED? I THINK WHEN YOU COMMIT YOURSELF TO TREATING EVERYBODY WITH RESPECT AND TREAT THEM HOW YOU WOULD HOPE TO BE TREATED UNDER THE SAME CIRCUMSTANCES, EVEN THE MENTALLY ILL OR SUICIDAL PERSON – MAYBE, **ESPECIALLY** THE MENTALLY ILL OR EMOTIONALLY DISTURBED – THEY RESPOND IN A POSITIVE MANNER.

I THINK IN HORACE'S CASE, I ENCOUNTERED HIM IN A VULNERABLE STATE OF MIND. HE WAS GIVEN NO QUARTER BY THE HOSPITAL STAFF, WHO I THINK VIEWED HIM AS A VIOLENT, DANGEROUS, AND MENTALLY DISTURBED THREAT. MAYBE EVEN A THUG. I ALLOWED HIM TO FEEL AS IF HE WAS BEING HEARD. MAYBE EVEN VALUED.

HERE'S ANOTHER THING. I COULD HAVE ACCOMPLISHED MY MISSION OR DUTY BY SIMPLY SUMMONING MY GUYS TO RUSH IN HERE AND HOOK HIM UP. EITHER WAY, HE WOULD HAVE ENDED UP COMMITTED. OF COURSE, I DON'T THINK I AM GOING OUT ON THE

PROVERBIAL LIMB HERE WHEN I SPECULATE THAT SOMEONE, MAYBE EVERYONE WOULD HAVE GOTTEN HURT. MAYBE WORSE.

AND ANOTHER THING. WHEN THIS THING ENDED WITH COOP BEING SAFELY COMMITTED, MY TROOPS AND I WERE TREATED LIKE HEROES MARCHING THROUGH A NEWLY-LIBERATED TOWN. THINK ABOUT IT. IMPROVED RELATIONSHIP WITH THE HOSPITAL, NO INJURIES, NO LAWSUITS, NO FUNERALS. JUST A FEW EXTRA MINUTES OF LISTENING AND CHATTING.

THE THIRD-PERSON SOLUTION TO DE-ESCALATING THE MENTALLY ILL & EMOTIONALLY DISTURBED

SERGEANT SHULL IS TOO MODEST TO SAY THIS OUT LOUD, BUT THE METHODS HE USED TO CALM AND RESOLVE THE SAFETY-RELATED ISSUES THAT HORACE COOPER PRESENTED AT THE EASTON HOSPITAL BORDERS ON GENIUS. ONE OF THE MOST SUCCESSFUL CALMING METHODS SUGGESTED FOR DEALING WITH MENTALLY ILL, SUICIDAL AND/OR SEVERELY EMOTIONALLY DISTURBED PEOPLE IS EXACTLY WHAT SGT. SHULL CREATED IN THE ABOVE SCENARIO (THE BUD SHULL STORY).

The **Third-Person De-escalation Approach** is similar to techniques used is hostage crisis negotiations, in which a ("neutral") third-person is brought in to negotiate a solution. Usually, it is easier for this third-person to take a neutral stance and to allow time and space for the disturbed person to calm down. The third-person is not an arbiter trying to decide right from wrong, but a **non-judgmental facilitator of (tactical) communications.**

The Third-Person in a hospital setting (psychiatric facility) should be a trained staff member who was not present at the start of a conflict (like Bud Shull). A staff member, or officer, who was there at the start of the incident, may be seen as part of the problem. In a hospital setting, the ideal third-party would be someone who knows the patient and enjoys a degree of rapport.

And, finally, research suggests that ineffective personal relationships and interactions are major factors in the escalation of a volatile mental health subject. Intolerant environments, of which nurses and cops are a big part of, and ineffective interactions influence behavior **more than even severe psychiatric symptoms.**

CHAPTER 6. WHY THEYATTACK?

"THE THING THAT I ASK YOU TO UNDERSTAND ABOUT DE-ESCALATION TECHNIQUES IS
THAT WHEN A PERSON IS UNDER STRESS, THE RAREST COMMODITY IS
COMMON SENSE."

HARRY HAMMER RESPONDING TO CRITICISM FROM A STUDENT AT ONE OF HIS ADVANCED DE-ESCALATION TECHNIQUES SEMINARS (CIRCA 2013) THAT 'ALL THESE TECHNIQUES AND STUFF ARE NOTHING MORE THAN COMMON SENSE."

OKAY. HOW ABOUT IT, CLASS? CAN YOU NAME SOME OF THE REASONS WHY PEOPLE ATTACK US?

I ASK THIS QUESTION AT SOME POINT DURING MY ADVANCED DE-ESCALATION TECHNIQUES SEMINARS. I USUALLY HAVE A FLIPCHART OR WHITEBOARD CLOSE BY AND WRITE ALL THE RESPONSES. I GET SIMILAR RESPONSES AND I WRITE THEM ALL. MANY, IF NOT ALL, THE RESPONSES ARE IN SOME WAY REASONABLE. AND THEN, AFTER THE RESPONSES PETER OUT, I WRITE AN EXAGGERATEDLY LARGE AND RED QUESTION MARK.

?

THE FACT IS, OFTENTIMES WE DO NOT HAVE A CLUE WHY A PERSON DECIDES TO PHYSICALLY ATTACK US. ONLY HE KNOWS WHAT IS IN HIS HEAD AT THAT TIME. ONLY HE KNOWS WHAT CONTRIBUTED TO THAT DECISION. MAYBE, SOMEHOW, SOMEWAY, THE SENSITIVE AND PRECOCIOUS WIRES, FIBERS AND DENDRITES'FIBERS GET CROSSED SENDING A FLURRY OF FIERY IMPULSES THROUGH THE SYNAPSES, AND BANG, WE HAVE AN ATTACK.

SOUNDS LIKE I AM SAYING THAT WE CAN EXERCISE NO OR LITTLE CONTROL OVER EVENTS? WHICH IS THE FURTHEST THING FROM REALITY. WHAT I AM SAYING IS THAT THERE MAY BE SCORES OF REASONS WHY SOMEONE ELECTS TO ATTACK US,

*BUT BY USING **MEASURED, DELIBERATE AND PROFESSIONAL LANGUAGE AND TACTICS** WHILE MAINTAINING CONTROL OF OURSELVES, WE CAN, IN OVER 97% OF SCENARIOS, SEE THE ATTACK COMING BEFORE THE FIRST PUNCH IS LAUNCHED AND MINIMIZE THE CHANCES THAT THE PUNCH WILL EVER BE LAUNCHED.*

*BUT, BEFORE WE EXAMINE SOME OF THE UNIVERSAL FACTORS BEHIND ALL ATTACKS AGAINST LAW ENFORCEMENT AND CITIZENS-AT-RISK, MAYBE WE PEER INTO THE MIRROR AND DO SOME SELF-EXAMINATION. WE ARE GOING TO LOOK AT SOME OF THE ATTITUDES, WORDS AND/OR ACTIONS THAT ALMOST ALWAYS **PISS OFF PEOPLE**. THINGS THAT WE (COPS, CORRECTION OFFICERS, SECURITY AND LAY CITIZENS) DO OR SAY THAT COULD INFLAME AN ALREADY COMBUSTIBLE PERSON TO PHYSICALLY ATTACK US, OR EVEN THINGS THAT MAY EVEN MOTIVATE A TOTALLY COOPERATIVE PERSON TO VERBALLY RESIST AND/OR LODGE A COMPLAINT AGAINST US.*

P.O.P LIST – THINGS THAT PISS OFF PEOPLE

"GIVING YOUR UNDIVIDED ATTENTION TO AN AGGRESSIVE PERSON – LISTENING ATTENTIVELY WITHOUT BEING JUDGMENTAL,
MAKING GOOD EYE CONTACT, GIVING VERBAL CUES SHOWING THAT
YOU ARE INTERESTED IN WHAT HE IS SAYING, GIVING OFF SOME OPEN BODY
LANGUAGE AND WHEN YOU SPEAK, SPEAKING IN A CALM VOICE, HAS A COMFORTING EFFECT BECAUSE TYPICALLY
THE BELLIGERENT PERSON FEELS VALIDATED AND LESS LIKELY TO TURN TO VIOLENCE."

THE COMMUNITY POLICING DISPATCH, AUGUST 14, 2016 ISSUE.

*WAR PHRASES OR WORDS. THERE ARE WORDS THAT YOU CAN USE THAT CAN BRING CALM TO A SITUATION. WE WILL TALK ABOUT THOSE A LITTLE LATER. THERE ARE ALSO WORDS THAT CAN INFLAME AND INCENSE PEOPLE. THESE WORDS I CALL **WAR WORDS**, BECAUSE THEY WILL ALMOST ALWAYS TRIGGER, OR ESCALATE EMOTIONS. COMBUSTIBLE EMOTIONS NO COP OR COUNSELOR WISHES FOR, UNLESS, OF COURSE, HE IS INSANE. OR A MASOCHIST, ONE...*

WAR OR TRIGGER WORDS

➢ *"WE CAN DO THIS THE EASY WAY OR THE HARD WAY!" TO MANY, IF NOT ALL BAD GUYS I HAVE DEALT WITH, THESE WORDS ARE A CHALLENGE. IF HE IS ALONE, HE VERY WELL MIGHT DECIDE NOT TO TEST YOU. BUT IF HE IS WITH OTHERS – ESPECIALLY SOMEONE WHOSE OPINION MEANS SOMETHING,*

HE WILL FIGHT YOU DAMN NEAR EVERY TIME. AND THE THING IS, HE MAY KNOW THAT, IN THE END, HE WILL END UP IN JAIL, THE HOSPITAL, OR EVEN WORSE, BUT TO MOST BAD GUYS THE IMPORTANT THING IS TO SOUND GOOD AND LOOK GOOD TO WHOEVER IT IS LOOKING ON. REMEMBER. ALL ARRESTS ARE PUBLIC EVENTS AND MAYBE THE ONLY THING THAT THE BAD GUY HAS LEFT IN HIS LIFE – MAYBE THE ONLY THING THAT HE HAS SOME CONTROL OVER – IS HIS REPUTATION. HIS STREET CRED. YOU TAKE THAT AWAY, YOU ARE TAKING HIS "FACE," AND FACE IS ALWAYS A FIGHTING ISSUE!

SHORT TALE FROM THE STREET

AL DALE WAS A FRIEND OF MINE AS WELL AS A PA. STATE P.O. WORKING OUT OF THE ALLENTOWN DISTRICT. AL WAS ON THE LOOK FOR A PAROLE VIOLATOR. ON THE NIGHT OF THIS STORY, HE LEARNED FROM A RELIABLE SOURCE THAT THE PAROLEE (CHRISTIAN COLTER) WAS SEEN AT A PRIVATE CLUB IN DOWNTOWN ALLENTOWN, SO AL, WHO LATER ADMITTED TO ME THAT HE LET HIS EGO GET THE BETTER OF HIM, ROCKETED IN HIS STATE CAR TO THAT CLUB AND WAITED OUTSIDE FOR COLTER TO SAUNTER BY.

DALE HAD HIMSELF A WHEEL GUN BACK IN THE DAY. A SMITH OR A PYTHON, I THINK. HE WAS A WANNA-BE COP, WHICH IS WHY WE CALLED HIM "TROOPER AL." KNOWING TROOPER AL AS I DID, I WOULD BET ALL MY JACK REACHER BOOKS THAT HE SPENT MOST OF THE TIME WAITING FOR COLTER SLAPPING A HAND ACROSS THE CYLINDER AND WATCHING THE DULL GOLD EYES OF THE SIX BULLETS SPIN IN A SLOW CIRCLE. MAYBE IMAGINING HOW HE WOULD TAKE THE BIG PAROLEE DOWN AND HOOK HIM UP.

Not more than 15-minutes passed, and sure enough, Colter did saunter by, unfortunately, with a gorgeous woman, dressed to the nines, at his side. If it was me, the first thing I would have thought was, crap, this bad boy is not going to want to go back to The Wall easy-like. But, hell, that was me. Trooper Al was something else.

So, as Colter strolled past the state car, Dale pushed a button and the passenger window descended with a whirring sound.

"Yo, Colter," Dale called sharply.

"Yo, parole man," Colter responded, without slowing his gait.

"You are under arrest for technical parole violations," Dale told me he said to Colter, who was a huge man with black belt martial arts skills.

"Not a good time, parole man," said Colter. "Tomorrow works swell for me."

Again, if this was me and I was by myself, that might have been good enough for me. "Okay, Colt. See me in my office sometime in the morning. Have fun tonight." And then drive the hell off.

But this was Trooper Al we are talking about. So, he said what he always said in these type of situations. "Listen, man, we can do this the easy way or the hard way. What's it going to be?"

Dale told me that Colter stopped, leaned over and whispered something in the woman's ear, and then casually sidled over to the state car. He leaned his big shoulders and face inside the open window and smiled. Alan could clearly see traces of white powder – probably cocaine – around the big black man's nose and mouth.

COLTER LOOKED AROUND THE INSIDES OF THE CAR, PERHAPS CHECKING TO MAKE SURE THAT THE CHUBBY PAROLE MAN DIDN'T HAVE HIMSELF ONE OR MORE PAROLE AGENTS LURKING AND WAITING IN THE BACK SEAT. THEN, HE SAID, IN WHAT DALE DESCRIBED AS A CASUAL, SINGSONG VOICE: "OKAY, PAROLE MAN. THAT'S PRETTY FUNNY. HOW ABOUT YOU SHOWING ME THE HARD WAY?"

DALE JUST SAT THERE, TAPPING A FINGERNAIL ON HIS STEERING WHEEL AND STARING BLANKLY AT HIS RADIO DIAL.

COLTER CHUCKLED AND SAID, "WHAT I THOUGHT," TURNED AND TOOK THE HAND OF THE WOMAN AND STROLLED OFF INTO OBLIVION.

IT WAS YEARS BEFORE CHRIS COLTER EVER WAS SEEN AGAIN BY ANY AUTHORITY FIGURE. THAT AFTER HE WAS BUSTED FOR AN ARMED ROBBERY IN A TOWN OUTSIDE BERLIN, MARYLAND.

BACK TO THE P.O.P. LIST

CALM DOWN!" TELLING A PERSON WHO IS UPSET TO CALM DOWN ALMOST ALWAYS HAS THE OPPOSITE EFFECT. WHY? THINK ABOUT IT A SECOND. HAVE YOU EVER BEEN TRYING TO MAKE A POINT OR ARGUING WITH ANOTHER PERSON AND THAT PERSON SAYS, "HEY, CALM DOWN!" I KNOW IT HAS HAPPENED TO ME AND MY REACTION WAS "I **AM CALM!**" HERE YOU ARE, THINKING YOU ARE ARGUING RATIONALLY, DOING YOUR BEST TO KEEP YOUR EMOTIONS IN CHECK, AND THIS JERK IS REPRIMANDING YOU (HE MAY NOT BE, BUT IT SURE FEELS LIKE IT) AND CHIDING YOU TO KEEP CALM. BOTTOM LINE: AVOID TELLING THE OTHER PERSON TO CALM DOWN. INSTEAD, **MODEL, OR MIRROR CALM.** SHOW HIM "CALM," INSTEAD OF TELLING HIM TO CALM DOWN. **OR, SILENCE** FOR A FEW MINUTES MAY HAVE A CALMING EFFECT. GIVE HIM TIME TO COLLECT HIS THOUGHTS.

CULTURAL STEREOTYPES. MANY YEARS BACK, I WAS ACCOMPANIED BY A YOUNG COP ON AN ARREST. THE PAROLEE IN QUESTION HAD VIOLATED TWO TECHNICAL VIOLATIONS AND HAD NO HISTORY OF VIOLENCE. I HAD ASKED THE LOCAL POLICE DEPARTMENT FOR BACKUP BECAUSE NONE OF THE OTHER PAROLE AGENTS

WERE AVAILABLE AND OUR PROTOCOL DISCOURAGED US FROM RETRIEVING VIOLATORS BY OUR LONESOME.

THE PAROLEE IN QUESTION WAS BLACK AND THE OFFICER WAS WHITE. THIS WAS A RURAL AREA AND THE COPS HAD A NASTY REDNECK REPUTATION IN THOSE DAYS. ANYWAY, WE APPROACHED THE FARMHOUSE WHERE MY GUY WORKED, AND AS WE WERE CLOSING IN FROM BOTH SIDES, UP PULLS MY GUY ON A TRACTOR. TEUBOLLT (HIS NAME) SHOUTED OUT AT ME AND WAVED, EVEN THOUGH HE COULD CLEARLY
SEE THE OFFICER, WHO NOW WAS JOGGING TOWARD HIM, ONE HAND INDEXING THE BUTT OF HIS SMITH.

HE HAD TO KNOW I WAS CARRYING BAD NEWS WITH ME, BUT STILL, HE GAVE NO SIGN OF RESISTING AND MADE NO MOVE TO RUN.

BEFORE I COULD SAY ANYTHING TO THE PAROLEE, HOWEVER, THE OFFICER APPROACHED AND SAID PRECISELY THESE WORDS: "HEY, LEROY, HOW ABOUT PEELING YOUR ASS OFF THAT TRACTOR BEFORE I YANK YOU OFF IT, HOMEBOY!"

I FROZE RIGHT THERE. BUT MY PAROLEE STILL DID NOT RESIST, HE JUST DROPPED HIS HEAD AGAINST THE STEERING WHEEL AND WAITED FOR ME TO APPROACH, REACH OUT MY HAND AND SAY, "COME ON, BOLT, " I GOTCHA."

WE MADE THE ARREST, THAT RACIST COP AND I, BUT I AM SURE BAKER TEUBOLLT NEVER FORGOT THE WORDS THAT OFFICER USED THAT DAY, SO MANY YEARS AGO.

HOMEBOY AND LEROY ARE EXAMPLES OF CULTURAL STEREOTYPES EXACERBATED BY BAD TONE.

I'VE WITNESSED MANY CULTURAL STEREOTYPES UTTERED BY LAW ENFORCEMENT, CORRECTIONS, SECURITY AND PAROLE OFFICERS. NOT ALL OF THESE RESULTED IN PHYSICAL ATTACKS. MANY RESULTED IN THE SUBJECT GRITTING HIS TEETH BUT COOPERATING. HOWEVER, YOU'D BETTER BELIEVE THAT, DEEP DOWN, HE RESENTED THE INSULT.

I HAVE WITNESSED SEVERAL OTHER SIMILAR INSULTS THAT I KNOW PISS OFF PEOPLE (POP), INCLUDING:

- ➤ *"PEPE, PEDRO OR JUANITA FOR A LATIN, SPANISH OR MEXICAN.*
- ➤ *"AUNT JEMIMA (AS IN, "WHY DON'T YOU GO IN THE KITCHEN AND RUSTLE US UP SOME PANCAKES AND LET US DO OUR JOBS HERE, AUNT JEMIMA?" WHICH WAS PROBABLY THE MOST EGREGIOUS AND RACIST CULTURAL STEREOTYPE I HAD EVER WITNESSED)!*
- ➤ *"YO, EINSTEIN!" SPOKEN SARCASTICALLY TO SOMEONE WHO HAS SAID OR DONE SOMETHING THE OFFICER THOUGHT TO BE STUPID OR DUMB*
- ➤ *DICKHEAD, DICKWAD, ASSHOLE, AND SO MANY OTHER SIMILAR INSULTS TAGGED SOMEWHERE AT THE BEGINNING, MIDDLE OR END OF AN ORDER, ET AL.*
- • *"WHY? BECAUSE I JUST TOLD YOU SO. THAT'S WHY!"* I REFERENCE THE FIVE-STEP HARD STYLE DETAILED EARLIER IN THIS BOOK. IN THE FIVE-STEP, OFFICERS ARE ENCOURAGED TO *ASK INSTEAD OF COMMANDING A SUBJECT TO DO SOMETHING, AND IF THAT SUBJECT ASKS "WHY?," OFFICERS ARE ENCOURAGED TO ALWAYS "SET CONTEXT," MEANING TO EXPLAIN WHY.*
- • *"HEY, WHAT'S YOUR PROBLEM?" INSTEAD OF THIS WAR PHRASE, TRY "WHAT'S THE MATTER, SIR? HOW CAN I HELP?"*
- • *"WHATEVER?" THIS "WHATEVER" IS NOT A CULTURAL STEREOTYPE, OF COURSE, BUT IT CAN BE PARTICULARLY COMBUSTIBLE (A WAR WORD), IF UTTERED TO A SUBJECT, SUSPECT, OR CITIZEN WHO MAY BE QUESTIONING AN OFFICER'S ACTIONS OR WORDS, OR WORSE, WHEN AN OFFICER USES THIS WAR WORD ("WHATEVER") WHEN A SUBJECT IS TRYING TO EXPLAIN HIS FEELINGS OR REASONS FOR HIS ACTIONS OR "ATTITUDE."*
- • *"YOU, GET OVER HERE!"*
- • *"I AM NOT GOING TO TELL YOU AGAIN!"*
- • *"DID YOU HEAR WHAT I SAID?"*
- • *"SHUT UP AND LET ME TALK!"*
- • *"DO YOU WANT TO GO TO JAIL?"*

- *"SIT DOWN!" THESE WAR WORDS WERE UTTERED BY A PA. STATE PAROLE AGENT WITH A PHD FROM A RESPECTED UNIVERSITY. BUT THE PAROLEE WHOM SHE WAS ADDRESSING HAD VERBALLY ATTACKED HER IN FRONT OF SEVERAL OTHER PAROLE OFFICERS AND I BELIEVE SHE WAS INFLUENCED BY PEER PRESSURE (I WILL GO INTO **INFLUENCES,** LIKE PEER PRESSURE, IN A SUBSEQUENT CHAPTER) TO PUT THE PAROLEE IN HIS PLACE. THIS IS AN UNDERSTANDABLE REACTION BECAUSE IT IS A **NATURAL REACTION.** THE THING IS, HOWEVER, A* NATURAL REACTION IS USUALLY A DISASTROUS REACTION, *BECAUSE THE PAROLEE WAS IN **HIS OWN HOME AT THE TIME** FACING UNWELCOME INVADERS. THIS WAS A TERRITORIAL ISSUE.*

- *"'CAUSE THOSE ARE THE RULES. THAT'S WHY!" IN A LATER CHAPTER I WILL GO INTO HOW TO ARTFULLY EXPLAIN TO A BELLIGERENT SUBJECT WHY* THOSE ARE THE RULES. *IT IS BETTER TO PATIENTLY AND PROFESSIONALLY EXPLAIN TO A PERSON, SUCH AS SAYING SOMETHING LIKE, "*SIR, LET ME TELL YOU WHY THIS RULE IS IN EFFECT..."

- *"HEY, PAL, IT'S NONE OF YOUR BUSINESS (WHAT HAPPENED TO YOUR BUDDY)." VERBAL JUDO SUGGESTS THAT, UNLESS IT PRESENTS A SAFETY HAZARD, ALWAYS GIVE AN EXPLANATION. AFTER ALL, WE DERIVE OUR AUTHORITY FROM THE PUBLIC TRUST, SO EVERYTHING WE DO IS EVERYBODY'S BUSINESS.*

- **FAILING TO TAKE CONTROL OF THE INTERACTION.** *THE NUMBER ONE REASON WHY COPS GET KILLED, ACCORDING TO AN FBI STUDY, IS THAT THE OFFICER DID NOT TAKE CONTROL OF AN INTERACTION. THE SECRET TO CALMING AN **EDP (EMOTIONALLY DISTURBED PERSON) IS** TACTICAL EMPATHY. LISTEN ACTIVELY TO WHAT THE DISTURBED PERSON IS SAYING AND INTERVENE PROFESSIONALLY BASED UPON WHAT YOU INTERPRET IS THE PROBLEM AS HE (EDP) SEES IT, AND OF COURSE, HOW YOU (THE OFFICER) UNDERSTANDS IT.*

- **PROFANITY.** *I SAVED THIS TRIGGER (WAR WORD) FOR LAST. NOT BECAUSE IT IS THE WORST MISTAKE AN OFFICER CAN MAKE, BUT BECAUSE I BELIEVE PROFANITY IS A GIVEAWAY (SIGN) THAT AN OFFICER IS BEGINNING TO LOSE*

CONTROL OF HIS WORDS (WORDS MATTER). CURSE WORDS USED BY AN OFFICER SCARES THE BEJESUS OUT OF ME! I AM SERIOUS ABOUT THIS. TO ME, PROFANITY BY AN OFFICER IS A VIOLATION OF ONE OF THE CRUCIAL RULES OF THE MANAGEMENT OF AGGRESSIVE PEOPLE, WHICH TEACHES THIS GOLDEN RULE: "AN OFFICER MUST NEVER GIVE VOICE TO HIS INNER-VOICE. THE INNER-VOICE IS THE NATURAL INNER VOICE THAT WHISPERS TO YOU, "HERE COMES ANOTHER FUCKING ASSHOLE."

ANOTHER OBVIOUS DRAWBACK IS THE OPTICS OF PROFANITY IN THE CONTEXT OF THE SCENARIO. MEANING, DARN NEAR EVERYBODY HAS A SMART OR CELL PHONE. ERGO, IN ANY INTERACTION WITH A SUBJECT OR A SUSPECT, THERE IS AN EXCELLENT CHANCE THAT THE INTERACTION WILL BE VIDEOTAPED OR FILMED. FOLLOWING THAT TO ITS LOGICAL CONCLUSION, IS ANYTIME YOU INTERACT WITH ANOTHER PERSON IN PUBLIC THERE IS A GOOD CHANCE THAT INTERACTION – YOUR WORDS AND YOUR BODY LANGUAGE – WILL BE FILMED AND MADE PUBLIC TO POTENTIALLY THE ENTIRE WORLD! *THIS COULD BE EMBARRASSING AND EVEN LEGALLY CATASTROPHIC IF THAT INTERACTION TURNS PHYSICAL AND YOU COMBINE VIGOROUS FORCE WITH THE USE OF PROFANITY.*

WHICH BRINGS UP ONE OF MY PRIMARY DE-ESCALATION POWER PRINCIPLES: "ALWAYS CONDUCT YOURSELF IN PUBLIC AS IF YOUR WORDS AND ACTIONS ARE BEING PRESERVED FOR EVERYONE TO SEE AND HEAR (BEING FILMED OR TAPED)."

ANOTHER DRAWBACK OF PROFANITY, ESPECIALLY IN A CRISIS, IS THAT PROFANITY IS USUALLY PERSONAL AND EMOTIONAL AND RARELY PROFESSIONAL. IN MANY CASES, THE PERSONAL USE OF PROFANITY OFTEN BUILDS GROUND FOR THE SUBJECT TO ATTACK THE OFFICER, EITHER ON THE SCENE, OR LATER, IN COURT AND/OR IN THE MEDIA!

FOR INSTANCE, IN ONE MEMORABLE SCENARIO (AT LEAST MEMORABLE TO ME), DURING AN ARREST OF A PAROLE VIOLATOR, THE PAROLEE VERBALLY ATTACKED ONE OF THE OFFICERS ON MY ARREST TEAM WITH WHOM HE (THE PAROLEE) HAD SOME PERSONAL

ISSUES. THE PAROLE OFFICER WENT BERSERK, LOST CONTROL, AND CALLED THE MAN A "GUTLESS MOTHERFUCKER" IN THE PRESENCE OF HIS FAMILY.

THE SCENE PREDICTABLY EXPLODED AND THE FAMILY INTERVENED PHYSICALLY AND WE PLAYED HELL GETTING THE PAROLEE SAFELY OUT OF THE HOUSE. TWO WEEKS LATER, AT HIS PROBATION VIOLATION HEARING BEFORE A COMMON PLEAS JUDGE, THE SUBJECT'S MOTHER TESTIFIED THAT A PAROLE OFFICER CALLED HER SON A MOTHERFUCKER IN FRONT OF HER. SHE THEN STATED THAT HER SON HAD NEVER HAD SEX WITH HER AND SHE THEN BROKE DOWN IN TEARS.

THE JUDGE THEN REPRIMANDED ME AND MY ARREST TEAM FOR THEIR LACK OF PROFESSIONALISM AND FOUND THAT THE PROBATIONER SHOULD BE RELEASED.

*THERE ARE A ZILLION OF THESE EXAMPLES OF CATASTROPHIC AND ESCALATING WAR WORDS USED BY NOT ONLY POLICE AND OTHER LAW ENFORCEMENT OFFICERS. USED ALSO BY HEALTH CARE, EDUCATION AND OTHER (NON-LAW ENFORCEMENT) PROFESSIONALS. THE ABOVE ARE ONLY SAMPLES OF WORDS OR PHRASES I HAVE PERSONALLY WITNESSED. THE IMPORTANT THING IS THAT EACH OF THE ABOVE WORDS OR PHRASES ARE ENDED WITH A **PARENTHETICAL** "ASSHOLE" IN THE MIND OF THE RECIPIENT OR VICTIM OF THESE WAR PHRASES.*

WE ARE OFTEN RESPONSIBLE FOR THE DEEP RIFT BETWEEN US (LAW ENFORCEMENT, ET AL) AND THE PUBLIC. WE GO IN FOR AN ARREST BUT OFTEN DISRESPECT EVERYBODY ELSE IN THE AREA. IN SOME SCENARIOS IN WHICH I WAS INVOLVED, WE BAG THE GUY, BUT WHEN A RELATIVE – IN ONE CASE THE PROBATIONER'S MOTHER – TRIES TO ASK US WHY WE ARE TAKING HER GUY AWAY, WE TELL HIM OR HER TO GET THE HELL OUT OF OUR WAY, "IT'S NONE OF YOUR BUSINESS."

GAVEN DEBECKER ON WHY THEY ATTACK US

"THERE IS ONE MAIN PRINCIPLE THAT UNDERLIES ALL DE-ESCALATION TECHNIQUES
RANGING FROM
INTERPERSONAL COMMUNICATIONS TO MANAGING BELLIGERENT PEOPLE: EMPATHY
ABSORBS TENSION."

DR. GEORGE THOMPSON, FOUNDER OF VERBAL JUDO, ON "THE LANGUAGE OF CALMING
PEOPLE."

J.A.C.A AND DE-ESCALATION

"WHEN A PERSON IS UPSET AND RAVING ON, YOU CAN ALWAYS
FIND THE SOLUTION IN HIS OWN WORDS."

JACA IS THE ACRONYM USED BY DE BECKER IN "THE GIFT OF FEAR" SUGGESTING SEVERAL KEY FACTORS UNDERLYING WHY PEOPLE ATTACK OTHER PEOPLE. HERE WE GO:

JUSTIFICATION

ALTERNATIVES

CONSEQUENCES &

ABILITY

*J*USTIFICATION.

DE BECKER POSTULATED THAT A MAJOR REASON WHY A PERSON WILL ATTACK AN AUTHORITY FIGURE IS THE BELIEF THAT THE AUTHORITY PERSON SAID OR DID SOMETHING THAT JUSTIFIED AN ATTACK. THE THING TO REMEMBER IS THAT EVERYBODY HAS THEIR OWN INTERPRETATION OF "JUSTIFICATION" IN EVERY SITUATION. NEVERTHELESS, A PHYSICAL ATTACK WILL PROBABLY NOT BE PERPETRATED UNLESS THE ELEMENT OF JUSTIFICATION EXISTS.

UNDERSTANDING THAT ALMOST ANYTHING CAN REPRESENT JUSTIFICATION TO AN AGGRESSIVE PERSON, I BELIEVE ONE OF OUR OBJECTIVES MUST BE TO ELIMINATE OR AT LEAST MINIMIZE THE LIKELIHOOD OF JUSTIFICATION.

HERE ARE A FEW TACTICS DESIGNED TO MINIMIZE THE POSSIBILITY OF JUSTIFICATION:

<u>ALWAYS BE NICE UNTIL YOU CAN NO LONGER BE NICE!</u> YES, I AM AWARE THAT MANY OF US BELIEVE THAT BEING NICE IS BEING WEAK. BUT I BELIEVE THE EXACT OPPOSITE IS TRUE. BEING NICE IS PROBABLY THE LAST THING A BAD GUY EXPECTS FROM FIVE-OH WHEN HE IS ACTING LIKE A COLOSSAL ASSHOLE. IT CREATES SURPRISE AND THE FACT IS, SURPRISE WEAKENS RESISTANCE. BEING NICE ALSO SURPRISE IN MANY CASES, WEAKENS RESISTANCE. ANOTHER KEY FACTOR IS THAT ELEVATES THE ELEMENT OF

*JUSTIFICATION BECAUSE BYSTANDERS – EVEN THOSE CLOSE TO THE SUBJECT – CAN SEE THE CONTRAST BETWEEN THE BAD GUY ACTING LIKE A MANIAC AND THE OFFICER, WHO IS LISTENING, OPEN, FLEXIBLE, AND BEING EMPATHIC IN RESPONSE TO THE MANIACAL BAD GUY. THIS IS IMPORTANT BECAUSE OFTEN, MEMBERS OF THE AUDIENCE WILL GOAD THE BAD GUY INTO ATTACKING OR RESISTING AN OFFICER WHO IS ACTING LIKE A HARD-ASS. IN THIS CASE, BEING THE HARD-ASS **BUILDS GROUND THAT JUSTIFIES RESISTANCE AND RETALIATION!***

YOU MAY HAVE WITNESSED THIS PHENOMENON. A FRIEND OR FAMILY MEMBER OR EVEN A STRANGER WITNESSING THE INTERACTION (REMEMBER: ARRESTS OR INTERACTIONS ARE ALL PUBLIC EVENTS!) WILL SAY SOMETHING TO ENCOURAGE THE SUBJECT TO COOPERATE FOR HIS OWN GOOD. I HAVE SEEN IT ON SEVERAL OCCASIONS.

DEPERSONALIZE. *EXPECT VERBAL HOSTILITY, EVEN THREATS AND ATTEMPTS TO INTIMIDATE. GIRD YOURSELF EVEN BEFORE THE INTERACTION TO KEEP YOUR COOL AND TO AVOID TAKING VERBAL HOSTILITY PERSONALLY. ONE WAY TO LOOK AT IT IS THAT THIS IS ONLY A JOB. THE WAY I LOOK AT IT, THOUGH, IS THAT I GET WHAT THE BAD GUY IS TRYING TO GOAD ME INTO DOING, AND I WILL BE DAMNED IF I AM GOING TO ALLOW THAT SONOFABITCH TO GET AWAY WITH IT!*

SEPARATE AND SUPPORT. *VERBAL JUDO CALLS THIS TACTIC THE CUT & HERD. EITHER WAY, THE IDEA IS TO SEPARATE THE SUBJECT OR SUSPECT FROM HIS AUDIENCE. WITHOUT HIS AUDIENCE, WHOM OFTENTIMES OFFER HIM SUPPORT AND COURAGE, JUSTIFICATION MELTS AWAY.*

SEPARATING ALSO SUPPORTS THE CLIENT, SUBJECT OR SUSPECT BY ELIMINATING EMBARRASSMENT OR HUMILIATION THAT OFTEN COMES WITH AN INTERACTION WITH LAW ENFORCEMENT.

AND POSSIBLY, THE MOST DISASTROUS TACTIC(S) THAT UNSKILLED COPS USE WHEN CONFRONTING RESISTANT PEOPLE BECOMES APPARENT WHEN YOU LOOK AT THE FOLLOWING SEMINAL STUDY...

THE LA STUDY ON THE 10 AWFUL TACTICS OFFICERS USE WITH RESISTANT PEOPLE.

"WHEN WE SEE OURSELVES ONLY AS A HAMMER, WELL, EVERYONE ELSE HAS TO LOOK LIKE A NAIL."

JAMES O. SMITH, FORMER TRAINING DIRECTOR, PA. BOARD OF PROBATION AND PAROLE

"10 CATASTROPHIC STEPS."

THIS 2000 STUDY EXAMINED TACTICS THE "AVERAGE POLICE OFFICER" USES WHEN CONFRONTING A PERSON WHO RESISTS HIS ORDERS OR COMMANDS.

1). THE OFFICER ISSUES A COMMAND, OR ORDER, TO THE SUBJECT.

2). THE SUBJECT OFFERS SOME RESISTANCE.

3). THE OFFICER REPEATS THE COMMAND.

4). THE SUBJECT AGAIN REFUSES TO OBEY AND/OR OFFERS VERBAL RESISTANCE.

5). THE OFFICER NOW <u>ESCALATES TO THREATS.</u>

6). THE SUBJECT BECOMES MORE ADAMANT IN HIS REFUSAL/RESISTANCE.

7). THE OFFICER NOW <u>ESCALATES TO PHYSICAL FORCE.</u>

8). THE SUBJECT RESISTS.

9) THE OFFICER <u>HESITATES.</u>

10. HESITATION GETS THE OFFICER IN A LEGAL JACKPOT, INJURED, OR
 KILLED!

ALTERNATIVES. RESEARCH SHOWS THAT EVEN WHEN A PERSON BELIEVES HE HAS JUSTIFICATION, HE MIGHT NOT ATTACK IF WE INTRODUCE GOOD OPTIONS INTO THE EQUATION. YOU MAY RECALL THAT IN VERBAL JUDO'S MAGICAL FIVE-STEP HARD STYLE, OFFICERS ARE ENCOURAGED TO ASK INSTEAD OF COMMAND, SET THE CONTEXT; AND GIVE THE SUBJECT ALTERNATIVES. GIVING GOOD OPTIONS IS AN IMPORTANT STEP IN THE PROCESS OF DEFUSING DIFFICULT AND AGGRESSIVE PEOPLE.

IN EFFECT, THIS MEANS THAT A PERSON WITH WHOM WE INTERACT IS FAR MORE LIKELY TO ATTACK WHEN HE IS **UNDER THE INFLUENCE** OF DRUGS, ALCOHOL, CULTURAL INSENSITIVITY, PREJUDICE, ANGER, PSYCHOLOGICAL, HEAVY-HANDED TACTICS BY AN OFFICER OR MENTAL/ EMOTIONAL ISSUES AND OTHER TRIGGERS OF VIOLENCE, **IF HE IS PRESENTED WITH NO OTHER ALTERNATIVE(S) TO VIOLENCE.**

THE FIVE STEP IN ACTION

A GREAT EXAMPLE OF THIS CONCEPT IN ACTION IS A MT. LEBANON (PA) POLICE OFFICER WHO HAD RECEIVED A COMPLAINT OF EXCESSIVE NOISE. I HAPPENED TO BE WITH HIM BECAUSE THE OFFICER SUSPECTED THAT A FUGITIVE I HAD BEEN TRACKING WAS HIDING IN THAT BUILDING. THE OFFICER KNOCKED ON THE DOOR AND WHEN THE

HOST OF WHAT TURNED OUT TO BE A WILD PARTY ANSWERED, THE OFFICER PROCEEDED TO APPLY THE VERBAL JUDO FIVE-STEP YEARS BEFORE I HAD EVER HEARD OF THE STRESS-REDUCTIVE TECHNIQUE (NOR, BY THE WAY, HAD THIS OFFICER).

(1) THE OFFICER **INTRODUCED HIMSELF**, A COMMON COURTESY, WHICH I ADVOCATE ALL OFFICERS AND CITIZENS DO AT THE BEGINNING OF ALL CAR STOPS AND MOST OTHER INTERACTIONS. THE OFFICER THEN **ASKED** THE HOST IF HE WOULDN'T MIND STEPPING AWAY FROM THE PARTY AND INTO THE HALLWAY.

(2) THE OFFICER **EXPLAINED THE REASON FOR HIS VISIT** (RECEIVED A COMPLAINT ABOUT EXCESSIVE NOISE).

(3) THE OFFICER OBSERVED THE OTHERS INSIDE THE ROOM. SAW THAT THE ROOM WAS HIGHLY VOLATILE. EVERYONE APPEARED TO BE DRUNK AND EVERYONE SEEMED TO BE TALKING LOUDLY. UNDERSTANDING THE EFFECT OF INTERVIEWING THE HOST IN FRONT OF THESE POSSIBLY BELLIGERENT WITNESSES, THE OFFICER **SEPARATED THE SUBJECT FROM THE POTENTIALLY EXPLOSIVE GUESTS** BY NICELY **ASKING** THE HOST IF HE WOULDN'T MIND STEPPING INTO THE HALLWAY?

(4) THE OFFICER THEN GAVE THE HOST **OPTIONS**. HE COULD CONTINUE WITH THE PARTY, IF HE WOULD AGREE TO KEEP THE NOISE DOWN. IF HE (OFFICER) HAD TO RETURN BECAUSE OF ANOTHER COMPLAINT, HE WOULD HAVE NO CHOICE BUT TO SHUT DOWN THE PARTY (CONSEQUENCES).

(5) THE OFFICER THEN CLOSED THE EXCHANGE WITH SEVERAL APT **PEACE PHRASES,** INCLUDING: *"SIR, IT IS UP TO YOU, BUT REALLY, DO YOU NEED THAT KIND OF PROBLEM HERE TONIGHT?"*

(6) **THE HOST** THANKED THE OFFICER AFTER ASSURING THE OFFICER THAT HE WOULD LOWER THE MUSIC, TAKE BETTER CONTROL OF THE PARTY, AND GUARANTEED THAT THE OFFICER WOULD NOT BE REQUIRED TO RETURN THAT NIGHT.

CONSEQUENCES

ANOTHER IMPORTANT FACTOR IN OUR QUEST TO UNDERSTAND WHY PEOPLE ATTACK US IS THE FACT THAT OFTEN AN AGGRESSIVE PERSON, WHO IS UNDER THE INFLUENCE, *WILL IGNORE THE* **IMPLICIT CONSEQUENCES OF HIS ACTIONS UNLESS THE OFFICER OR CITIZEN (AUTHORITY FIGURE) APTLY REMINDS THE SUBJECT OF THEM.** BEFORE WE GO TOO MUCH FURTHER, ALLOW ME TO CLARIFY WHAT I MEAN BY UNDER THE INFLUENCE.

I USE THE TERM "UNDER THE INFLUENCE" TO *DESCRIBE THE EMOTIONAL STATE A PERSON IS IN. THE TERM MEANS, BASICALLY, THAT A PERSON'S ACTIONS AND THOUGHTS ARE BEING INFLUENCED AND/OR CHANGED BY ONE OR MORE STRESSORS, LIKE DRUGS, ALCOHOL, ANGER, RAGE, FEAR, HUMILIATION, EMBARRASSMENT, JEALOUSY, RACISM, MENTAL OR EMOTIONAL DISTURBANCE, DOMESTIC STRIFE, FINANCIAL STRESS, DEPRESSION, ET. AL. BECAUSE OF THOSE INFLUENCES, THE PERSON ACTS, THINKS, AND SPEAKS IN SUCH A WAY THAT HE CAN BE CONSIDERED* **BRAIN DAMAGED!**

RESEARCH SHOWS THAT WHEN A PERSON IS UNDER THESE INFLUENCES, HE OR SHE IS UNABLE TO ACCESS HIS NEO CORTEX. OFTENTIMES, WHEN HE IS UNDER THESE KIND OF STRESSORS, HE WILL HAVE TRIGGERED SNS ACTIVATION, AND

*ACCORDINGLY, ESPECIALLY WHEN DEALING WITH POLICE IN CRISIS SCENARIOS, WILL BE ACTING AND THINKING FROM HIS **PRIMITIVE BRAIN.***

*STUDIES SHOW THAT MANY OF THESE INFLUENCES AFFECT PEOPLE IN SUCH A WAY THAT THEIR SYSTEM IS FLOODED WITH STRESS HORMONES, CAUSING AN SNS NERVOUS SYSTEM ACTIVATION. IMPORTANTLY, RELATIVE TO **CONSEQUENCES,** ONE OF THE MANY NEGATIVE IMPACTS OF SNS IS THAT THE SUBJECT LOSES THE **ABILITY TO PROCESS THE CONSEQUENCES OF HIS ACTIONS!***

*SO, WHAT WE HAVE HERE ARE OFFICERS AND CITIZEN AUTHORITY FIGURES DEALING WITH BRAIN DAMAGED PEOPLE. TO DE-ESCALATE THAT PERSON, THEN, IT IS INCUMBENT ON US TO **THINK AND ACT FOR THAT PERSON** AS WE HOPE HE WOULD ACT 24-HOURS OR SO FROM NOW WHEN HE IS NO LONGER "UNDER THE INFLUENCE," OR BRAIN DAMAGED.*

***PRESENTING THE CONSEQUENCES OF A SUBJECT'S ACTIONS,** THEREFORE, IS ONE OF THE ESSENTIAL STEPS TO PREVENTING AN ATTACK. CONSEQUENCES MIGHT INCLUDE ASKING THE SUBJECT IF HE IS AWARE THAT CONTINUING ON THIS PATH COULD LEAD TO HIM LOSING HIS JOB, LOSING THE ABILITY TO BE WITH HIS WIFE, GIRLFRIEND, CHILDREN, ETC. CONSEQUENCES SHOULD NOT BE STATED IN A PROVOCATIVE OR THREATENING WAY, BUT INTERJECTED IN A MEASURED WAY. IT IS ESSENTIAL TO UNDERSTAND THAT WE ARE NOT BEING JUDGMENTAL. PUNISHMENT IS THE PROVIDENCE OF THE COURT SYSTEM. WE ARE SIMPLY TELLING THE PERSON WHAT LIKELY WILL BE THE CONSEQUENCES OF HIS ACTIONS, AND HOPEFULLY, PRESENTING HIM WITH VIABLE ALTERNATIVES SO HE MIGHT AVOID THOSE CONSEQUENCES.*

ALWAYS REMEMBER. IF THE SUBJECT HAS SOMETHING TO LOSE, YOU HAVE SOMETHING TO USE.

ABILITY

TO REVIEW, THE FOUR KEY PRINCIPLES OF JACA ARE JUSTIFICATION, ALTERNATIVES, CONSEQUENCES, AND NOW,

ABILITY. _This is a simple factor proposing that even if the three other factors are present, if the_

person believes that he does not have the **ability to successfully attack and overcome the officer or citizen, he will not attack.**

In my experience, however, I have witnessed antisocial people who have waged battle against officers when it was obvious they had no chance to win. And I do mean, No Chance. No Way! _They attacked despite the almost impossible odds because they would rather lose a fight than be thought of as a coward, or a "pussy." Their street cred is a powerful influencer. They fought despite the lack of_ Ability, _despite the possibility that they would be soundly beaten, maybe even shot._

Remember, when confronted in the presence of an audience, the subject will often do whatever he perceives he needs to do to **look good and sound good.** It is important to understand that **peer pressure** is one of the most powerful influencers on most types of assaults, because losing _one's street-cred, or in some cases, honor, is humiliating to some people and as I have already documented,_ humiliation is the only emotion that crosses all cultures! _Which is why being able to separate the subject from his audience is important, but failing that ability, it becomes so important for officers to act and speak in a way as to show respect. To make sure that they do not tip over that crucial "Dignity Domino!"_

A good example of a subject maintaining his Dignity Domino is a man fighting the police, losing, being cuffed and dragged away to lockup, and later returning to his friends and family and bragging that" "I didn't take no guff from five-oh. It took damn near six of them to put me in that cell!"

Despite what I just wrote in the previous paragraph, however, those cases of attacks in the face of great odds

(INABILITY), REPRESENT LESS THAN THREE PER CENT OF INTERACTIONS. I THINK ANY OFFICER OR CITIZEN WOULD ACCEPT 97% SUCCESS AGAINST ATTACKS.

ESSENTIALS OF ESTABLISHING "INABILITY!"

MODEL NON-VERBAL COMMANDS, INCLUDING, BUT NOT LIMITED TO

CONTROLLED BREATHING – SLOW AND CENTERED IN THE ABDOMINAL AREA -CONTROLLED VOICE, CONTROLLED POSITIVE BODY LANGUAGE, CONTROLLED VOCABULARY.

ESTABLISH AND MAINTAIN SAFE PROXEMICS, INCLUDING KEEPING ONE'S HANDS OUT OF THE SUBJECT'S FACE (THREATENING AND A TRIGGER MOVE). MAINTAIN DISTANCE/DO NOT "TRAP" THE SUBJECT.

TACTICAL POSITIONING, INCLUDING GOOD CONTACT AND COVER, TRIANGULATION, RELATIVE POSITIONING, ALL OF WHICH PROMOTES THE REALITY OF POSITIONING FOR SAFETY.

NEAREST WEAPON/NEAREST TARGET, WHICH INVOLVES POSITIONING ONE'S HANDS OPPOSITE OF WHERE THE SUBJECT'S HANDS ARE. GOOD PROXEMICS ARE KEY TO THE ABILITY TO DEFUSE AGGRESSION. HOW WE STAND, WHAT WE DO WITH OUR BODY, THE DISTANCE WE ESTABLISH DURING A CONTACT. EVERYTHING. NEUTRAL FACIAL EXPRESSION, YES, BUT MAKE SURE WE MAINTAIN A "LISTENING FACE (NODDING, SMILE, ETC.)."

EXCELLENT OFFICER PRESENCE. ABILITY IS DIMINISHED WHEN MORE THAN ONE OFFICER, MAYBE EVEN THREE, ARE PRESENT. ALWAYS REMEMBER, HOWEVER, THAT POORLY USED MANPOWER ESCALATES IF POSITIONING IS POOR AND IF MORE THAN ONE OFFICER IS GIVING COMMANDS AT THE SAME TIME. OR, EVEN WORSE, WHEN CONFLICTING COMMANDS ARE YELLED SIMULTANEOUSLY. THIS LEADS TO CONFUSION ON THE PART OF

*THE SUBJECT AND CONFUSION LEADS TO FEAR OR ANGER, EACH OF WHICH CAN BE A **TRIGGER!***

*TACTICAL OFFICER PRESENCE. **TOP** MEANS THAT THE OFFICER(S) CREATE THE PERCEPTION OF BEING COORDINATED AND **IN CONTROL OF THE SCENE.** I HAVE SEEN SIX OR SEVEN OFFICERS TRYING TO CONTROL A SCENE BUT BEING SO UNCOORDINATED THAT THEY ESCALATE EMOTIONS AND RESISTANCE.*

PRECISE TACTICAL COMMANDS MAXIMIZE TOP (TACTICAL OFFICER PRESENCE) ONLY WHEN THE OFFICER GIVING COMMANDS COMMUNICATES THE FOLLOWING (WHEN TACTICALLY POSSIBLE AND SAFE TO DO SO)."

- ✓ ***WHO AM I? WHO ARE WE? IDENTIFICATION OF RELEVANT OFFICER(S) AND THEIR DEPARTMENT.***
- ✓ **WHY ARE WE HERE?** WHAT IS THE REASON FOR THE STOP, CONTACT AND/OR INTERACTION? WARRANTS? UNDER WHAT AUTHORITY?
- ✓ ***WHAT DO YOU HAVE TO DO TO REMAIN SAFE?*** DIRECTIONS AND/OR REQUEST AS TO WHAT THE SUBJECT MUST DO AND HOW TO DO IT, IF THAT IS IN QUESTION.
- ✓ ***RAM? DESCRIBE A REASONABLE ARC OF MOVEMENT.*** DESCRIBE PRECISELY WHAT EACH PERSON MUST DO IN A SCENARIO TO BE CONSIDERED "COOPERATIVE" AND TO STAY SAFE.
- ✓ **ANSWER RELEVANT QUESTIONS ON THE SCENE.** IF UNABLE (WHEN PRACTICAL) EXPLAIN WHY. POSSIBLY LEAVE A CARD WITH YOUR CONTACT INFORMATION.
- ✓ **TREAT EVERYONE ON THE SCENE WITH RESPECT.**

A TALE FROM THE STREET.

"DE-ESCALATION IS LIKE VERBAL CHESS. GETTING A PERSON WHO IS UNDER THE INFLUENCE, OR BRAIN DAMAGED, TO DO WHAT YOU WANT HIM TO DO, EVEN THOUGH IT IS OBVIOUS THAT HE DOES NOT WANT TO DO IT. AND THE TRICK IS TO MAKE

THE FOLLOWING TRUE STORY INVOLVES A CHARISMATIC POLICE OFFICER NAMED BOB FROM THE HUNTSVILLE, ALABAMA PD WHO I MET AT AN ADVANCED VERBAL JUDO INSTRUCTOR COURSE IN JACKSONVILLE, FLORIDA. I WISH I COULD REMEMBER THE LAST NAME OF THIS COLORFUL OFFICER WHO WAS TRULY AMAZING. BUT THIS WAS BACK IN 1998, MAYBE EVEN BEFORE THAT, SO 20-SOME YEARS HAVE GONE BY AND MY NOTES FROM THAT SESSION ARE UNCLEAR. NEVERTHELESS, THIS STORY REFLECTS MANY OF THE KEY PRINCIPLES, CONCEPTS AND TACTICS CENTRAL TO VERBAL JUDO, AND OF COURSE, DE-ESCALATION TECHNIQUES.

ALABAMA LIGHTNING

I HAPPENED TO BE ROLLING THROUGH MY TOUR AND HAVING ME AN UNUSUALLY UNEVENTFUL NIGHT. STILL, I HAD THIS FEELING THAT ALL COPS GET FROM TIME TO TIME. THE FEELING THAT SOMETHING BAD WAS COMING. WHICH WAS WEIRD, I GUESS, BECAUSE RIGHT ABOUT THEN, AN HOUR BEFORE GOING OFF DUTY, I ROLL ACROSS THIS VIRTUAL GIANT WEARING DENIM OVERALLS AND NOTHING ELSE. HE WAS ROARING WORDS THAT I COULDN'T UNDERSTAND AND THROWING FURNITURE OUT OF HIS HOUSE AND ONTO NOT ONLY HIS FRONT YARD BUT THE YARD OF HIS NEIGHBOR'S, AND HARD TO BELIEVE, INTO THE STREET, WHICH WAS AT LEAST 60-SOME FEET FROM HIS HOUSE.

AND WHEN I SAY "FURNITURE," I AM TALKING PRETTY HEAVY DUTY SHIT. LIKE A BIG COUCH, A RIPPED-UP EASY BOY AND EVEN A FRIGGING REFRIGERATOR. THE MAN HAD MUSCLES ON HIS MUSCLES.

ME, I HAD NEVER RUN ACROSS THIS GIANT BEFORE, AND AS I SAT IN MY CRUISER, WATCHING AND THINKING, I KNEW SURE AS I KNEW ANYTHING THAT IF I HAD TO FIGHT THIS HOMBRE, EVEN WITH LOADS OF BACKUP, SOMEONE WAS GOING TO GET HURT AND HURT BAD.

BUT THEN, I COULDN'T EXACTLY DRIVE OFF. THE MONSTER HAD SEEN ME, AS DID A FEW OF THE NEIGHBORS, EVEN THOUGH IT WAS THE MIDDLE OF THE NIGHT. SHIT! OKAY, SO I TOOK A DEEP BREATH, UNFOLDED MYSELF FROM THE CRUISER. AND APPROACHED THE GUY. I DIDN'T LIGHT HIM UP OR ANYTHING. WHY? IT OCCURRED TO ME

THAT, MAYBE, LIGHTING UP THE SCENE COULD BRING DOWN SOME BAD JUJU ON ME.

THE FIRST THING I TRIED WAS INTRODUCING MYSELF AND MY DEPARTMENT, EVEN THOUGH IT WAS WRITTEN IN BOLD BLUE ON THE DOOR OF MY CRUISER. HE SAID NOTHING IN RESPONSE. JUST CROSSED THOSE LOG-LIKE ARMS ACROSS HIS CHEST AND GAVE ME A SIDEWAYS FELONY STARE.

OH, YEAH. I HAD CALLED THIS SCENARIO IN. ASKED FOR BACKUP, BUT WHERE I PATROL, THE NEAREST OFFICER WAS LONG MINUTES AWAY. TOO LONG, BY MY RECKONING.

FIRST THING I TRIED WAS A RATIONAL APPROACH. SOMETHING LIKE, "SIR, YOU CAN'T BE DOING WHAT YOU'RE DOING. DON'T YOU KNOW?"

"YEAH MAN, I ALREADY DID IT, SO THE FUCK WHAT?" HE SAID, HIS BIG ARMS STILL CROSSED ON HIS CHEST, BUT NOW HE WAS ROCKING BACK AND FORTH ON HIS HEELS, WHICH I TOOK AS A BAD SIGN. HE SPAT A WAD OF TOBACCO JUICE CLOSE TO MY BOOTS AND SAID, "PLUS, HOW ABOUT THIS? I GOT ME SOME MORE SHIT IN THAT HOUSE OVER YONDER THAT I AM ABOUT TO TOSS, SO WHAT THE FUCK ABOUT THAT?"

AND THEN HE JUST TURNED AROUND AND SHAMBLED TO HIS PORCH AND SAT HIMSELF ON A SWING AND ROCKED BACK AND FORTH. LIT HIMSELF UP SOMETHING AND HEFTED HIMSELF A JUG FULL OF SOMETHING THAT SURE SMELLED LIKE GASOLINE. WHITE ALABAMA LIGHTNING, MAYBE.

I SAUNTERED OVER TO THE PORCH AND ASKED IF IT WOULD BE OKAY FOR ME TO SIT NEXT TO HIM. HE SHOT ME A LOOK THAT TOOK ME IN FROM HEAD TO FOOT AND MADE A SUCKING SOUND WITH HIS LIPS AND TEETH. HE TOOK ANOTHER LONG PULL AT THE JUG, THEN LOOKED AT ME AGAIN. GIVING ME THE DISTINCT IMPRESSION THAT HE WAS TAKEN ABACK THAT I WAS STILL HERE, STANDING IN FRONT OF HIM. HE SHOOK HIS BIG, SHINY BALD HEAD AND THEN HE HEFTED THE JUG TO HIS SHOULDER, TURNED HIS HEAD AND TOOK HIMSELF ANOTHER LONG PULL.

"THE FUCK I CARE, TACO?" HE GROWLED, FINALLY, NOT LOOKING AT ME. JUST EYEING THE JUG.

"WELL, I DON'T SUSPECT YOU DO CARE, SIR, BUT I SURE WISH I COULD SHARE THAT JUG WITH Y'ALL," I SAID.

WHICH MADE HIM LOWER THE JUG TO HIS LAP AND TURN HIS ATTENTION TOWARD ME. HE MADE A GESTURE WITH ONE OF HIS REAR-TIRE SIZED HANDS TOWARD A LAWN CHAIR NEXT TO HIM. AND HE ACTUALLY SMILED. IT WAS A TOOTHLESS SMILE, BUT A WELCOME SMILE NONETHELESS.

I SAT IN THE LAWN CHAIR AND AGAIN HE SMILED. AFTER A FEW MORE SECONDS, HE GENTLY PLACED THE JUG ON THE GROUND AND PUT BOTH HIS THUMBS IN HIS OVERALLS. ROCKING BACK IN THE SWING, HE ASKED ME, "WHERE'D YOU GET THEM FANCY DRIVING GLOVES, TACO?"

I KNOW BIG GEORGE (GEORGE THOMPSON, THE FOUNDER OF VERBAL JUDO) ALWAYS SAYS WHEN A PERSON IS UPSET AND STARTS RAVING, HE WILL GIVE YOU EVERYTHING YOU NEED TO KNOW TO DE-ESCALATE HIM IN HIS WORDS. SO, EVEN THOUGH HE DIDN'T SEEM TOO UPSET AT THE MOMENT, I BELIEVE WHAT GEORGE ALWAYS SAYS IS TRUE.

"DRIVING GLOVES? NO, SIRREE. ACTUALLY, THESE AIN'T DRIVING GLOVES. I HEARD SOMEONE IN THE NEIGHBORHOOD WAS MOVING STUFF, SO I PUT THESE WORK GLOVES ON. SO, WHAT DO YOU SAY, PAL? HOW ABOUT LETTING ME HELP YOU MOVE ALL THIS STUFF BACK INTO YOUR HOUSE, SO NOBODY CRASHES INTO IT. WHAT DO YOU SAY?"

"YOU'D DO THAT?" THE GUY ASKED, RAISING THE JUG TOWARD ME AND GESTURING WITH HIS HEAD FOR ME TO PARTAKE. "I'D SURELY LIKE TO SEE YOU WORK THEM PRETTY GLOVES, TACO."

I WAVED MY HAND IN FRONT OF THE JUG. "NOT NOW, IF YOU DON'T MIND, PARDNER, MAYBE AFTER WE'RE DONE, BUT HECK, YEAH," I ALMOST SANG AS I WORKED THE FINGERS OF MY GLOVES TOGETHER. "FOR SURE, YEAH, ABOUT THE FURNITURE. JUST TURN ME LOOSE. YOU AND ME."

IT'S LIKE I HAVE ALWAYS SAID. SOME COPS ARE JUST NATURAL TALKERS AND HEART-CHANGERS. YOU CAN LEARN A LOT FROM THESE TALES FROM THE STREETS, EACH OF WHICH COMPOUNDS THE CENTRAL GOAL OF DE-ESCALATION, WHICH IS TO GENERATE VOLUNTARY COMPLIANCE WITH THE MASTERY OF LANGUAGE AND ADAPTATION.

ABOUT ADAPTATION. IT IS AN ART. VERBAL JUDO PREACHES THAT TO CONNECT WITH OTHERS THROUGH TACTICAL COMMUNICATIONS, WE MUST THINK OF OURSELVES AS TACTICAL CHAMELEONS. IT IS CRUCIAL TO BE ABLE TO CHANGE, LIKE THE CHAMELEON. TO CHANGE AND ADAPT TO THE PEOPLE WE ENCOUNTER AND THE ENVIRONMENT IN WHICH WE FIND OURSELVES. TACTICAL CHAMELEONS MIGHT EVEN TALK DIFFERENTLY – USING SLANG AND JIVE IN SOME SETTINGS, REGIONAL COLLOQUIALISMS IN ANOTHER AND LOFTY AND ESOTERIC LANGUAGE IN ANOTHER.

CHAPTER 7.

"UNIVERSALS."

TACTICS THAT ALWAYS DE-ESCALATE.

"MOTHER FUCKER, IF YOU DIDN'T HAVE THAT BADGE AND GUN, I'D KICK YOUR ASS
ALL THE WAY FROM HERE TO THE FUCKING OHIO RIVER."
"I HEAR YOU, SIR. BUT THE FACT IS, I DO, AND I AM HOPING YOU AND I
CAN GET ALONG OKAY SO I DON'T HAVE TO USE EITHER. THAT WOULD
BE GOOD FOR YOU, GOOD FOR ME. GOOD FOR EVERYBODY."

PLU-PERFECT DE-ESCALATION TACTICS

*LET'S BEGIN THIS SECTION WITH **THE FIVE THINGS EVERYBODY WANTS.** BE HE A VIOLENT GANG BANGER, A POWER-RAPIST, OR A CHURCH-GOING EXECUTIVE HAVING HIMSELF A BAD DAY, IT IS ALL THE SAME. WITHOUT EXCEPTION, EVERYBODY WANTS TO BE...*

- ✓ *TREATED FAIRLY.*
- ✓ *TREATED HONESTLY.*
- ✓ *TREATED CONSISTENTLY.*
- ✓ *TREATED EQUALLY, AND PROBABLY MOST IMPORTANTLY*
- ✓ *TREATED WITH RESPECT.*

STUDIES REVEAL, YOU GIVE THE PEOPLE WITH WHOM YOU ARE DEALING THOSE FIVE THINGS, YOU GOT NO PROBLEMS. YOU TREAT A PERSON FAIRLY, CONSISTENTLY, MEANING YOU ARE STEADY AND RELIABLE ON HOW YOU TREAT PEOPLE, REGARDLESS OF THEIR SOCIAL STATUS, RACE, CRIMINAL RECORD, EQUAL TO HOW YOU TREAT OTHERS AND SHOW HIM RESPECT, WHY, HECK, YOU ARE GOLDEN. I DIDN'T MENTION HONESTY, MAINLY BECAUSE WE CANNOT ALWAYS BE HONEST WITH A CRIMINAL OR DANGEROUS PERSON IN CASES WHERE BEING HONEST MIGHT ENDANGER A

CONFIDENTIAL SOURCE, OR TIP HIM OFF ON YOUR PLANNED TACTICS.

HOW TO DE-ESCALATE ANYONE, ANYTIME, ANYWHERE

"THERE ARE SCORES OF AMAZING TACTICS, PRINCIPLES AND CONCEPTS CRITICAL TO THE DE-ESCALATION OF CASCADING VIOLENCE. BUT I THINK FIRST AND FOREMOST, YOU MUST TRULY <u>BELIEVE</u> THAT YOU CAN DE-ESCALATE ANYONE, ANYTIME. THE MIND IS AN AMAZING THING..."

HARRY HAMMER WIGDER. AUGUST, 2016, CONDUCTING AN ADVANCED DE-ESCALATION TECHNIQUES SEMINAR, TREATMENT TRENDS, ALLENTOWN, PA.

IN TRUTH, NOTHING, EVEN MY DE-ESCALATION STRATEGIES, WORKS 100% OF THE TIME. BUT, STILL, I CONTINUALLY SUGGEST THAT THE FOLLOWING (AND OTHER) TACTICS WILL WORK ALL THE TIME FOR SEVERAL REASONS. ONE OF THE MOST IMPORTANT REASONS IS, BY EMPLOYING THESE TACTICS WE ARE FIRST AND FOREMOST MAINTAINING CONTROL OF OUR OWN EMOTIONS, ELIMINATING ASSUMPTIONS AND PREJUDICE WE MIGHT HAVE CONCERNING THE PERSON OR PEOPLE WE ARE DEALING WITH, AND BY DOING THAT WE ARE CREATING AN OPEN AND FLEXIBLE APPROACH TO PROBLEMS AND DANGERS WE MAY CONFRONT. WE ARE DE-ESCALATING OURSELVES FIRST BY CREATING WHAT VERBAL JUDO CALLS A HABIT OF MIND.

ANOTHER REASON I BELIEVE THAT DE-ESCALATION NEVER FAILS IS BECAUSE, IF WE MUST USE FORCE WE ARE ALWAYS JUSTIFIED BECAUSE WE CAN SHOW WE TRIED

VERBAL PERSUASION - LIKE THE 5-STEP, DEFLECTORS, PEACE PHRASES, AND OTHER DE-ESCALATION TACTICS. THESE ARE TIME AND BATTLE PROVEN TECHNIQUES AN TACTICS THAT WILL ALLOW US TO WIN IN THE STREETS, IN THE COURTS, AND IN THE MEDIA.

THE MEDIA INFLUENCES AND AFFECTS HOW THE COURTS DECIDE OUR CASES AND THAT AFFECTS OUR SAFETY AND SUCCESS ON THE STREETS.

IN THE CONTEXT OF THIS BOOK, UNIVERSALS ARE TACTICS AND TECHNIQUES THAT HAVE PROVEN TO WORK ABOUT 97 TO 98% OF THE TIME. WHILE I KNOW THAT 98% IS NOT 100% OF THE TIME, I STILL CALL THE TECHNIQUES UNIVERSALS BECAUSE, EVEN IF THE PERSON YOU ARE ATTEMPTING TO DEFUSE CONTINUES TO ACT AGGRESSIVELY, YOU HAVE DONE ALL THAT CAN BE EXPECTED OF A PROFESSIONAL AND HAVE ESTABLISHED PRECLUSION AND JUSTIFICATION WHEN THE BAD GUY FORCES YOU TO RESORT TO FORCE. ALSO, IN YOUR ATTEMPTS TO CONNECT WITH THE OTHER PERSON, YOU ARE DE-ESCALATING THE SCENE AROUND THE SUBJECT AND THE OTHERS WHO MAY BE WITNESSING THE INTERACTION.

A TALE FROM THE STREET

OUR WORDS MATTER – WE HAVE TO "SOUND GOOD!"

A FEW YEARS BEFORE BECOMING A PA. STATE PAROLE AGENT, RAYMOND HARTMAN WAS A SECURITY SPECIALIST AT A COMMUNITY COLLEGE NEAR WILLIAMSPORT, PA. I TRAINED AND CERTIFIED RAY BACK IN THE LATE '90'S AS A PPCT DEFENSIVE TACTICS (DT) AND AS A SPONTANEOUS KNIFE DEFENSE (SKD) INSTRUCTOR. RAYMOND WAS ALSO ONE OF MY FIREARMS INSTRUCTORS, AND IN ORDER TO MAINTAIN HIS INSTRUCTORSHIP, RAY HAD TO ATTEND MY ADVANCED DE-ESCALATION AND VERBAL JUDO CLASSES. DURING ONE OF MY VJ CLASSES, RAY SHARED THE FOLLOWING STORY.

IT WAS ON ONE OF MY STROLLS THROUGH ONE OF THE CO-ED DORMITORIES THAT I RAN INTO TIGER BURWELL, WHO HAPPENED TO BE ONE OF THE COLLEGE'S TOP ATHLETES. BURWELL WAS HIGH OR DRUNK OR SOME SORT OF CONTROLLED SUBSTANCE AND WAS GOING ABOUT DESTROYING HALF OF THE DORMITORY. EVERYBODY WAS AFRAID OF TIGER – FOR GOOD REASON – SO I FOUND MOST OF THE STUDENTS – THIS WAS THE MIDDLE OF THE NIGHT, BY THE WAY – HUDDLED IN A CLUSTER AT ONE END OF THE DORM WHILE TIGER WAS THROWING RANDOM OBJECTS LIKE GARBAGE CANS, CHAIRS,

TABLES, AND BOTTLES AT THEM AND THREATENING TO BURN DOWN THE BUILDING.

I APPROACHED SLOWLY AND CAREFULLY. HE SNARLED AT ME AND GOT HIMSELF INTO A BOXER'S STANCE AND I TOLD HIM THAT HE LOOKED LIKE HE WAS THINKING OF KICKING MY ASS, AND LOOKING AT HIM, HE PROBABLY COULD DO THAT. I ASKED HIM WHY WOULD YOU WANT TO DO THAT AND JEOPARDIZE YOUR SCHOLARSHIP AND YOUR FUTURE AT THE SCHOOL? BUT HE NEVER RESPONDED. JUST TURNED AND RAN INTO THE LAVATORY.

I WAS RELUCTANT TO GO AFTER THE DRUNKEN BEAST, BUT, FRANKLY, COULD THINK OF NO ALTERNATIVE ACTION. SO, I FOLLOWED HIM INTO THE HEAD AND HE GREETED ME WITH A SLOW-MOVING HAYMAKER, WHICH I EASILY BLOCKED AND FOLLOWED THAT BY SMASHING HIM SEVERAL TIMES (TORSO, ARMS AND LEGS) WITH A COLLAPSIBLE BATON THAT I HAD BEEN ISSUED.

TIGER STUMBLED BACKWARDS, CALLED ME A MOTHERFUCKER AND TOLD ME HE WAS GOING TO RIP OFF MY ARM AND BEAT ME CONTINUOUSLY OVER MY HEAD WITH IT. HE SCREAMED SOME OTHER INCOMPREHENSIBLE THREATS INTO THE AIR, GROWLED, PICKED UP A LARGE WASTE CAN AND THREW IT AT ME.

UNDERSTANDING THAT TIGER WAS BOTH WILLING AND CAPABLE OF RIPPING OFF BOTH MY ARMS AND DRUMMING THE STAR SPANGLED BANNER ON WHAT WAS LEFT OF MY BODY, PLUS BEING STUNNED THAT FOUR OR FIVE FLUID SHOCK WAVE STRIKES TO HIS LEGS HAD LITTLE OR NO EFFECT –I BUM RUSHED HIM, BLOCKED ANOTHER PUNCH AND PUMMELED HIM WITH A SERIES OF PUNCHES AND BATON STRIKES, BEFORE TACKLING HIM AND SLAMMING THE BACK OF HIS HEAD AGAINST A SINK, AND IT WAS OVER.

THE THING IS, DURING THE ENTIRE FIGHT IN THE LAVATORY, I VERBALIZED THAT I DID NOT WANT TO GET HURT AND THAT THE LAST THING I WANTED TO DO WAS TO FIGHT WITH HIM. I EVEN GAVE HIM SOME ALTERNATIVES TO FIGHTING, LIKE, "LOOK, TIGER, WE DON'T HAVE TO FIGHT, YOU KNOW? DO WHAT I ALWAYS DO WHEN THINGS GO TO SHIT. TAKE A DEEP BREATH AND GET CONTROL OF YOURSELF AND YOU AND I CAN CLEAN UP THE MESS WE

MADE AND THEN GO OUR SEPARATE WAYS. YOU CAN DO THAT AND
ALL THAT WILL HAPPEN IS I WRITE YOU A SIMPLE CITATION THAT
WILL HAVE NO EFFECT ON YOUR COLLEGE EDUCATION OR YOUR
SPOT ON THE BASEBALL TEAM. HOW'S THAT SOUND, DUDE?"

THE BOTTOM LINE IS THAT TIGER, DESPITE BLEEDING FROM HIS
HEAD, BIT A HUGE CHUNK OF FLESH OUT OF MY CHEEK, CLIPPED ME
WITH ONE OR TWO ROUNDHOUSES BEFORE MY BACKUP ARRIVED
AND SUBDUED HIM. ULTIMATELY, WE ENDED UP IN COURT BECAUSE
I WAS FORCED BY THE COLLEGE TO CHARGE HIM WITH AGG
ASSAULT. HIS ATTORNEY COMPLAINED THAT I HAD USED
EXCESSIVE FORCE AND IT LOOKED LIKE THE CASE WOULD BE
THROWN OUT AND/OR I WOULD BE FIRED OR SUSPENDED. THAT IS,
UNTIL A COLLEGE STUDENT WHO HAD WITNESSED TIGER'S
INSANITY OF THAT NIGHT PRIOR TO MY ARRIVAL, TESTIFIED THAT
SHE COULDN'T SEE WHAT WAS HAPPENING IN THE LAVATORY BUT
HEARD TIGER, WHO HAD ME BY SIX INCHES AND ABOUT 75-POUNDS,
THREATENING TO RIP MY ARM OFF AND BEAT ME OVER THE HEAD
WITH IT, WHILE, AT THE SAME TIME, HEARING ME "BEING SO NICE
AND POLITE AND PROFESSIONAL THAT I WAS AMAZED. MR.
HARTMAN ASKED TIGER TO STOP FIGHTING AND CONTINUALLY
URGED HIM TO THINK ABOUT WHAT HE WAS DOING AND EVEN
SUGGESTED THAT TIGER THINK ABOUT HIS COLLEGE CAREER, HIS
FUTURE AND OTHER THINGS.'

I REMEMBER THINKING, EVEN BACK THEN, YEARS BEFORE I EVER
HEARD OF VERBAL JUDO OR DE-ESCALATION, THAT **WORDS
MATTER**. OF COURSE, I WON THE CASE AND THE CHARGES WERE
CARRIED OVER TO CRIMINAL COURT AGAINST BURWELL.

THINGS THAT (ALMOST) ALWAYS WORK

PEACE PHRASES. *I HAVE BEEN TEACHING MY VERSION OF WORDS AND PHRASES THAT ARE DESIGNED TO REDUCE STRESS AND TENSION FOR OVER ALMOST 30-YEARS. I CALLED THESE PHRASES "REDUCERS" BACK THEN. THEY WERE OKAY,*
BUT, ADMITTEDLY, NOWHERE AS GOOD AS VERBAL JUDO'S PEACE PHRASES.

PEACE PHRASES *ARE DESIGNED TO – LIKE* **EMPATHY** *– ABSORB STRESS AND TENSION IN CONFRONTATIONAL SCENARIOS. PERHAPS MORE IMPORTANTLY, THEY ARE ALSO ENGINEERED TO* COMMUNICATE CONCERN AND **RESPECT** FOR THE SUBJECT THAT WILL LEAD TO THE GENERATION OF **VOLUNTARY COMPLIANCE, THE GOAL OF DE-ESCALATION TACTICS.** I URGE YOU *TO CONSIDER USING ONE OR TWO OF YOUR FAVORITE PHRASES IN SITUATIONS WHEN YOU SENSE AND BELIEVE THAT CIRCUMSTANCES ARE STARTING TO ESCALATE. HERE IS A LIST OF* REDUCTIVE *PEACE PHRASES YOU MIGHT CONSIDER USING WHEN THINGS ARE BEGINNING TO GO SOUTH, OR, SIMPLY TO KEEP THINGS FRIENDLY:*

PEACE PHRASES DESIGNED TO GENERATE VOLUNTARY COMPLIANCE

"THERE ARE BASICALLY TWO WAYS, IN MY OPINION, TO MANAGE AGGRESSIVE AND HOSTILE PEOPLE. YOU CAN STAND TOE-TO-TOE AND EYE-TO-EYE AND PIT YOUR 200-POUNDS AGAINST HIS 200-POUNDS – OR, WORSE, YOUR 120-POUNDS AGAINST HIS 200-POUNDS. BEST MAN WINS! OR, YOU CAN USE MY WAY -WINOLOGY. USE HIS STRENGTH, ANGER, RAGE, AGGRESSION AGAINST HIM. STAY AT A WINNING-ANGLE AND STEP ASIDE. LET HIM EXPEND HIMSELF AGAINST NOTHING BUT AIR AS YOU TAKE CONTROL.
I HAVE TRIED BOTH WAYS AND WINOLOGY ROCKS!

HARRY HAMMER, OCTOBER 26, 2016, DSM SEMINAR, CALVARY BAPTIST CHURCH, EASTON, PA.

"SIR, FOR YOUR SAFETY AND MINE, PLEASE…"

"MR. SMITH, HELP ME HELP YOU."

"THANK YOU FOR COOPERATING. YOU COULD HAVE MADE THINGS TOUGH FOR US."

"SIR, IS THERE ANYTHING I CAN SAY TO GET YOU TO GO ALONG WITH THE PROGRAM TODAY? I SURE HOPE THERE IS."

"SIR, I WONDER IF WE COULD CHAT FOR A MOMENT?"

"SIR, REALLY, DO YOU NEED THAT KIND OF PROBLEM TONIGHT?"

"MISS, IT WILL BE GOOD FOR YOU, GOOD FOR ME, GOOD FOR EVERYBODY."

"I CAN SEE YOU ARE UPSET. TELL ME THIS, IF YOU WERE IN MY PLACE, WHAT WOULD YOU DO?"

"MR. HUGHES, YOU HAVE SOME GOOD OPTIONS HERE…"

"I APPRECIATE YOUR DOING WHAT YOU WERE ASKED (THANKING HIM FOR DOING WHAT HE WAS REQUIRED TO DO)."

"JAKE, I WONDER IF IT WOULD BE OKAY TO ASK YOU A QUESTION?"

"HELP ME UNDERSTAND WHAT YOU ARE FEELING HERE, SIR."

"IF YOU TAKE A DEEP BREATH OR TWO, YOU WILL BEGIN TO FEEL A LOT BETTER (I USED THIS PP AFTER TAKING THE GUY DOWN TO THE GROUND HARD AND HOOKING HIM UP. HE WAS SCREAMING THAT HE WAS GOING TO SUE ME AFTER HE KILLED ME. I WAS TALKING TO MAYBE DE-ESCALATE HIM, BUT ALSO FOR THE CROWD THAT HAD GATHERED AROUND US)."

"SIR, STOP FIGHTING ME. I DON'T WANT TO GET HURT (IN REALITY, YOU MAY NOT REALLY BE CONCERNED ABOUT GETTING HURT. YOU MAY BE IN TOTAL CONTROL. JUST TRYING TO CALM HIM, FEED HIS EGO, AND ARE ALSO TALKING FOR THE CROWD. WORDS MATTER)."

"SIR, YOU MAY BE RIGHT, BUT…"

"MISS, I CAN SEE THAT YOU ARE UPSET. LET'S TALK."

"DON'T WORRY, SIR. LET'S CHAT ABOUT THIS. TWO HEADS ARE ALWAYS BETTER THAN ONE."

"SIR, WOULD YOU MIND TAKING A SEAT SO WE CAN CHAT ABOUT THIS? (A FAR BETTER APPROACH THAN WHAT I WITNESSED A PAROLE OFFICER TELLING A MAN, WHO WAS IN HIS OWN HOME: "SIT DOWN, DUDE!")?

"MR. JONES, I KNOW YOU ARE UPSET. UNDER THE SAME CIRCUMSTANCES, I MAY HAVE BEEN ALSO, BUT..."

"SIR, I WONDER IF WE COULD CHAT FOR A SECOND?" (A LOT BETTER THAN, "HEY, YOU, COME HERE!").

"JOHN, YOU DON'T NEED TO FEEL ALONE. I CAN REMEMBER DOING THE SAME THING YEARS BACK..." (TELL A STORY)

"SIR, HELP ME HELP YOU." OR, "HELP ME HELP YOUR SON..."

"SIR, SEEMS YOU'VE GOTTEN YOURSELF IN A REAL SITUATION HERE. HELP ME HELP YOU."

"SIR, LOOKS LIKE YOU'RE HAVING YOURSELF A BAD DAY. WE ALL HAVE BAD DAYS. I KNOW I HAVE."

"JAKE, I WOULD FEEL THE SAME WAY, IF I WERE YOU..."

"MISS, I MAY NOT BE ABLE TO HELP YOU WITH YOUR COMPLAINT, BUT LET ME ASK MY SUPERVISOR. TWO HEADS ARE ALWAYS BETTER THAN ONE... (THIS IS A GREAT INTELLECTUAL DELAYING TACTIC. THE SUBJECT IS ANGRY AND YOU ARE DISENGAGING FOR A FEW SECONDS OR A MINUTE. GIVES HIM TIME TO CALM AND THINK THINGS OVER)."

"YOU MAY BE RIGHT, MR. DAVIS. DO YOU HAVE ANY SUGGESTIONS ON HOW WE CAN BETTER HELP YOU?"

"SIR, PLEASE BE CAREFUL MERGING BACK INTO TRAFFIC. YOUR SAFETY IS IMPORTANT TO US."

"I HEAR THAT, JOHN, BUT CAN YOU TELL ME EXACTLY WHAT I SAID OR DID THAT GOT YOU SO UPSET?"

"IT WILL BE GOOD FOR YOU, GOOD FOR ME, GOOD FOR EVERYBODY."

"SIR, YOU ARE RIGHT. I AM LATE GETTING HERE, BUT, ME, I'VE BEEN LATE FOR EVERYTHING SINCE I WAS BORN. THE THING IS, THOUGH, I AM HERE NOW AND, IF YOU LET ME IN, I BET I CAN HELP YOU WITH YOUR PROBLEM..."

THESE ARE BUT A FEW EXAMPLES OF PEACE PHRASES. THERE IS NO BLUEPRINT. YOU CAN COME UP WITH YOUR OWN, I AM SURE. THE THING ABOUT THESE STATEMENTS OR ASSERTIONS IS THAT THEY ALMOST ALWAYS REDUCE STRESS!

THE LANGUAGE OF REASSURANCE. *THIS PRINCIPLE OR TACTIC IS CRITICAL TO CALMING PEOPLE. VERBAL JUDO POINTS OUT THAT "THERE ARE HUNDREDS OF WAYS TO CALM PEOPLE, BUT **THERE IS ONLY ONE MAIN PRINCIPLE THAT UNDERLIES ALL TECHNIQUES. EMPATHY ABSORBS TENSION!"***

WHAT FOLLOWS IS WHAT I FEEL IS AN EXCELLENT REAL-LIFE EXAMPLE OF THE LANGUAGE OF REASSURANCE AND EMPATHY:

REAL LIFE EXAMPLE OF THE LANGUAGE OF REASSURANCE & EMPATHY.

IT WAS IN 1986. MY ARREST TEAM AND I PICKED UP A BIKER NAMED HARDY FOR A TECHNICAL PAROLE VIOLATION. AS WE WERE LEADING THE GUY TO THE STATE CAR, HIS WIFE BEGAN YELLING OBSCENITIES AT US AND A FEW OF THE NEIGHBORS STARTED EMERGING FROM THEIR HOMES. THEY DID NOT LOOK HAPPY AND TENSIONS WERE PICKING UP A BIT.

I PULLED ONE OF MY BUSINESS CARDS FROM MY WALLET WHILE TWO OF MY GUYS FOLDED THE PAROLEE INTO THE BACK SEAT. I WROTE MY PHONE NUMBER ON THE BACK AND WALKED TO WHERE

SHE STOOD ON HER PORCH AND OFFERED HER MY CARD, WHICH SHE REFUSED TO ACCEPT.

"HELLO, MRS. HARDY. I AM HARRY WIGDER, YOUR SON'S P.O. I AM WITH THE ALLENTOWN D.O. WE ARE TAKING YOUR SON BACK FOR TECHNICAL VIOLATIONS. THESE ARE NOT NEW CHARGES. TRUTH IS, MA'M, IF I DON'T ARREST HIM, THEY WILL ARREST ME.

"I DON'T BLAME YOU FOR BEING UPSET. BUT, IF YOU WANT, I WILL CALL YOU TOMORROW AND EXPLAIN EVERYTHING."

THE PAROLEE'S MOTHER ACTUALLY SMILED AS SHE REACHED OUT AND TOOK MY CARD.

JUMP OR STRIP PHRASES. ALL OFFICERS AND CITIZENS WHO WORK WITH MARGINAL PEOPLE EXPERIENCE VERBAL HOSTILITY. AS A MATTER OF FACT, POLICE AND CORRECTIONAL OFFICERS FACE VERBAL ABUSE DAILY. THE IMPORTANT THING IS HOW WE RESPOND. IT IS CRUCIAL BECAUSE, FACING RELENTLESS VERBAL ATTACKS CAUSES PERSONAL AND PROFESSIONAL STRESS. REMEMBER. PEOPLE IN OUR FIELDS SUFFER TREMENDOUS PENALTIES FOR UNDERGOING ABUSE. STUDIES SHOW WE LEAD THE WORLD IN DIVORCES, ALCOHOLISM, SUICIDES AND OTHER CONSEQUENCES OF ABSORBING THESE KINDS OF ATTACKS WITHOUT THE ABILITY AND OPPORTUNITY TO RESPOND IN A SATISFACTORY MANNER. AS A MATTER OF FACT, KAREN SOLOMON STATED, IN AN ARTICLE IN CALIBRE PRESS (11/21/16), "AN OFFICER COMMITS SUICIDE EVERY 22-HOURS."

THE JUMP AND STRIP PHRASE TACTICS ARE INGENIOUS AND EFFECTIVE METHODS DESIGNED TO **STRIP THE POWER AND IMPACT** OF A VERBAL ATTACK AND TO **JUMP OVER** INSULTS, THREATS, PROFANITY, WHILE CONCOMITANTLY ACHIEVING AN OFFICER'S PROFESSIONAL OBJECTIVE(S). IF YOU RECALL, IN CHAPTER TWO, I DISCUSSED THE **D.E.F.U.S.E** EQUATION. ONE OF THE KEY PRINCIPLES OF DEFUSING AGGRESSIVE WAS TO DEPRECIATE THE VERBAL ICON. WELL, BY USING THESE PHRASES WHEN CONFRONTED BY AGGRESSIVE PEOPLE WHO ARE ATTEMPTING TO CAUSE THE OFFICER TO ACT-OUT THE PRESCRIBED RESPONSE – TO

LOSE HIS PROFESSIONALISM AND HIS COOL – THE OFFICER IS
ELIMINATING THAT
POSSIBILITY.

HOW STRIP (JUMP) PHRASES WORK

"REMEMBER, PEOPLE ARE RARELY LOGICAL UNDER STRESS. THE RULE IS, NEVER USE
LOGIC WHEN HE IS UNDER STRESS. BETTER TO CALM THE PERSON FIRST, THEN TRY
TO REASON.

*THE WAY STRIP PHRASES WORK IS SIMPLY TO DEFLECT VERBAL
ABUSE INSTEAD OF ABSORBING THE WICKED ARROWS OF VERBAL
HOSTILITY. TOO MANY OF US TAKE THESE ATTACKS PERSONALLY
AND, UNFORTUNATELY SPEND THEIR ENERGY REACTING TO THESE
ATTACKS. THIS IS MISGUIDED, AS IT GETS THE EGO INVOLVED IN
THE INTERACTION. WHICH, BY THE WAY, IS EXACTLY WHAT THE
ATTACKER IS HOPING FOR. TOO OFTEN OFFICERS TURN THEIR
ATTENTION INWARD TO GET IN TOUCH WITH THEIR EMOTIONS, SO
THEY CAN VERBALLY REACT AND RETORT TO THE VERBAL ATTACK.*

*INSTEAD, THE RECOMMENDED TACTIC IS TO STRIP THE VERBAL
ATTACK OF ALL POWER BY MAINTAINING OUR CENTER AND CALM
AND BY JUMPING OVER THESE ATTACKS AND MOVING ON TO
ACHIEVE OUR PROFESSIONAL GOAL WITHOUT
GETTING FOOT SWEPT, OR MANIPULATED, BY THE BAD GUY.*

DEFLECTING VERBAL HOSTILITY – THE EQUATION:

*STEP 1. THE AGGRESSOR VERBALLY ATTACKS THE OFFICER OR
AUTHORITY FIGURE. MAYBE AN INSULT, A THREAT, AN ATTEMPT TO
INTIMIDATE, OR A PERSONAL ACCUSATION.*

*STEP 2. THE TARGET-OFFICER DEFLECTS THE ATTACK DEFTLY, THE
SAME AS HE MIGHT BLOCK AN INCOMING PUNCH. HE USES WORDS
DESIGNED TO MINIMALLY ADDRESS THE SUBJECT'S INSULTS, ETC.,
USING A.....*

STRIP OR JUMP PHRASES DESIGNED TO DEFLECT MIGHT INCLUDE:

180

✓ "I HEAR THAT, SIR, BUT..."
✓ "I 'PRECIATE THAT, BUT..."
✓ "YOU COULD BE RIGHT, BUT..."
✓ "YOU GOT SOME BAD DATA THERE, BUT..."
✓ "THAT MAY BE TRUE, BUT..."
✓ "YOU COULD SAY THAT AGAIN, BUT..."

STEP 3. IN THIS STEP, THE OFFICER WILL USE THE WORD <u>**"BUT."**</u>
"BUT" ACTS AS A SPRINGBOARD INTO THE NEXT PHASE OF THIS
DEFUSING STRATEGY – WHICH IS THE USE OF **PROFESSIONAL
LANGUAGE.** EVERY WORD AFTER "BUT" MUST BE PROFESSIONAL
LANGUAGE DESIGNED TO ACHIEVE THE OFFICER'S PROFESSIONAL
OBJECTIVE.

STEP 4. IN THIS STAGE, THE OFFICER SHOULD USE PROFESSIONAL
LANGUAGE WHICH INCLUDES WHATEVER IT IS THE OFFICER NEEDS
THE SUBJECT TO PERFORM.

AN EXAMPLE OF AN EFFECTIVE STRIP PHRASE MIGHT BE:

BAD GUY: *"TELL YOU WHAT, YOU UGLY BASTARD, I AIN'T GOING
WITH YOU, NO WAY!"*
OFFICER: *"I 'PRECIATE THAT, SIR (JUMP PHRASE), BUT
(SPRINGBOARD) I STILL NEED YOU TO TURN AROUND SLOWLY AND
PUT YOUR HANDS BEHIND YOUR BACK AND..."*

WHY ARE STRIP PHRASES EFFECTIVE?

❖ DEFLECTING VERBAL ABUSE FEELS GOOD. RELIEVES
   STRESS.
❖ DEFLECTING VERBAL ABUSE DISEMPOWERS THE ATTACKER.
❖ DEFLECTING VERBAL ABUSE ALLOWS THE OFFICER TO
   MAINTAIN A PROFESSIONAL IMAGE.
❖ DEFLECTING VERBAL ABUSE SOUNDS GOOD TO THE PUBLIC
   WHO DO NOT WISH TO HEAR THE OFFICER USING
   THREATS AND PROFANITY.
❖ AND, FRANKLY, DEFLECTING VERBAL ABUSE IS PLAIN FUN! I
   KNOW THIS MIGHT SOUND UNPROFESSIONAL, BUT, HECK,

THE TRUTH IS, IT IS ENJOYABLE PLAYING THIS GAME WITH A PERSON WHO IS TRYING TO CAUSE YOU TO LOSE YOUR COOL. INSTEAD, IN THIS GAME, YOU ARE THE ONE WHO IS COOL AND IN CONTROL AND HE IS FLABBERGASTED!

THE FIVE-STEP HARD STYLE. *THIS VERBAL JUDO TECHNIQUE IS EFFECTIVE IN 99% OF CASES WHERE IT IS EMPLOYED. HOWEVER, WE HAVE ALREADY DISCUSSED IT IN A PREVIOUS CHAPTER.*

EMPATHY. *WE HAVE ALREADY DISCUSSED EMPATHY IN A PREVIOUS CHAPTER IN THE DEFUSE EQUATION. HOWEVER, I CANNOT STRESS THIS ENOUGH: EMPATHY IS THE SINGLE, MOST POWERFUL CONCEPT IN THE SYNTAX AND LANGUAGE OF LAW ENFORCEMENT. IT IS EASILY THE MOST CRUCIAL SKILL IN BOTH PHYSICAL AND VERBAL INTERACTIONS WITH THE PUBLIC. EMPATHY, IN FACT, WORKS EVERY SINGLE TIME WITH NO EXCEPTIONS. EMPATHY ABSORBS TENSION. NOT ONLY THAT, USING EMPATHY IS EASY AND SIMPLE. ALL YOU HAVE TO DO IS REFLECT BACK TO THE SUBJECT WHAT YOU ARE HEARING, SEEING AND SENSING. THE SKILL HERE IS TO LISTEN REFLEXIVELY, STAY OPENMINDED AND FLEXIBLE. SIMPLE.*

5). THE CUT AND HERD. *THIS TACTIC CAN BE USED IN SITUATIONS WHEN ONE OR MORE OFFICERS NEED TO ADDRESS ONE PERSON, BUT THERE IS A CROWD OF PEOPLE AROUND THAT PERSON. OFTEN, ADDRESSING THAT INDIVIDUAL WITH HIS PEERS, ASSOCIATES, CONFEDERATES AND/OR LOVED ONES CLOSE BY CREATES A POTENTIAL HAZARD TO THE OFFICER(S). THE CUT AND HERD IS A COMMON-SENSE TACTIC (BE AWARE, OF COURSE, THAT, UNDER STRESS, COMMON SENSE IS THE RAREST OF COMMODITIES). THE STRATEGY INVOLVES ONE OFFICER DEALING WITH THE CROWD WHILE THE OTHER IS ABLE TO SAFELY ADDRESS THE TARGET-SUBJECT. IF THE OFFICER IS ALONE, AND, IF HE PERCEIVES THAT DOING SO WILL BE SAFE, HE CAN ASK THE SUBJECT TO STEP AWAY FROM THE CROWD.*

I'M SURE OFFICERS AND CITIZENS ARE ALREADY AWARE OF THIS, BUT I AM COMPELLED TO MENTION THE FACT THAT, OFTEN, YOUNG MEN FEEL THEY NEED TO PROVE THEIR MANHOOD IN FRONT OF THEIR WIFE, MOTHER, OR GIRLFRIEND. AS A MATTER OF FACT, MY EXPERIENCE WORKING WITH ANTISOCIAL PEOPLE FOR THE LAST 40-SOME YEARS SHOWS THAT THERE ARE FEW INDIVIDUALS MORE VOLATILE AND DANGEROUS THAN A DRUNK YOUNG MAN IN THE COMPANY OF A WOMAN. HELL, NOW THAT I THINK BACK ON IT, THE GUY DOESN'T HAVE TO BE UNDER THE INFLUENCE OF DRUGS OR ALCOHOL, HE IS ALREADY "UNDER THE INFLUENCE OF THE NEED TO IMPRESS HIS WOMAN AND THAT INFLUENCE TRUMPS THE HELL OUT OF DRUGS OR ALCOHOL!

THE TACTICAL (PROFESSIONAL)-10 CAR STOP.

STOPPING A VEHICLE, EVEN FOR A MINOR VIOLATION, IS RIFE WITH POTENTIAL DANGER. TOO MANY OFFICERS HAVE BEEN SLAYED BY MOTORISTS AND/OR THEIR PASSENGER(S) THROUGH NO FAULT OF THEIR OWN. MANY OF THESE OFFICERS USED SOUND TACTICS, BUT THE THING IS, THEY HAD NO IDEA WHOM IT WAS THEY HAD STOPPED. IN MANY CASES, THE MOTORIST WAS ON THE LAM FOR A HEINOUS CRIME, WAS EMOTIONALLY DISTURBED, OR, SADLY, A MONSTROUS BAD GUY WHO WAS LOOKING FOR A COP TO ASSASSINATE. JUST TO WATCH HIM DIE.

BESIDES THOSE REASONS, THE MOTORIST HAS JUST BEEN LIT UP AND HE IS SITTING ON TOP OF SEVERAL THOUSAND POUNDS OF FUELED DYNAMITE. HE MAY BE UNDER THE INFLUENCE OF FEAR, ANGER, FRUSTRATION. ANY NUMBER OF EMOTIONS. OR, MAYBE WORSE, HE MAY BE SUICIDAL AND LOOKING AT THE APPROACHING OFFICER AS A MEANS OF COMMITTING SUICIDE, WHICH NOWADAYS, IS FAR FROM A RARE OCCURRENCE..

INTRODUCING THE TACTICAL-10 CAR STOP, WHICH INVOLVES A SERIES OF STEPS DESIGNED TO HELP AN OFFICER ASSESS THE LEVEL OF DANGER THE MOTORIST PRESENTS WHILE DE-ESCALATING HIMSELF, HIS PARTNER AND EVERYBODY INSIDE THE VEHICLE.

1). SLOW AND MEASURED APPROACH. THIS IS A TACTIC DESIGNED TO ASSESS THE MOTORIST AND THE SURROUNDINGS. THE OFFICER SHOULD BE AWARE OF HIS BODY LANGUAGE. ELIMINATE THE "GORILLA WALK," IF THAT IS HIS STYLE. SLOW IT DOWN, LOOK AND LISTEN FOR ANY DANGER SIGNS. YOU MIGHT EVEN TOUCH THE TRUNK AS YOU SLOWLY PASS. YOU NEVER KNOW. MAYBE THE TRUNK IS AJAR AND SECRETING AN ASSASSIN INSIDE, READY TO POP OUT AND BLAST YOU. IT HAS HAPPENED. IF YOU ARE CARRYING A CITATION BOOK OR ANYTHING ELSE, REMEMBER TO ALWAYS KEEP YOUR GUN HAND FREE.

2). CLEAR YOUR HEAD. REMOVE ANY ASSUMPTIONS OR PREJUDICES ABOUT THE MOTORIST OR ANYONE ELSE YOU SEE IN THE VEHICLE. REMAIN OPEN AND FLEXIBLE. ASSUMING A PERSON MIGHT BE DANGEROUS SIMPLY BECAUSE OF HIS APPEARANCE COULD CAUSE YOU TO OVERREACT IF HE BECOMES BOISTEROUS OR RESISTANT IN SOME WAY. DEFUSE YOURSELF AND ALWAYS REMEMBER TO ORDER YOU TACTICS FROM **LIGHT TO HEAVY!** *ONCE YOU PULL YOUR FIREARM AND START ORDERING THE SUBJECT(S) AROUND IT IS IMPOSSIBLE TO GO BACK TO BEING NICE. I DISCUSS THIS OPEN, FLEXIBLE AND ALERT ATTITUDE WHEN I TALK ABOUT THE BEGINNER'S MIND.*

3). GREETING. GREETING THE INDIVIDUAL IS A COMMON COURTESY, BUT, ALONG WITH A SMILE, WILL DISARM THE DRIVER. "GOOD EVENING, SIR."

4). INTRODUCTION. ALONG WITH THE GREETING, INTRODUCE YOURSELF, YOUR RANK, AND YOUR DEPARTMENT. "GOOD EVENING, SIR. I AM TROOPER DALY FROM THE DALLAS HIGHWAY PATROL...". THERE IS A GOOD REASON FOR EVERYTHING. BY GIVING A GREETING AND INTRODUCING YOURSELF AND YOUR DEPARTMENT, YOU ARE MAKING IT TOUGH FOR THE MOTORIST TO GIVE YOU VERBAL CRAP. AS GEORGE THOMPSON ALWAYS SAID, "WE ARE IN THE CRAP-TAKING BUSINESS." *NEVERTHELESS, THAT ADAGE DIDN'T STOP BIG GEORGE FROM COMING UP WITH TECHNIQUES AND STRATEGIES – LIKE THIS 10-STEP – DESIGNED TO MINIMIZE OR ELIMINATE COPS TAKING CRAP DURING CAR STOPS.*

5). THE REASON FOR THIS STOP. THEN STATE THE REASON YOU STOPPED THIS INDIVIDUAL. *"THE REASON I STOPPED YOU, SIR, IS THAT YOU BLEW RIGHT THROUGH THAT STOP SIGN BACK YONDER A MILE OR SO..."*

6). "JUSTIFIED REASON?" <u>ASK</u>: *"SIR, LET ME ASK YOU, IS THERE ANY <u>JUSTIFIED</u> REASON FOR YOU DOING THAT?"* THE THING IS, THERE CAN BE ONLY A RARE CIRCUMSTANCE WHERE BLOWING THROUGH A STOP SIGN CAN BE JUSTIFIED. MAYBE HE IS A COP ON THE JOB, MAYBE THERE IS A MEDICAL EMERGENCY. BUT, MORE LIKELY THAN NOT, THE MOTORIST WILL HAVE NO JUSTIFICATION FOR THE VIOLATION. BUT, IF HE DOES TRY TO JUSTIFY OR EXPLAIN AWAY THE VIOLATION, WELL, HECK, HE JUST GAVE YOU AN ADMISSION OF GUILT. ONCE AGAIN, THESE STEPS WILL ELIMINATE ANY REASON FOR THE DRIVER, OR ANY OF HIS PASSENGERS, FROM GIVING YOU ANY CRAP.

7). ASK FOR HIS DRIVER'S LICENSE AND/OR REGISTRATION WHILE ASKING HIM WHERE THE REGISTRATION IS LOCATED (AND IS THERE ANYTHING IN THAT GLOVEBOX I HAVE TO WORRY ABOUT AS FAR AS MY SAFETY IS CONCERNED).

8). ADVISE THAT YOU ARE GOING TO YOUR PATROL CAR TO CHECK OUT HIS INFORMATION.

9). INVOKE RAM. RAM IS A VERBAL JUDO TERM AND IT MEANS A REASONABLE ARC OF MOVEMENT. THE OFFICER SHOULD DESCRIBE WHAT THE SUBJECT SHOULD DO TO BE CONSIDERED COOPERATIVE, AND, THEREFORE SAFE. IN THIS CASE, IT WOULD BE, *"SIR, FOR YOUR SAFETY AND MINE (PEACE PHRASE), PLEASE REMAIN SEATED. YOU UNDERSTAND, IF YOU COOPERATE, EVERYTHING WILL BE FINE?"* ANOTHER GREAT EXAMPLE OF *RAM* MIGHT BE SOMETHING LIKE: *"SIR, FOR YOUR SAFETY AND MINE, PLEASE KEEP YOUR HANDS ON YOUR STEERING WHEEL UNTIL I CAN CHECK THIS OUT."*

AN IMPORTANT TACTICAL CONSIDERATION OF INVOKING RAM. YOU HAVE APTLY DESCRIBED TO THE SUBJECT WHAT HE MUST DO TO BE CONSIDERED COOPERATIVE AND, THEREFORE SAFE. IMPLICITLY, THIS MEANS THAT, IF HE VIOLATES *RAM*, YOU SHOULD CONSIDER HIM IN AN ATTACK MODE. TO BE SURE, WHEN DEALING

WITH A MOTORIST, BE CERTAIN TO INSTRUCT HIM – BEFORE YOU RETURN TO YOUR CRUISER TO CHECK OUT HIS PAPERWORK - TO REMAIN IN HIS VEHICLE, SO THAT IF HE STEPS OUT OF HIS VEHICLE AND APPROACHES YOU, YOU NOW HAVE JUSTIFICATION FOR USING FORCE OR WHATEVER ACTION IS CALLED FOR.

*10). **WRITE THE TICKET OR OTHERWISE TAKE NECESSARY ACTION.** BE SURE TO END THE INTERACTION ON A POSITIVE NOTE. A GREAT PEACE PHRASE MIGHT BE, "SIR, PLEASE BE CAREFUL MERGING BACK INTO TRAFFIC. YOUR SAFETY IS IMPORTANT TO US."*

BACK TO UNIVERSAL TACTICS THAT ALWAYS WORK

"THE MORE ANTISOCIAL THE PERSON, THE MORE
PROFESSIONAL WE MUST BE."
VERBAL JUDO'S DOUBLE EDGED SWORD

*6). **I-STATEMENTS (OVER YOU-STATEMENTS).** WORDS MATTER, SURE, BUT EVEN MORE IMPORTANT IS HOW WE USE OUR WORDS. FOR INSTANCE, OUR **TONE** MAY REFLECT PREJUDICE OR DISDAIN, WHICH CAN LIGHT UP AN AGGRESSIVE PERSON AS IF HE WERE A STICK OF TNT AND YOU WERE THE MATCH! ANOTHER WAY WE MIGHT LIGHT UP SOMEONE IS THROUGH **YOU-STATEMENTS.** THESE STATEMENTS ARE OFTEN PERCEIVED BY THE SUBJECT AS PREJUDICIAL AND JUDGMENTAL. NO ONE LIKES BEING JUDGED. MEANING THAT THESE YOU-STATEMENTS CAN CLOSE DOWN COMMUNICATIONS FASTER THAN DAMN NEAR ANYTHING ELSE! I HAVE ALSO FOUND THAT MANY YOU-STATEMENTS ARE FOLLOWED BY THE PARENTHETICAL "ASSHOLE!" THIS IS PROBLEMATIC BECAUSE OFTEN YOU-STATEMENTS HAVE BEEN KNOWN TO **TRIGGER** VERBAL OR PHYSICAL RESISTANCE, EVEN ATTACKS. INSTEAD, USE I-STATEMENTS, WHICH PUT THE ONUS ON THE OFFICER, OR SPEAKER.*

I-STATEMENTS VS YOU-STATEMENTS

➢ *YOU STATEMENT: "WHAT THE HELL IS WRONG WITH YOU, MAN?"*

- I-STATEMENT: *"SIR, I CAN HEAR FEAR IN YOUR VOICE AND I CAN SEE HURT IN YOUR EYES (THIS IS FROM A REAL SCENARIO INVOLVING A MEDICAL SECURITY OFFICER TALKING TO A MENTALLY ILL PATIENT). TELL ME WHAT I CAN DO TO HELP."*
- YOU-STATEMENT: *"YOU ARE ALWAYS LATE, TED."*
- I-STATEMENT: *"TED, I FEEL A LITTLE FRUSTRATED WHEN YOU ARE LATE BECAUSE IT MAKES **ME** LATE FOR ALL THE OTHER THINGS I HAVE TO DO."*
- YOU-STATEMENT: *"WHY DON'T YOU EVER LISTEN, HANK?"*
- I-STATEMENT: *"HANK, I HAVE TO ADMIT, IT IS DISAPPOINTING WHEN YOU DON'T LISTEN.."*
- YOU-STATEMENT: *"KIT, YOUR ATTITUDE IS PISSING ME OFF!"*
- I-STATEMENT: *"KIT, I FEEL DISSED. LET'S TALK."*

HOW TO CONSTRUCT AN EFFECTIVE I-STATEMENT.

STEP 1. USE THE WORD "I."
STEP 2. WHAT YOU FEEL OR WANT.
STEP 3. THE EVENT THAT PROVOKED THE FEELING OR DESIRE.
STEP 4. THE EFFECT THAT EVENT HAS ON ME.

OR: "KATHY, I FEEL DISRESPECTED BECAUSE YOU SEEM TO ALWAYS DO THE EXACT OPPOSITE OF WHAT I ASK YOU TO DO. CAN WE TALK?"

*7). WHEN IN DOUBT, TELL A "STORY." WHEN CONFRONTED WITH A PROBLEM PERSON OR A PROBLEM ISSUE, I OFTEN RESORTED TO RELATING A STORY ABOUT A SIMILAR INCIDENT THAT MIGHT TEACH A LESSON. I AM A STORY-TELLER BY NATURE, AS ARE MANY COPS OR COUNSELORS, SO THESE STORIES ALWAYS SEEMED TO HELP GET MY MESSAGE ACROSS. THE SINGULAR INGREDIENT TO AN EFFECTIVE "STORY" IS THAT IT **MUST CROSS THE SUBJECT'S EXPERIENCE OR SITUATION WITH MINE OR SOMEONE ELSE'S (EXPERIENCES).** IT DIDN'T REALLY MATTER THAT THE STORY MIGHT BE SOURCED IN MY IMAGINATION OR A TRUE EVENT(S), IF IT SEEMED TRUE, IT USUALLY WORKED (REMEMBER, NOTHING WORKS 100% OF THE TIME WITH 100% OF THE PEOPLE).*

ON USING STORIES TO CREATE CHANGE OR REDUCE AGGRESSION

"STORIES," IN ONE WAY OR ANOTHER HAVE ALWAYS WORKED FOR ME. I BET THEY CAN WORK FOR YOU, TOO. HOW DO I KNOW THAT? FIRST, EVERYONE LOVES TO BE TOLD STORIES. EVEN EVIL MOTOR SCOOTERS WHOM YOU HAVE LIKELY HAD TO DEAL WITH FROM TIME TO TIME. IT IS JUST THE WAY HUMAN BEINGS HAVE RELATED TO THE WORLD AROUND THEM SINCE THE BEGINNING OF TIME. OR, AT LEAST SINCE THE BEGINNING OF HUMAN COMMUNICATIONS. STORIES. EITHER HEARING THEM OR TELLING THEM, ARE PART OF OUR DNA. SECONDLY, TELLING STORIES THAT RELATE DIRECTLY OR INDIRECTLY TO ANOTHER PERSON OR THAT PERSON'S ISSUES OR PROBLEMS CONNECTS YOU, THE TELLER, TO THE OTHER PERSON. AND, OF COURSE, A CONNECTION HAPPENS TO BE ONE OF THE CRITICAL PRINCIPLES OF DE-ESCALATING AND/OR EFFECTIVELY COMMUNICATING WITH ANOTHER PERSON!

WHEN IT COMES TO TELLING STORIES TO CONNECT OR TO REDUCE AGGRESSION, I BELIEVE THAT THERE ARE A FEW COMPONENTS THAT ARE REQUIRED TO MAKE YOUR STORY AN EFFECTIVE CHANGE AGENT. FIRST, AND PROBABLY MOST IMPORTANT, IS YOUR STORY'S RELEVANCE. MEANING, THE TALE YOU TELL MUST CROSS YOUR EXPERIENCE(S) WITH HIS. SECOND, YOUR STORY DOESN'T HAVE TO REALLY ORIGINATE IN YOUR TRUE EXPERIENCES. AS IN MANY OF MY WINOLOGY

PRINCIPLES, TRUTH IS IRRELEVANT. TRUTH CAN HELP, OF COURSE, BUT IT REALLY DOESN'T MATTER, SO LONG AS WHAT YOU SAY HITS THE RIGHT NERVE.

YOUR STORY MUST HAVE A GOAL. GOES WITHOUT SAYING, BUT I'M SAYING IT ANYWAYS. FOR INSTANCE, HERE IS A TRUE STORY THAT'S

GOAL IS THE VALUE OF TACTICAL RESPECT, WITHOUT WHICH COMES DEATH (DISSIM IS DEATH).

"DISSIM IS DEATH"

A Law Enforcement "Story"

IT WAS IN EUREKA, KANSAS, BACK IN THE 80'S. TWO OFFICERS WENT OUT TO BUST A BAD GUY. TIM, ONE OF THE OFFICERS, HAD BUILT HIMSELF UP A GIANT HATRED FOR THIS PARTICULAR BAD GUY AND EVEN THOUGH OTHER OFFICERS HAD OFFERED TO MAKE THIS ARREST, TIM WANTED TO BE THE FIRST TO HIT THE FRONT DOOR. WHICH IS EXACTLY WHERE HE WAS WHEN HE WAS SHOT THROUGH THE NECK AND KILLED. THE OTHER OFFICER WAS SHOT THROUGH A TESTICLE AS HE CROUCHED BEHIND A TRUCK.

LATER, IN COURT, THE BAD GUY APOLOGIZED FOR WOUNDING THE 2ND OFFICER. HE HAD THOUGHT HE WAS THE FIRST OFFICER – TIM – WHO HE HAD NO RESPECT FOR. AND TELLS THAT OFFICER (THE SURVIVOR) THAT HE HAD ALWAYS TREATED HIM WITH RESPECT AND DIGNITY, WHICH HE HAD ALWAYS APPRECIATED. HE HAD EVEN TOLD OTHER BAD GUYS NOT TO SHOOT HIM (OFFICER NUMBER 2), IF THEY COULD HELP IT.

"I KILLED THAT BASTARD (TIM) BECAUSE OF HIS DISRESPECT. DISRESPECT IS DISSIM AND ON THE STREETS, DISSIM IS DEATH!"

I TOLD THIS STORY TO THREE OFFICERS ON MY ARREST TEAM DURING A PRE-ARREST PRACTICE SESSION. WE WERE DISCUSSING CONTACT AND COVER ROLES AND DOING SOME HANDCUFFING PRACTICE. MY YOUNGEST OFFICER WAS ALL GEEKED-UP ABOUT ARRESTING THE BAD GUY BECAUSE THE BAD GUY HAD GIVEN HIM "A LOT OF DISRESPECT" THE PREVIOUS YEAR WHEN HE WAS THE GUY'S PROBATION OFFICER. THERE WAS A LOT OF EGO AND PERSONALIZATION GOING ON. TOO MUCH, FAR AS I WAS CONCERNED. THE STORY SEEMED TO WORK AS THAT OFFICER AGREED TO TAKE A LOW-PROFILE ROLE IN THE ARREST AND TRANSPORTATION AND TREATED THE PAROLEE WITH "SOME" RESPECT.

8). PARAPHRASING. I CONFESS THAT I DID NOT OFTEN RESORT TO THE ART OF PARAPHRASING WHEN I WAS WORKING THE STREETS. THAT DOES NOT MEAN THAT PARAPHRASING WOULDN'T HAVE WORKED. ON THE CONTRARY, VERBAL JUDO INSISTS IT CAN AND WILL WORK FOR OFFICERS AND CITIZENS ALIKE. VJ DESCRIBED PARAPHRASING AS "TAKING WHAT YOU BELIEVE THE PERSON IS SAYING, INTERPRETING WHAT HE MEANS, FRAMING THAT MEANING AND GIVING IT BACK TO HIM. THAT PERSON, IN TURN, WILL THE EITHER CONFIRM, CLARIFY, OR CORRECT YOUR WORDS WITH WHAT HE REALLY MEANS UNTIL WORDS AND MEANINGS ARE CO-EQUAL."

FOR INSTANCE, WE MIGHT HAVE WHAT IS CALLED THE SWORD OF INSERTION, OR INTERRUPTION: "HEY, SIR, HOLD ON A SECOND. LET ME SEE IF I HEARD YOU RIGHT. YOU ARE UPSET BECAUSE YOU THINK I DISSED YOU IN FRONT OF YOUR FRIENDS. RIGHT?"

THE OTHER PERSON CAN NOW CORRECT OR MODIFY YOUR MEANING WITH HIS RESPONSE. *BUT, I THINK, THE IMPORTANT THING IS THAT YOU ARE COMMUNICATING AND ALL THE TIME THAT IS GOING ON, YOU ARE ACTIVELY ALLOWING TIME TO TICK BY, AND THAT TIME CREATES AN* INTELLECTUAL DELAY, *WHICH CALMS AND SOOTHES. OF COURSE, NOT ONLY THAT, BUT YOU APPEAR TO BE CONCERNED ABOUT GETTING THINGS RIGHT.*

ONE LAST THING. WHEN YOU ASK "LET ME SEE IF I HEARD YOU RIGHT," YOU ARE ACTUALLY HOOKING *THE OTHER PERSON WITH A GREAT PEACE PHRASE (PLUS, EMPATHY). OFTEN, THE PERSON WILL STOP IN MID-RANT TO SEE IF YOU DID GET WHAT HE SAID RIGHT!*

9) DISTRACTIONS. THESE ARE TACTICS DESIGNED TO WEAKEN AGGRESSION BY CHANGING THE BAD GUY'S THOUGHT PROCESS. THE TRICK IS TO USE WORDS AND GESTURES TO REDIRECT A SUBJECT'S FOCUS AWAY FROM WHOM HE INTENDS TO ATTACK. MAYBE THE BEST EXAMPLE OF A DISTRACTION WAS USED A DECADE AGO ON A DANGEROUS PAROLEE WHOM WE HAD HEARD WAS CARRYING AN EDGED WEAPON AND INTENDED TO SLICE UP HIS PAROLE AGENT. HE REPORTED TO OUR DISTRICT OFFICE ON HIS AGENT'S DUTY DAY – AS EXPECTED – AND, AS PER THE ROUTINE, HE WAS ESCORTED TO THE MEN'S ROOM

WHERE HE GAVE UP A URINE SAMPLE. AS HE WAS LED FROM THE RESTROOM, HE WAS DIRECTED TO PLACE THE URINE BOTTLE ON THE SAMPLE DESK, AND, AS HE DID SO, HIS PAROLE AGENT SUDDENLY APPEARED, POINTED AT THE PAROLEE'S CROTCH AND SAID, "LOOK IT, JAKE, YOU PISSED YOURSELF."

JAKE, THE PAROLEE, LOOKED DOWN AT HIS CROTCH AND PLACED BOTH HANDS OUT TO HIS SIDES, AT WHICH TIME- AS PLANNED – TWO OFFICERS QUICKLY APPROACHED AND HANDCUFFED JAKE. THE DISTRACTION TECHNIQUE WORKED THE WAY A DISTRACTION TECHNIQUE IS DESIGNED TO WORK. DIVERTED THE SUBJECT'S ATTENTION AWAY FROM WHAT HE INTENDED TO DO, WEAKENED HIS MOTOR ACTIONS, AND, BY THE WAY, SAVED THE DAY. WE SEARCHED JAKE AND FOUND A UTILITY KNIFE SECRETED BEHIND HIS BELT BUCKLE.

PPCT TRAINING SYSTEMS DEFINES A DISTRACTION TECHNIQUE AS A CONTROL TECHNIQUE(S) THAT WEAKENS RESISTANCE BY CHANGING THE BAD GUY'S THOUGHT PROCESS.

THERE ARE HUNDREDS OF THINGS YOU CAN DO AND SAY TO DISTRACT AND RE-DIRECT A BAD GUY. I HAVE USED MAYBE A DOZEN. SUCH AS:

THE COUGH AND POINT. A BAD GUY IS FOCUSED ON ME WITH THAT FELONY GLARE. SUDDENLY HE MAKES HIS MOVE TOWARD ME AND I START COUGHING AND HOLDING MY HAND OUT, AS IF TO SAY, STAY BACK! HE STOPS IN HIS TRACKS EVERY TIME. NOT KNOWING WHAT TO DO.

WHAT'S THAT? A BAD GUY SEEMS ANGRY, HE IS COMING TOWARD ME. JUST AS HE GETS CLOSE I POINT AT A LOGO ON HIS SHIRT AND SAY, "WHAT THE HELL IS THAT?" OR, WHERE'D YOU GET THOSE BOOTS?" IT DOESN'T MATTER IF HE IS EVEN WEARING BOOTS. HE WILL STOP AND LOOK AT HIS FEET OR HIS SHIRT AND THAT IS ALL YOU NEED TO BREAK HIS RHYTHM. CHANGE THE MOMENTUM TO YOUR SIDE.

HANDCUFFING-DISTRACTIONS. HERE ARE A FEW GOOD ONE'S I LEARNED FROM DANGEROUS DAN SOLLA, A PPCT INSTRUCTOR

TRAINER, AND SUPER-JACK LEONARD, A PPCT STAFF INSTRUCTOR AND LEGEND. JUST AS HE IS ABOUT TO HANDCUFF A SUBJECT, ESPECIALLY IF THE GUY APPEARS JUMPY OR GEEKED-UP, LEONARD OR SOLLA WILL ASK HIM: "OK, SIR, GOT A QUESTION FOR YOU. WHO WON THE CIVIL WAR, THE EAST OR THE WEST?" BELIEVE IT OR NOT, THE SUBJECT ALWAYS TRIES TO ANSWER THE QUESTION. I WILL OFTEN ASK THE SUBJECT HIS NAME, OR BIRTH DATE JUST BEFORE I HOOK HIM UP. OR, PERHAPS, WHEN I HAVE A SUBJECT PRONED-OUT, JUST BEFORE I MOVE IN TO HANDCUFF, I WILL ASK HIM TO LOOK AT HIS HAND AND WIGGLE HIS FINGERS. THAT WAY, I KNOW HE IS OBEYING MY COMMANDS.

THE EXACT WORDS MATTER LITTLE. THE IMPORTANT THING IS TO CHANGE THE BAD GUY'S CHANNEL FROM THE ONE HE WANTS TO WATCH TO THE ONE YOU NEED HIM TO WATCH. TO REDIRECT HIS FOCUS AND WEAKEN HIS ABILITY TO RESIST.

CHAPTER 8

THREE RULES FOR THE MANAGEMENT OF AGGRESSIVE BEHAVIOR (MOAB).

ANGER MANAGEMENT

I. KNOW THE ENVIRONMENT.
II. KNOW THE OTHER PERSON.
III. KNOW YOURSELF.

THESE THREE "RULES" OR GUIDELINES COME FROM THE M.O.A.B TRAINING SYSTEM. THESE ARE SIMPLE AND EASY-TO-APPLY PRINCIPLES OF OFFICER SAFETY. HOWEVER, MAYBE MORE IMPORTANTLY, IF ADHERED TO, THESE PROTOCOLS CAN BE CRUCIAL FOR THE EFFECTIVE REDUCTION OF STRESS IN ANY CONFRONTATIONAL INTERACTION. YOURSELF.

"KNOW THE ENVIRONMENT."

"THUS, WHAT ENABLES THE WISE SOVEREIGN AND THE GOOD GENERAL TO STRIKE AND CONQUER, AND ACHIEVE THINGS BEYOND THE REACH OF ORDINARY MEN, IS FOREKNOWLEDGE."

- *SUN TZU, "THE ART OF WAR*

SAD AUTHOR'S NOTE. *JUST TODAY – DECEMBER 2, 2016 – A TACOMA, WASHINGTON DEPUTY WAS SHOT AND KILLED RESPONDING TO A DOMESTIC DISTURBANCE CALL. THE OFFICER WAS PART OF A TEAM ATTEMPTING TO BRING A PEACEFUL RESOLUTION INSIDE A HOME IN A TACOMA NEIGHBORHOOD OF SINGLE-FAMILY HOMES. I DO NOT REPORT THIS TRAGEDY TO ELEVATE THE NEED FOR DE-ESCALATION SKILLS. AS FAR AS I KNOW, THE OFFICERS DID EVERYTHING IN THEIR POWER TO PREVENT THIS TRAGEDY, BUT, AS I HAVE ILLUSTRATED NUMEROUS TIMES IN THIS BOOK, WE ARE DEALING WITH SOME VERY DISTURBED AND DANGEROUS PEOPLE. ONE MORE THING. SINCE I BEGAN WRITING THIS BOOK, I HAVE KEPT COUNT. IN ONLY A FEW MONTHS, WE HAVE LOST 9 OFFICERS!*

INSIDE OF THE ESTABLISHMENT. *OBVIOUSLY, IF YOU ARE ON AN ARREST TEAM, YOU ARE GOING TO ENTER ONLY AFTER COMMUNICATING AN ACTION PLAN WITH ALL MEMBERS OF THE TEAM, APPROACHING THE BUILDING IN AN OBLIQUE AND TACTICALLY SAFE MANNER, THEN PERFORMING A QUICK PEEK, OR CUTTING THE PIE. YOUR TEAM WILL ENTER IN SUCH A WAY TO AVOID THE FATAL FUNNEL, ET AL. MOREOVER, YOU ARE GOING TO UNDERSTAND WHAT YOUR SPECIFIC ROLE MIGHT BE. CONTACT? COVER? INSIDE? OUTSIDE?*

*RELATIVE TO **DE-ESCALATING THE** SCENE, THE CRUCIAL ELEMENTS WE NEED TO DEAL WITH ARE OBSERVING AND ASSESSING. QUESTIONS THAT NEED TO BE ANSWERED INVOLVE THE NUMBER OF PEOPLE – BESIDES YOUR TARGET PERSON(S) – THAT ARE ON THE SCENE? HOW ARE THEY ACTING – DRUNK, HIGH, ANGRY, LOUD,*

QUIET, ARMED, UNARMED, AGITATED? IS THE SCENE OVER-STIMULATED? POTENTIAL WEAPONS? PEOPLE WHO ARE CAUSING THIS OVER-STIMULATION – MAYBE ENCOURAGING THE SUSPECT OR SUBJECT TO ESCAPE OR FIGHT?

ONE TACTIC THAT IS A MUST. IF YOU ENCOUNTER ANYONE WITH INSIDE INFORMATION ABOUT THE ENVIRONMENT, YOU MUST ASK QUESTIONS AND FIND OUT THE FACTS! YOU MAY BE THINKING, OF COURSE, BUT THE FACT IS, TACTICAL TEAMS OR INDIVIDUAL OFFICERS HAVE IMPERILED THEMSELVES BY RUSHING THROUGH OR PAST WHOEVER ANSWERS THE DOOR OR WHO ARE OUTSIDE THE LOCATION. TOO MANY OFFICERS HAVE DIED BECAUSE THEY LACKED THE NECESSARY INTELLIGENCE THAT SIMPLE QUESTIONS OF THE HOST WOULD HAVE ANSWERED. QUESTIONS LIKE: ARE THERE WEAPONS? WHERE IS THE SUBJECT? IS HE ALONE? WHAT IS HIS DISPOSITION?

ANOTHER TACTICAL QUESTION MIGHT BE WHAT OR WHOM CAN YOU REMOVE FROM THE SCENE THAT MIGHT DEFUSE OR DE-ESCALATE THE SCENE? THAT MIGHT INCLUDE YOU. THERE MIGHT BE A SITUATION WHERE DISENGAGING, SECURING THE SCENE, ETC., MIGHT WORK BEST.

WHAT ABOUT THE AUDIENCE? *ALWAYS BE AWARE OF THE PEOPLE ON THE SCENE OTHER THAN THE SUBJECT. THE AUDIENCE CAN BE A PROVOCATIVE FACTOR. OFTEN, THE SUBJECT WILL BELIEVE HE WILL **LOSE FACE** IF HE COMPLIES WITH A DIRECT COMMAND WITH FRIENDS, CONFEDERATES AND LOVED ONES LOOKING ON. ALWAYS REMEMBER THAT **FACE IS ALWAYS A FIGHTING ISSUE** AND ANYTIME OFFICERS RISK HUMILIATING OR EMBARRASSING A SUBJECT WITH AN AUDIENCE LOOKING ON, THEY ARE RISKING **TOPPLING THE FIRST OF MANY DIGNITY DOMINOS.***

BUT, FOR THE MOMENT, LET'S FORGET THINGS LIKE THE "DIGNITY DOMINO" AND PEER PRESSURE AND OTHER INFLUENCES. MAYBE EVEN MORE IMPORTANT, THOUGH, IS UNDERSTANDING THE PHYSICAL SUPPORT THAT CAN EMERGE FROM MEMBERS OF AN "AUDIENCE." WHO KNOWS WHAT PEOPLE MAY HAVE A WEAPON(S) IN THEIR POSSESSION? OR, WHO KNOWS WHO WILL SUDDENLY ATTACK OFFICERS OUT OF NOWHERE?

ON THE OTHER HAND, BE AWARE OF ANYONE ON OR AROUND THE
SCENE WHO CAN PROVIDE YOU WITH VALUABLE INFORMATION
ABOUT THE LOCATION, THE SUBJECT OR ANY WEAPONS. BE AWARE,
ALSO, OF ANYONE ON THE SCENE WHO IS WILLING AND ABLE TO
HELP YOU TALK THE BAD GUY DOWN OR PROVIDE YOU OR THE
SUBJECT WITH POSITIVE SUPPORT THAT CAN LEAD TO A PEACEFUL
RESOLUTION.

OFFICERS, THEREFORE, WHEN ENTERING A SCENE WHERE THERE IS
AN AUDIENCE, MIGHT CONSIDER USING THE CUT AND HERD TACTIC
(DISCUSSED EARLIER), WHERE THE ARREST-TARGET IS SEPARATED
FROM THE AUDIENCE.

AND OFFICERS NEED TO ALSO MAKE THEMSELVES AWARE OF
POTENTIAL ESCAPE ROUTES AND BARRICADES – TABLES, DESKS,
BEDS, TELEVISIONS, ETC. - IN THE ENVIRONMENT THAT THEY MIGHT
USE TO SEPARATE THEMSELVES FROM ATTACK. ALSO, ALWAYS BE
AWARE OF REAL AND POTENTIAL WEAPONS ON THE SCENE (WITHIN
REACH OF THE SUBJECT AND/OR OTHERS ON THE SCENE.

KNOW THE OTHER PERSON(S)

"THE MORE ANTISOCIAL A BAD GUY IS,
THE MORE PROFESSIONAL WE MUST BE."

VERBAL JUDO'S DOUBLE-EDGED SWORD.

LET ME PRESENT YOU WITH A REAL-LIFE SCENARIO WHERE NOT
"KNOWING" A STRANGER IN HIS WORKPLACE GOT A PROBATION
OFFICER SLICED UP. AS A MATTER OF FACT, IF THIS OFFICER WOULD
HAVE KNOWN THE 3 RULES FOR THE MANAGEMENT OF AGGRESSIVE
BEHAVIOR, HE WOULD HAVE NEVER BEEN WITHIN SHOUTING
DISTANCE OF THE MANIAC WHO SLICED HIM UP!

I AM NOT USING THE OFFICER'S NAME BECAUSE, LIKE SEVERAL
OFFICERS WHOSE STORIES I HAVE WRITTEN ABOUT, STILL WORK IN
THE SYSTEM, AND MIGHT BE EMBARRASSED TO HAVE THEIR STORIES
READ.

THIS OCCURRED IN A PHILADELPHIA (PA) JUVENILE PROBATION OFFICE BACK IN THE LATE 90'S. THE PROBATION OFFICER REPORTED TO HIS OFFICE AS WAS HIS HABIT ABOUT A HALF-HOUR BEFORE THE START OF "BUSINESS". HE ENJOYED RELAXING, DRINKING A CUP OF JOE, AND READING THE PAPER BEFORE DEALING WITH HIS CASELOAD AND PAPERWORK. THIS MORNING, HOWEVER, JUST AS HE FLIPPED HIS INQUIRER ONTO HIS DESK, HE HEARD A SCREAM FOLLOWED BY A FELLOW PROBATION OFFICER RUNNING BLINDLY PAST HIM.

OUR PROBATION OFFICER, OBVIOUSLY ALARMED BY THE SCREAMING OFFICER, CHECKED OUT THE NEXT CUBICLE. WHERE HE SAW A MAN WHOM HE HAD NEVER SEEN BEFORE, RIFLING THROUGH THAT OTHER OFFICER'S FILING CABINET, THROWING PAPERS AND FOLDERS OVER HIS SHOULDERS.

"CAN I HELP YOU, SIR?" OUR P.O. ASKED THE STRANGER.

NOTHING. THE MAN LOOKED BRIEFLY AT THE P.O., THEN CONTINUED THROWING OBJECT OVER HIS SHOULDER.

"SIR, I ASKED YOU IF I CAN HELP YOU."

NO VERBAL RESPONSE. HOWEVER, THE STRANGER TURNED AND FACED THE P.O. FOR A FEW SECONDS, GAVE HIM WHAT I CALL A FELONY STARE AND TOOK A PAIR OF SCISSORS OUT OF HIS COAT POCKET AND, WHILE CONTINUING TO STARE AT THE OFFICER, PLACED IT ON A NEARBY DESK. THE STRANGER CAST ANOTHER BALEFUL STARE AT THE OFFICER, THEN CASUALLY TURNED AND RESUMED TEARING THE FILING CABINET APART.

THE P.O. LATER DESCRIBED THE STRANGER AS BEING ENTIRELY DRESSED IN BLACK. A BLACK WATCH CAP, BLACK SUNGLASSES, BAGGY BLACK SWEATPANTS AND A HEAVY BLACK OVERCOAT (EVEN THOUGH THIS OCCURRED IN JULY).

"SIR, I AM GOING TO HAVE TO DEMAND THAT YOU STOP DOING WHATEVER IT IS YOU THINK YOU ARE DOING AND LEAVE THIS OFFICE."

AGAIN. NOTHING.

SO, THE P.O. APPROACHED THE STRANGER AND REPEATED HIS COMMAND AND AS HE GOT WITHIN TOUCHING DISTANCE, THE STRANGER RETRIEVED THE SCISSORS AND STABBED THE OFFICER ABOUT TEN TIMES BEFORE HIDING BEHIND THE DESK WHERE SECURITY LOCATED AND HANDCUFFED HIM.

WHEN INTERVIEWED LATER BY COUNTY DETECTIVES, THE STRANGER STATED THAT HE WAS AN OUTPATIENT AT THE MENTAL HEALTH UNIT LOCATED ON THE FLOOR BELOW. HE HAD GOTTEN LOST AND PANICKED. HE WANDERED INTO THE PROBATION OFFICE THROUGH A BACK DOOR THAT WAS AJAR AND ENCOUNTERED A MAN, AND THAT MAN STARTED YELLING AND SCREAMING AT HIM. AGAIN, HE PANICKED – HIS WORD – AND GRABBED SOME SCISSORS OFF A NEARBY DESK AND WAVED IT AT THE MAN, WHO SCREAMED AND RAN OUT OF THE OFFICE.

AFTER THE JUVENILE P.O. RAN AWAY, THE STRANGER TRIED TO FIND HIS WAY OUT OF THE BUILDING AND STARTED SCRATCHING HIS WAY THROUGH THE FILING CABINET, BELIEVING IT WAS A WAY OUT. HE CONFIDED TO THE DETECTIVE THAT HE "FELT LIKE ALICE IN WONDERLAND AND WAS CERTAIN THE QUEEN OF HEARTS WAS GOING TO HAVE MY HEAD CUT OFF..." HE WAS FRIGHTENED AND TRYING TO "DIG MY WAY OUT OF WHEREVER I WAS TO JUST GO BACK HOME" WHEN ANOTHER MAN – THE SECOND PROBATION OFFICER – CONFRONTED HIM AND STARTED ASKING HIM CONFUSING QUESTIONS.

LET'S CONSIDER SOME OF THE **IMPLICATIONS** RELATIVE TO **KNOWING THE OTHER PERSON**. KNOWING WITH WHOM YOU ARE DEALING IS IMPORTANT. IN THE ABOVE SCENARIO, IT WOULD HAVE SAVED THE JUVENILE PROBATION OFFICER PAINFUL WEEKS IN A PHILADELPHIA HOSPITAL AND SEVERAL MICRO-SURGERIES. HOW?

I WAS ASKED TO CONDUCT AN ADVANCED DE-ESCALATION TECHNIQUES SEMINAR FOR BOTH THE ADULT AND JUVENILE OFFICERS OF THE PHILADELPHIA COUNTY PROBATION SERVICES, PARTIALLY BECAUSE OF THE ABOVE INCIDENT, AS WELL AS

ANOTHER INCIDENT WHERE A SECURITY OFFICER HAD BEEN BADLY CUT. I DISCUSSED, AMONG OTHER ISSUES, THE THREE RULES FOR THE MANAGEMENT OF AGGRESSIVE BEHAVIOR AND HOW ADHERING TO THESE RULES CAN MAXIMIZE THEIR SAFETY. WHEN IT CAME TO KNOWING THE SUBJECT (THE STRANGER IN THE WORKPLACE), I ASKED THE CLASS WHAT DID THE P.O. IN QUESTION KNOW ABOUT THE STRANGER WHO HAD STABBED ONE OF THEIR OFFICERS.

"HE KNEW NOTHING ABOUT THE GUY," WAS THE MOST COMMON ANSWER. "THE GUY WAS A TOTAL STRANGER."

TRUE. HE WAS A STRANGER, BUT, DESPITE THAT, THERE ARE PLENTY OF VERBAL AND NON-VERBAL INDICATORS THAT, IF UNDERSTOOD, SHOULD HAVE TOLD THE PROBATION OFFICER ALL OF WHAT HE NEEDED TO KNOW ABOUT THE STRANGER IN HIS OFFICE. THESE INDICATORS WOULD HAVE TOLD THE OFFICER THAT THE STRANGER WAS DANGEROUS. FOR INSTANCE:

✓ ONE, THE STRANGER WAS INEXPLICABLY TEARING APART A FILING CABINET AND RECKLESSLY THROWING OBJECTS OVER HIS SHOULDER. FIRST THING THAT SHOULD OCCUR TO AN OFFICER IS THAT THIS IS NOT THE BEHAVIOR OF A PERSON IN HIS RIGHT MIND. THE SECOND THING IS THAT, EVEN IF THE MAN IS IN HIS RIGHT MIND, HE CERTAINLY IS A DESTRUCTIVE AND/OR A CRIMINAL (UNINVITED) PERSON. ANOTHER RELIABLE CLUE THAT THE STRANGER PRESENTS POTENTIAL DANGER TO THAT OFFICER AND OTHERS WHO MAY BE ON THE SCENE.

✓ TWO, HE MARKED HIS TERRITORY, MUCH LIKE A DANGEROUS ANIMAL URINATES IN A CIRCLE AROUND HIMSELF TO COMMUNICATE TO OTHERS THAT THEY SHOULD STAY OUT OF HIS PERSONAL AREA. THIS ACTION (PLACING THE SCISSORS ON THE DESK AND THE BALEFUL STARE) COULD HAVE TOLD THE P.O. THAT HE IS ALREADY TRIGGERED. INFLUENCED MAYBE BY ANGER, RAGE, FEAR. BIG CLUE. HE IS DANGEROUS!

- ✓ *Three, the stranger never verbally responded to the P.O.'s statements, questions, commands. That indicates that perhaps he is not right. Maybe emotionally disturbed, or severely mentally ill. Crazy. Likely dangerous.*

- ✓ *Four, this person has no place in this workplace. Moreover, he is destroying government property. A crime. Take note, that there are five times when words fail (detailed in a later chapter), meaning any officer or civilian should no longer use words when one or more of these conditions exist. Instead, the officer or civilian should choose physical actions, one of which should be disengaging. Words will likely fail, but, worse, closing distance is uber-dangerous!*

- ✓ *Five, the stranger's clothing should be a red flag! I mean, wearing black is not a crime. Otherwise Johnny Cash and I would have been locked up years ago. But, a thick overcoat in July. Seriously?*

- ✓ *And, then, what about the scissors? A dangerous and deadly edged weapon, which he placed a few feet away. He did so with a challenging stare. The fact that he was armed presents us with*

another factor that clearly tells us that words will fail. That factor is Attack. "Attack" tells us that it is time to abandon words and transition to physical actions. Usually, "attack" comes into play when a bad guy invades an officer's space. This time the officer did the closing of distance, which proved to be a near fatal mistake.

So, MOAB rule – Know the Bad Guy – is, in my opinion, a life preserving principle. But, also, the officer could have taken advantage of an escape route (Know the Environment), disengaged and either summoned security and/or notified others in the workplace that a potential threat existed. Disengaging was his best option, but,

*FAILING THAT, AND KNOWING WHAT HE SHOULD HAVE KNOWN
ABOUT THE STRANGER, HE SHOULD HAVE REALIZED THAT THERE
WAS A DEADLY EDGED WEAPON IN OR NEAR THE STRANGER'S
PERSON AND HE (KNOW YOURSELF) ALSO SHOULD HAVE KNOWN
THAT HE WAS UNARMED AND NO MATCH FOR SOMEONE WITH AN
EDGED WEAPON.*

*IF WE REALLY KNOW THE SUBJECT, GREAT. WE KNOW WHAT HAS
WORKED WITH THE SUBJECT IN THE PAST. ALSO, WHAT DIDN'T
WORK. MORE, WE MIGHT KNOW WHO THE SUBJECT'S SUPPORT
SYSTEM IS AND WE ALSO KNOW IF HE IS NORMALLY A VIOLENT
PERSON OR A USUALLY NICE PERSON. WE ALSO GO INTO ANY
SCENARIO KNOWING THE SUBJECT'S NAME. KNOWING AND USING
THE PERSON'S NAME AS OFTEN AS REASONABLE. AND USING YOUR
NAME IN THE INTERACTION HUMANIZES
BOTH YOU AND THE SUBJECT AND HAS BEEN KNOWN TO BE A
CALMING FACTOR.*

*USING BOTH YOUR NAME AND THE SUBJECT'S NAME ARE
SIGNIFICANT PEACE PHRASES!*

KNOWING THE PERSON'S VERBAL AND NON-VERBAL SIGNATURES IS
CRUCIAL TO OUR SAFETY. I SUGGEST THAT OFFICERS OBSERVE AND
ASSESS SOME OF THE FOLLOWING SIGNS:

VERBAL & NON-VERBAL
SIGNATURES OF DANGER

*BODY LANGUAGE. OVER 80% OF A SUBJECT'S ATTITUDE AND
INTENT CAN BE DERIVED FROM HIS NON-VERBAL ACTIONS. RED
FLAGS, OR SIGNATURES OF DANGER COULD INCLUDE FACIAL
FACTORS, INCLUDING HIS EYES. EYE MOVEMENTS CAN TELL YOU HE
MIGHT BE HEARING VOICES (LOOKING UP AND AROUND); INTENDING
TO ATTACK (STEADY STARE) AND PERHAPS THAT HE HAS LOST THE
ABILITY TO COPE WITH REALITY (THE DEAD-EYED THOUSAND-YARD-
STARE). LOOK FOR CHANGES IN FACIAL COLORING. CHANGES FROM
HIS NATURAL COLOR TO RED MIGHT BE INDICATIVE OF TENSION,
BUT GOING FROM RED TO PALE IS INDICATIVE OF ANGER, AND THEN
PALE TO WHITE IS A SIGN THAT THE SUBJECT HAS TRANSITIONED*

*FROM ANGER ALL THE WAY TO **RAGE**. PALE AND/OR WHITE COLORING INDICATES THAT THE SUBJECT IS UNDERGOING VASCULAR CONSTRICTION, WHICH IS A RESULT OF SNS ACTIVATION WHEN THE BLOOD RUSHES FROM HIS EXTREMITIES TO HIS LARGER MUSCLES IN PREPARATION FOR FIGHT OR FLIGHT. THIS IS A HIGHLY DANGEROUS CONDITION.*

OTHER NON-VERBAL INDICATORS MIGHT INCLUDE:

- ❖ *BODY TENSION.*

- ❖ *RAPID FOOT MOVEMENTS. IN SOME CASES WHEN THE SUBJECT IS PREPARING TO ATTACK, HE WILL SITUATE HIS FEET SO THAT THE DOMINANT FOOT IS REARWARD (BOXER STANCE). THESE LOWER APPENDAGE MOVEMENTS ARE PART OF A "DANCE" DURING CONFLICT WHERE THE SUBJECT IS EITHER LYING, OR SO TENSE THAT HE IS SUBCONSCIOUSLY RELEASING THE ENERGY CAUSED BY TENSION AND STRESS.*

- ❖ *A SPRINTER'S STANCE. THINK OF SOMEONE LEANING FORWARD, HIS HEAD DIPPED, READY TO SPRINT. THIS OFTEN IS THE BAD GUY'S FINAL NON-VERBAL CLUE TO AN ATTACK.*

- ❖ *PACING. THE SUBJECT IS PACING BACK AND FORTH. HE IS FULL OF ENERGY. RELATIVE TO PACING AND OTHER SIMILAR BODY MOVEMENTS, DURING THE PRE-COMBAT STAGE, A SUBJECT WILL – IF YOU ARE PAYING ATTENTION – GIVE AWAY EITHER HIS INTENT TO ATTACK, OR SUBCONSCIOUS WARNINGS THAT HE IS ABOUT TO ATTACK, OR RELEASING BUILT-UP ENERGY CAUSED BY TENSION AND HE IS TRYING TO RELEASE IT. SOME SERIOUS RED FLAGS MIGHT INCLUDE PACING LIKE A CAGED TIGER; THROWING OBJECTS AT OR NEAR THE OTHER PERSON; DIPPING INTO HIS INTENDED-VICTIM'S SPACE AND BACK OUT AGAIN; RAISED VOICE; RAPID SPEECH, ETC.*

- ❖ *THE BOXER STANCE, INCLUDING BALLED FISTS, THE POWER-SIDE SHOULDER DIPPED, THE STRONG HAND MAY BE SECRETED BEHIND HIS BACK. THIS MIGHT OCCUR RIGHT*

AFTER THE PRE-ASSAULT SIGNS I DETAILED ABOVE. THIS IS A SERIOUS WARNING, OR SIGNATURE OF DANGER!

❖ *LOOK FOR FACIAL CHANGES, SUCH AS THE MOUTH HANGING SLIGHTLY OPEN, THE TEETH BARED, EYES GROWING LARGER. THIS IS THE 1000-YARD STARE, WHICH THE STRANGER IN THE ABOVE SCENARIO SEEMED TO BE EXHIBITING.*

❖ *NINETY-SEVEN PER CENT OF ASSAULTS (ON OFFICERS) ARE PRECEDED BY CERTAIN VERBAL AND NON-VERBAL CUES, INCLUDING, AMONG OTHER CUES:*

PRE-ASSAULT CUES

"IF YOU CAN GET YOUR MIND RIGHT DURING THE DANCE WE ALL DO JUST BEFORE A FIGHT, YOU CAN EASILY SEE AND HEAR A PUNCH COMING A MILE AWAY..."

MARK KRUG, FORMER BOUNCER, EXECUTIVE PROTECTION EXPERT

THE TARGET STARE – A BAD GUY WILL OFTEN TIP OFF HIS INTENTIONS WITH A PREDICTABLE SCRIPT.

1) *THIS "SCRIPT" INCLUDES THE BAD GUY GOING FROM LOUDLY ARGUING, CURSING, THREATENING, ETC. TO A SUDDEN CESSATION OF ALL VERBAL CONTENT. YOU CAN APTLY CALL THIS "THE QUIET BEFORE THE STORM."*

2) *THIS PHENOMENON IS OFTEN SEEN AS A RESOLUTION, BUT, PLEASE DO NOT BE FOOLED BY THIS. IT IS A RESOLUTION IN SOME WAYS, BUT ONLY BECAUSE THE BAD GUY HAS RESOLVED IN HIS MIND THAT HE IS GOING INTO ASSAULT MODE.*

3) *OFTEN, THE NEXT STEP IN THE "SCRIPT" IS THE SUBJECT WILL TURN HIS ATTENTION AWAY FROM HIS TARGET – THIS IS CALLED "THE HIATUS." IN MANY CASES, THE BAD GUY TURNS HIS BACK ON THE OFFICER.*

4) *THE NEXT STEP IS OFTEN THE OFFICER'S LAST CHANCE TO RECOGNIZE AND PREVENT AN*

ATTACK. THE SUBJECT WILL RETURN HIS ATTENTION TO THE OFFICER AND WILL NOW LOOK AT THE PART OF THE BODY HE INTENDS TO ATTACK. THIS WILL NOT BE A LONG-LOOK, BUT, INVARIABLY, BEFORE HE PUNCHES, BUTTS, STABS OR KICKS, HE WILL CAST A TARGET STARE AT HIS INTENDED TARGET. THIS IS PART OF A HIGHLY-PREDICTABLE SCRIPT.

HOW TO "HEAR" A PUNCH COMING A MILE AWAY –

*OTHER CUES TO AN INCOMING PUNCH MIGHT INCLUDE SUDDENLY INVADING AN OFFICER'S SPACE. OFFICERS SHOULD CONSIDER THIS MOVEMENT AN EARLY STAGE OF AN ASSAULT. I ALWAYS ADVOCATE THAT THE OFFICER ESTABLISH **PRECLUSION** BY DIRECTING THE SUBJECT TO "GET BACK!;" "STAY WHERE YOU ARE!;" OR, "FOR YOUR SAFETY AND MINE, SIR, DO NOT COME ANY CLOSER!" OF COURSE, OFFICERS SHOULD ALSO BE MINDFUL OF KEY BODY PARTS THAT ARE MICRO-MOVEMENTS INDICATIVE OF AN INCOMING ASSAULT. FOR INSTANCE, A BAD GUY DIPPING HIS POWER-SIDE SHOULDER MIGHT BE, WHEN COMBINED WITH OTHER MICRO-MOVEMENTS – LIKE A BOXER'S STANCE, THE POWER FOOT SHIFTED TO THE REAR, ETC., THE NEXT-TO-LAST MOVEMENT (THE LAST ONE WOULD BE FOOTWORK) BEFORE A PUNCH OR AN EDGED WEAPON THRUST OR SLASH IS LAUNCHED!*

THE FINGER-JAB OR POKE. MAKE NO MISTAKE, ANYONE WHO COMBINES THE SPACE INVASION WITH A FINGER-JAB HAS ESSENTIALLY LAUNCHED AN ASSAULT. THESE ACTIONS MUST BE CONSIDERED AS GENUINE SIGNATURES OF DANGER. THINK OF IT THIS WAY. ANYBODY WHO INVADES ANOTHER PERSON'S PSZ (PERSONAL SAFE ZONE) AND THEN TOUCHES OR JABS THE OTHER PERSON WITH A FINGER (INTO THE CHEST) IS BASICALLY "TESTING THE WATERS." SIGNIFICANT HERE IS THAT, IF THE OFFICER FAILS TO RESPOND WITH SOME KIND OF COUNTERMEASURE, HE IS ESSENTIALLY TELLING THE BAD GUY, "COME ON IN, THE WATER'S FINE."

ABOUT THE THREAT. I KNOW IN PREVIOUS CHAPTERS I URGED OFFICERS TO DEFLECT AND/OR VERBALLY DISARM ALL THREATS AND

ATTEMPTS TO INTIMIDATE. HOWEVER, OFFICERS SHOULD TAKE ALL THREATS SERIOUSLY. IF A BAD GUY
THREATENS AN OFFICER WITH A STATEMENT LIKE "COME ANY CLOSER, PIG, AND I WILL LIGHT YOUR ASS UP! THAT STATEMENT CAN BE DEFLECTED WITH AN APT JUMP OR STRIP PHRASE, BUT I WOULD ADMONISH OFFICERS TO **TRUST THEIR GUT FEELINGS!** CONSIDER A THREAT AN "ATTACK," AND, AN ATTACK IS ONE OF THE FIVE TIMES WHEN VERBAL JUDO SUGGESTS WORDS WILL NO LONGER WORK AND ONLY USE OF FORCE AND/OR DISENGAGING IS CALLED FOR.

KNOW YOURSELF IS THE THIRD RULE FOR THE MANAGEMENT OF AGGRESSIVE BEHAVIOR. THIS RULE, I BELIEVE, IS OF SUCH IMPORTANCE, THAT I AM DEDICATING THE NEXT CHAPTER TO IT.

CHAPTER 10.
YOU HAVE TO KNOW YOURSELF?

"A POLICE OFFICER'S JOB IS 97% MENTAL. ATTITUDE IS
EVERYTHING. A GOOD OFFICER COMMUNICATES
WITH PRO COM (PROFESSIONAL COMMUNICATIONS),
WITH ALL MEMBERS OF THE PUBLIC AND WITH
OTHERS ON HIS ARREST TEAM..."

VETERAN POLICE CAPTAIN, RICHARD WHITEHEAD.

ALL COPS HAVE WEAKNESSES. PROBLEM IS, MANY DENY THE
WEAKNESS. ACCORDING TO VERBAL JUDO, INC., AS MANY AS EIGHT
OUT OF TEN OFFICERS ARE IN DEEP DENIAL. THE LEGENDARY
CHINESE WARRIOR AND PHILOSOPHER, SUN TSU, IN "THE ART OF
WAR," PROPOUNDED THAT "THE PATH OF A SAMURAI'S STRENGTH
LIES IN RECOGNIZING (HIS) WEAKNESS." THAT BELIEF STILL RINGS
TRUE CENTURIES LATER.

THE THING IS, FRIENDS, **THE ONLY PERSON ON A SCENE THAT THE
AUTHORITY FIGURE OR POLICE OFFICER CAN CONTROL IS HIMSELF.**
THE OFFICER MUST KNOW HIS STRENGTHS AND LIMITATIONS. HE
MUST ALSO IDENTIFY HIS HOT BUTTONS, OR **TRIGGERS.** TRIGGERS
ARE ATTITUDES, PSYCHOLOGICAL ISSUES, AND OTHER THINGS THAT
WHEN ATTACKED, WILL ALWAYS CAUSE THE OFFICER TO LOSE
CONTROL OF HIS EMOTIONS. TRIGGERS ARE FEELINGS OR
EXPRESSIONS THAT CAN GET TO US PERSONALLY. AND THE THING
IS, IF THE OFFICER DOESN'T TAKE INVENTORY OF HIS TRIGGERS AND
TAKE STEPS TO CONTROL HIMSELF WHEN THOSE BUTTONS ARE
PUSHED, I GUARANTEE YOU THAT THE BAD GUY WILL!

THE IMPORTANT THING ABOUT UNDERSTANDING AND PROTECTING
OUR TRIGGERS IS THAT NO MATTER HOW AN OFFICER CAN MASTER
ALL THE SKILLS AND TECHNIQUES IN THE WORLD, IT WILL DO HIM

NO GOOD IF HE IS TOO DISTRACTED OR ANGRY TO REMEMBER THOSE SKILLS IN A PINCH. IF HE ALLOWS HIS EGO TO OVERTAKE HIS MASTERY OF TACTICS. HE WILL SURELY TAKE THOSE INEVITABLE ATTACKS PERSONALLY AND WILL BE UNABLE TO ACTIVATE THOSE SKILLS!

A BASIC TENET OF DEFUSING HOSTILITY IS ACCEPTING THE FACT THAT WE ARE RESPONSIBLE FOR OUR OWN CHOICES. INSTEAD OF BLAMING OURSELVES OR OTHERS, IT IS ESSENTIAL THAT WE MUST FIRST REALIZE AND WORK TOWARD GAINING CONTROL OF OURSELVES, AND, BY ACCOMPLISHING THAT, WE WILL GET THE **POWER** TO GET CONTROL OF ANY SITUATION!

SIMPLY PUT, **THE MORE UPSET WE ALLOW THE BAD GUY TO MAKE US, THE LESS LOGICAL WE BECOME.** AND THIS FACT EXPLAINS WHY MANY OF THE BAD GUYS WITH WHOM WE COME IN CONTACT USE ANGER, HOSTILITY, PROFANITY AND
INTIMIDATION TO GET WHAT THEY WANT, WHICH IN MANY INSTANCES IS FOR THE OFFICER TO LOSE HIS COOL AND BLOW HIS PROFESSIONALISM TO SMITHEREENS!

ALWAYS BE COGNIZANT THAT THE ANTISOCIAL PERSON AND THE CRIMINAL HARD CASE ARE EXPERTS AT PICKING OUT ANOTHER PERSON'S WEAKNESSES AND ATTACKING THEM. IF AN OFFICER TAKES NO EFFORT TO BECOME SELF- AWARE AND TO MAKE EFFORTS TO PROTECT HIS TRIGGERS, OR, BETTER YET, TO ELIMINATE THEM, IT COULD TURN OUT TO BE DISASTROUS.

I HAVE ALWAYS ADVOCATED THE SKILL OF RECOGNIZING THE THINGS THAT ALWAYS INFLUENCE US TO BECOME ANGRY, AND, IN TURN, LOSE CONTROL OF OUR EMOTIONS. TRIGGERS. DURING MY SEMINARS, I ASK THE AUDIENCE TO IDENTIFY FIVE OR TEN WORDS, ATTITUDES AND/OR OTHER THINGS WHICH ALWAYS PISS THEM OFF. I HAVE MY OWN LIST AND, WHEN I WAS ON THE STREET, I USED TO STUDY THAT LIST OVER AND OVER SO THAT I WAS INTIMATE WITH THOSE TRIGGERS. I UNDERSTOOD THE CHINESE PHILOSOPHY THAT TAUGHT, "TO KNOW YOUR ENEMY IS TO OWN YOUR ENEMY." EVENTUALLY, I GOT TO THE POINT WHEN I RECOGNIZED A TRIGGER, I COULD SAY TO MYSELF – "HEY, HERE GOES ONE OF MY TRIGGERS. IT DOESN'T MAKE A HILL OF BEANS TO ME ANY LONGER."

SO, WHAT ARE YOUR TRIGGERS?

"WHENEVER A BAD GUY CAN GOAD YOU INTO
ALLOWING YOUR PERSONAL FEELINGS TO
MAKE YOU MISUSE YOUR WORDS OR ACTIONS,
HE **OWNS YOU,** EITHER ON THE STREETS, MAYBE
NOT, BUT PROBABLY IN THE COURTS, OR IN THE
MEDIA...."

DR. GEORGE THOMPSON, FOUNDER, VERBAL JUDO, INC

MAYBE YOU CAN LOCATE ONE OR MORE OF YOUR TRIGGERS ON THIS LIST, MANY OF WHICH WERE MINE, BACK IN THE DAY. MANY ARE TRIGGERS SUGGESTED TO ME BY THE AUDIENCE(S) IN MY MANY SEMINARS.

THE OTHER PERSON ALWAYS PISSES ME OFF WHEN HE:

- *ROLLS HIS EYES WHEN I AM SPEAKING.*
- *IGNORES ME WHEN I AM SPEAKING TO HIM.*
- *TURNS HIS BACK ON ME AS I AM ADDRESSING HIM..*
- *SAYS BAD THINGS ABOUT ME AFTER WE HAVE CONCLUDED SPEAKING. USUALLY "UNDER HIS BREATH" WHILE HE IS WALKING AWAY, BUT LOUD ENOUGH FOR ME TO HEAR HIM. THESE ARE CALLED "HIDDEN OATHS."*
- *CURSES IN MY FACE.*
- *WHEN HE MOVES INTO MY SPACE. GETS TOO CLOSE.*
- *POKES ME IN MY CHEST OR OTHER AREA(S) WITH HIS FINGER.*
- *WHEN HE GETS HIS HANDS UP IN MY FACE.*
- *HE SPITS AT OR NEAR ME.*
- *TOBACCO JUICE SPAT NEAR OR AT ME.*
- *CALLS ME A BAD NAME.*
- *THREATENS ME OR ESPECIALLY A FAMILY MEMBER.*

- *LAUGHING AT OR ABOUT ME OR ANOTHER OFFICER.*
- *LIES TO ME.*
- *MAKES RACIST COMMENTS ABOUT ME OR SOMEONE ELSE.*
- *REFUSE TO DO WHAT I SAY.*
- *QUESTIONS MY AUTHORITY.*
- *QUESTIONS MY INTELLIGENCE.*
- *ARGUES WITH ME.*
- *DISAGREES WITH ME.*
- *RUNS AWAY FROM ME.*
- *SCREAMS AT ME. LOUD NOISES!*
- *DOESN'T ANSWER MY QUESTION(S).*
- *ACCUSES ME OF RACISM, CULTURAL INSENSITIVITY, ETC.*
- DOESN'T STOP SOON ENOUGH AFTER I LIGHT HIM UP.
- QUESTIONS MY COMPETENCY.
- MOVES AFTER I ORDER HIM TO "FREEZE!"

*THESE ARE MANY, BUT FAR FROM ALL, OF THE HOT BUTTONS MY AUDIENCES (AND I) HAVE IDENTIFIED. THE IMPORTANT CONCLUSION I HOPE OFFICERS TAKE AWAY FROM THIS TRIGGER EXERCISE IS THAT, WITHOUT EXCEPTION, WE ALL HAVE WEAKNESSES AND WE ALL HAVE THESE HOT BUTTONS. BAD GUYS WILL ALWAYS BE HUNTING FOR THESE TRIGGERS IN THAT ETERNAL SEARCH FOR **THAT EDGE** THAT CAN HELP THEM EITHER EVADE DETECTION OR ARREST, OR, WORSE, DEFEAT OR KILL THE OFFICER. AS I HAVE ALREADY MENTIONED, THE "WORST" BAD GUYS ARE THE BEST OBSERVERS. THEY ARE LIKE HAWKS, CIRCLING, ALERT FOR SOMETHING, MAYBE ONLY THEY CAN SEE. A WEAKNESS, AN OPENING, A VULNERABILITY, AND, ONCE THEY SPOT IT, QUICKLY AND BRUTALLY EXPLOIT IT.*

SO, I REITERATE. IF YOU DO NOT IDENTIFY YOUR TRIGGERS, FOR CERTAIN, THE BAD GUYS WILL!

IN THE END, THE BAD GUY'S PURPOSE IS TO FOOT SWEEP AN OFFICER. TO KNOCK HIM OFF BALANCE AND TO CAUSE HIM TO GIVE UP HIS PROFESSIONALISM. TO CAUSE HIM TO OVERLOOK EVIDENCE, OR CUES TO AN ONCOMING ATTACK. MAYBE TO GET HIM TO MISUSE HIS WORDS, MAYBE USE UNWARRANTED FORCE. SURE, OFTEN THE BAD GUY WILL END UP IN CUFFS, MAYBE EVEN IN AN EMERGENCY ROOM, OFTEN IN LOCKUP SOMEWHERE. BUT NOW HE HAS ACCOMPLISHED WHAT HE SET OUT TO DO AND THOSE SETBACKS ARE WELL WORTH THE PAIN AND THE TIME BEHIND BARS. BOTH ARE EIGHTS-OF-PASSAGE IN HIS LIFE, ANYWAYS.

Ho Hum. No big deal.

WHICH BRINGS US TO THIS NEXT POINT.

THERE IS AN IRONY IN ALL THIS. THE IRONY IS THAT, AT THE END OF THE DAY, THE UNSKILLED OFFICER, WHO IS THE PROFESSIONAL RESPONSIBLE FOR KEEPING THE PEACE AND CONTROLLING THE SCENE, ENDS UP BEING RESPONSIBLE FOR BUILDING GROUND. GROUND THAT UP UNTIL THEN DID NOT EXIST. THAT WILL ALLOW THE BAD GUY TO WALK UPON AND WREST CONTROL FROM THAT OFFICER(S) AND TAKE CONTROL OF THE SITUATION! THAT "GROUND" CAN GIVE THE BAD GUY <u>JUSTIFICATION</u> FOR ATTACKING THAT OFFICER. OR GIVE HIM AMMUNITION FOR SUING HIM AS WELL.

LOCATING AND "SQUEEZING" AN OFFICER'S TRIGGER(S) CAN WORK TO THE POINT THAT THE BAD GUY CAN WIN IN THE COURT, WIN IN THE MEDIA, MAYBE EVEN ON THE STREET!.

SPEAKING OF BRAIN-DAMAGED PEOPLE WHO ARE UNDER THE INFLUENCE

A TALE FROM THE STREETS

A BRIEF BUT TRAGIC TALE FROM THE STREETS

DAVENPORT, IOWA

JUDGE: "COP-SLAYING SUSPECT ATTACKED AND EXPLOITED MOM."
RYAN J. FOLEY AND DAVID PITT, ASSOCIATED PRESS

AN IOWA MAN CHARGED THURSDAY (NOVEMBER 3, 2016) WITH KILLING TWO POLICE OFFICERS WAS FACING **INTENSE MONEY PROBLEMS, HAD BEEN FOUND BY A JUDGE TO HIT AND** FINANCIALLY EXPLOIT HIS MOTHER AND WAS ORDERED TO
MOVE OUT OF HER BASEMENT <u>HOURS BEFORE THE SLAYINGS.</u>

SCOTT MICHAEL GREENE, 46, WAS ARRESTED THURSDAY AFTERNOON AFTER DETECTIVES QUESTIONED HIM AT THE POLICE STATION....

IN A LATER CHAPTER, I WILL DISCUSS SOME OF THE TIMES WHEN DE-ESCALATION FAILS. THE ABOVE NEWS ARTICLE, OBVIOUSLY, HAS LITTLE TO DO WITH THE ART OF DE-ESCALATING AGGRESSION. IF NOT UNCEREMONIOUSLY AMBUSHED, THESE UNFORTUNATE OFFICERS WOULD HAVE RIGHTFULLY AND JUSTIFIABLY RESPONDED QUICKLY, DECISIVELY AND WITH DUE FORCE. AND, LIKELY, WITHOUT UTTERING ONE WORD BEFOREHAND, SAVE PERHAPS FOR THE APPROPRIATE VERBAL WARNING PRIOR TO USING THEIR WEAPON(S).

*BUT, THEN AGAIN, WHEN WE ADDRESS DE-ESCALATION, WE ARE ALSO CONSIDERING THE ENTIRE PANOPLY OF SKILLS AND OTHER ASPECTS OF DEALING WITH AN ENTIRE CONTINUUM OF POTENTIALLY DANGEROUS PEOPLE. AND, IN THAT VEIN, I AM ASKING THE READER TO UNDERSTAND HOW PEOPLE WHOM YOU DEAL WITH, AND WHO MAY OR MAY NOT HAVE VIOLENT TENDENCIES, CAN BECOME **BRAIN DAMAGED** AND POSSIBLY DANGEROUS WHEN **UNDER THE INFLUENCE** OF THE FORCES THAT SCOTT MICHAEL GREENE OF DAVENPORT, IOWA APPEARS TO HAVE BEEN UNDER WHEN HE AMBUSHED AND TOOK THE LIVES OF THESE TWO FINE OFFICERS OF THE LAW!*

CHAPTER 11.

WHAT ABOUT OFFICERS WHO ARE "UNDER THE INFLUENCE?"

"...IN MANY CASES, BECAUSE OF MENTAL ILLNESS (UNDER THE INFLUENCE OF), THE CITIZEN CANNOT COMMUNICATE WITH POLICE. IN SOME CASES, THEY MAY APPEAR TO BE THREATENING OR UNCOOPERATIVE, WHEN IN FACT, THEY ARE UNABLE TO UNDERSTAND AN OFFICER'S QUESTIONS OR ORDERS."
PHILADELPHIA POLICE COMMISSIONER CHARLES RAMSEY, FEBRUARY, 2012

THE ABOVE NEWS STORY CONCERNING THE CITIZEN WHO ASSASSINATED TWO OFFICERS LIKELY BECAUSE OF THE POWERFUL "INFLUENCES" HE WAS UNDER, PLUS THE INVENTORY OF INFLUENCES (OR, TRIGGERS) LISTED IN CHAPTER 10 ILLUSTRATES HOW FACTORS BEYOND AN OFFICERS CONTROL CAN DRAMATICALLY IMPACT THEIR SAFETY. THESE *"INFLUENCES" CAN IMPACT HOW A CITIZEN OR PERCEIVED* BAD GUY *MAY REACT TO THE APPEARANCE AND/OR CONTACT WITH AN OFFICER (OR, A CITIZEN WHO IS AN AUTHORITY FIGURE).* HOWEVER, *LET'S NOT OVERLOOK ANOTHER IMPORTANT FACTOR IN ANY RELATIONSHIP OR INTERACTION BETWEEN A MEMBER OF A COMMUNITY AND LAW ENFORCEMENT. AND THAT IS...*

THE INFLUENCES *THE POLICE OR CORRECTIONS OFFICER IS UNDER AT ANY POINT IN A CONTACT.* LET'S *EXAMINE A FEW OF THESE:*

✓ *PEER PRESSURE. IT HAS LONG BEEN A CONTENTION OF MINE THAT OFFICERS WILL OFTEN REACT ONE WAY OR ANOTHER BECAUSE OF THE PRESENCE OF FELLOW OFFICERS. IT IS NOT UNUSUAL THAT AN OFFICER WILL GET TEASED AND MAYBE*

EVEN BELITTLED ("NANCY BOY," OR "PUSSY") BACK IN HEADQUARTERS AFTER OR EVEN DURING A CONFRONTATION WITH A RESISTIVE SUBJECT USING EMPATHY AND WORDS OF DE-ESCALATION INSTEAD OF IMMEDIATE ACTION.

✓ **WARRIOR-IMAGE.** *CONSIDER OUR OWN LANGUAGE AS A TRIGGER OR INFLUENCE. MORE OFTEN THAN NOT, POLICE CONSIDER THEMSELVES WARRIORS, NOT PEACE KEEPERS. I ATTEND TRAINING PROGRAMS ALL OVER THE COUNTRY AND ON ALMOST EVERY OCCASION, SPEAKERS ADDRESS COPS AS WARRIORS. I IMAGINE THAT THIS IMAGE THAT IS INCULCATED IN EVERY OFFICER INFLUENCES THEIR ACTIONS AND (LACK OF PEACE-PROMOTING) WORDS ON THE STREETS. WARRIORS RARELY USE REDUCTIVE LANGUAGE IN FICTION, IN MOVIES, ON TV. WHY WOULD IT BE ANY DIFFERENT ON THE STREETS? ALTHOUGH IT SHOULD. AFTER ALL, WE ARE DEALING WITH PEOPLE WE ARE SWORN TO PROTECT. IN MY WINOLOGY CONCEPT, HOWEVER, LAW ENFORCEMENT, CORRECTIONS, AND OTHER S ARE ENCOURAGED TO ALSO THINK OF THEMSELVES AS **PEACE WARRIORS**. PEACE WARRIORS UNDERSTAND THE NEED FOR **MINIMIZING THE USE OF FORCE UNLESS IT IS CALLED FOR**. PEACE WARRIORS CONSTANTLY SEARCH FOR FINDING WAYS FOR A PEACEFUL RESOLUTION.*

✓ **ACADEMY-TRAINING.** *AT A RECENT INTERNATIONAL LAW ENFORCEMENT CONFERENCE ATTENDING BY POLICE CHIEFS AND OTHER EXPERTS ON THE USE OF FORCE, CHICAGO POLICE DEPARTMENT SUPERINTENDENT EDDIE JOHNSON URGED OTHER DEPARTMENTS TO TRAIN OFFICERS TO CHANGE HOW THEIR ACADEMIES TEACH FORCE, NOTING THAT TRADITIONALLY ACADEMIES TEACH TACTICS AND PRINCIPLES FOR USING PROPER FORCE IN RESPONSE TO RESISTANCE AND AGGRESSION. "HOWEVER," HE NOTED, "IT IS RARE WHEN ACADEMIES TEACH THE USE AND MASTERY OF (REDUCTIVE) WORDS IN STRESSFUL SCENARIOS. RARE WHEN ACADEMIES TEACH THE MASTERY OF LANGUAGE INSTEAD OF GUNS, QUESTIONS INSTEAD OF ORDERS, PATIENCE INSTEAD OF IMMEDIATE ACTION..."*

✓ *COMMUNITY-RELATIONS. IT IS ALMOST IMPOSSIBLE FOR AN OFFICER NOT TO BE INFLUENCED BY THE ATTITUDES AND MENTALITY OF THE COMMUNITY WITHIN WHICH HE MUST WORK. CONSIDER FOR A MOMENT ATTITUDES IN CITIES SUCH AS FERGUSON, MISSOURI FOLLOWING THE CONTROVERSIAL SHOOTING AND DEATH OF MICHAEL BROWN. PHILADELPHIA POLICE COMMISSIONER RAMSEY NOTED RECENTLY THAT "THERE IS ANOTHER TYPE OF DE-ESCALATION. WE ALL OFTEN HAVE TO MANAGE HOW TO DE-ESCALATE TENSION IN OUR COMMUNITIES AFTER A (DEADLY) USE OF FORCE INCIDENT..." TENSE ENCOUNTERS WITH OUR COMMUNITIES ARE GOING TO CONTINUE TO ESCALATE WHEN LAW ENFORCEMENT CONTINUE TO REACT WITH FORCE, INSTEAD OF WORDS, WHEN A MEMBER OF THE COMMUNITY* "REFUSES TO COMPLY WITH AN ORDER WITHOUT ANY SIGN OF (ACTIVE) AGGRESSION OR HOSTILITY ACTIONS TOWARD AN OFFICER..."

✓ **Community-Hostility.** In fairness to law enforcement and the often-hostile relationship between them and the people in the communities they police, it is a fact, that, in many cases, officers who were determined to treat people – in many cases, minority citizens – with one, if not all of the "5 Things All People Want – **Fairness, Equity, Honesty, Consistency and Respect** –" have been greeted with hostility, verbal abuse, and, in many cases, outright belligerence, before they (officers) could even open up a dialogue. I must say that this type of hostility and hatred for authority has a direct influence on officers who are called upon to enforce laws and protect citizens in those communities. I, for one, cannot blame officers who enter such a community *Under the Influence* of anxiety, fear, maybe even hatred. Of course, once again, the officer is expected by our courts, their administrators, and those communities to **rise above**

215

those personal emotions and prejudice, but, still, reality is reality, is it not?

✓ *FEAR.* FEAR RANKS RIGHT NEAR THE TOP AS A MAJOR INFLUENCE ON HOW AN OFFICER WILL REACT UNDER PRESSURE. *PPCT TRAINING SYSTEMS PROPOSES THAT FEAR ACTS AS A TRIGGER FOR SYMPATHETIC NERVOUS SYSTEM (SNS) ACTIVATION. ALLOW ME TO REMIND YOU THAT SNS ACTIVATION AFFECTS OFFICERS' MOTOR SKILL ABILITY, CAUSES VISUAL DYSFUNCTIONS, AND THEIR ABILITY TO THINK UNDER SURVIVAL STRESS, WHICH IS SYNONYMOUS WITH SNS. FEAR IS A FORMIDABLE INFLUENCE OVER OUR ACTIONS, ESPECIALLY WHEN WE TAKE NO REMEDIAL STEPS TO RECOGNIZE AND MINIMIZE ITS EFFECT. NOT ONLY THAT, THERE ARE SEVERAL OTHER INFLUENCES WITHIN ITSELF, INCLUDING, BUT NOT LIMITED TO FEAR OF FEAR; FEAR OF KILLING; FEAR OF DEATH; FEAR OF INJURY; FEAR OF MAKING THE WRONG DECISION(S); FEAR OF LEGAL DIFFICULTIES (LITIGATION, EXCESSIVE FORCE ALLEGATIONS, ETC.); FEAR OF PEER DISRESPECT.*

✓ *ANGER. THIS IS ANOTHER EMOTION THAT RANKS NEAR THE TOP OF INFLUENCERS ON OUR EFFECTIVENESS. ANGER AND AGGRESSION WILL ALSO TRIGGER SNS ACTIVATION. OFTEN, SOME POLICE OFFICERS GET ANGRY AT THE FIRST SIGN OF RESISTANCE. OFTEN, THOSE SAME OFFICERS CONSIDER ALL RESISTANCE UNREASONABLE AND JUSTIFICATION FOR THEIR PERSONAL RAGE, WHICH, BY THE WAY, IS A POWERFUL REASON TO CONSIDER ADOPTING THE TWIN REDUCTIVE STRATEGIES OF REASONABLE PROFESSIONAL (TACTICAL) INDIFFERENCE AND/OR INTELLECTUAL DELAY! OFFICERS SHOULD REMEMBER THAT ANGER IS A PERSONAL AND VISCERAL REACTION, WHICH IN MANY CASES IS TRIGGERED BY WORDS AND ACTIONS BY A CITIZEN OR SUSPECT. ANGER, THEN, IS AN APPROPRIATE AND NATURAL REACTION TO PERCEIVED DISRESPECT BY A* PROFESSIONAL KEEPER OF THE PEACE, BUT AVENGING THAT ANGER IS NEVER ACCEPTABLE! DOING SO *IS EVIDENCE THAT AN OFFICER HAS TAKEN THOSE WORDS AND MISDEEDS BY THE OTHER PERSON* PERSONALLY.

*ANY TIME AN OFFICER REACTS EMOTIONALLY AND PERSONALLY TO THE OTHER PERSON'S ATTITUDE, WORDS AND ACTIONS, ALWAYS GETS THE **EGO** GETS INVOLVED, AND ANY TIME THE EGO GETS INVOLVED OFFICERS TEND TO REACT WITH PERSONAL RAGE.*

✓ ***EGO.*** *EGO IS AN INTEGRAL PART OF EVERY PERSON WALKING THIS GLOBE.* EGO IS <u>NATURAL</u>! *BUT I HOPE THAT THROUGHOUT THIS BOOK I HAVE MADE IT CLEAR THAT, FOR US (OFFICERS, SECURITY, AND CITIZENS WHO WORK WITH AGGRESSIVE PEOPLE),* **ACTING IN PROTECTION OF OUR EGO CAN BE CATASTROPHIC.** *EGO INFLUENCES US TO REACT TO PERSONAL VERBAL ATTACKS, EVEN RELATIVELY MINOR ONES, WITH* ANGER, RAGE, DEFENSIVENESS, HOSTILITY, AND SIMILAR ACTIONS. WHICH NOT ONLY FAIL TO ACHIEVE OUR TACTICAL OBJECTIVE(S), BUT, EVEN MORE DISASTROUSLY, **INFLATE THE BAD GUY'S INFLUENCERS AND CONCOMITANTLY ESCALATE THE CHANCES OF VIOLENCE AGAINST THE OFFICER!** *ALWAYS REMEMBER WHEN YOU ARE OUT THERE DEALING WITH HOSTILITY THAT* <u>**'THE MORE EGO YOU CARRY INTO ANY INTERACTION, THE LOWER YOUR SAFETY AND CONTROL IN THAT INTERACTION!'**</u>"

✓ ***SNS ACTIVATION.*** *ALMOST EVERY EMOTION OR PERCEPTION THAT INFLUENCES AN OFFICER'S ACTIONS CAN TRIGGER A CATASTROPHIC SURVIVAL STRESS OR SNS OVERLOAD. ONE OF THE KEY GOALS OF THIS BOOK AND OF ADVANCED DE-ESCALATION IS TO **TRICK THE SNS!** AGAIN, I NOTE THAT ALLOWING ONE'S EGO AND PERSONAL AGENDA TO DISORIENT YOU FROM YOUR DUTY TO PROTECT THE PUBLIC ENOUGH TO TRIGGER SNS WILL CAUSE YOUR HEART RATE TO ESCALATE, YOUR BREATHING TO GO BERSERK, YOUR VISION TO DEGRADE, AUDITORY EXCLUSION, AND, IF THAT ISN'T ENOUGH, WHEN YOUR RESTING HEART RATE SPIKES TO ABOUT 200 BPM, YOUR MIND TO SPIN INTO **IRRATIONAL** THOUGHTS, EVEN DELUSIONS. AGAIN, I REMIND OFFICERS OF THE REDUCTIVE TACTIC I CALL REASONABLE PROFESSIONAL INDIFFERENCE.*

WE CAN DISCUSS THESE INFLUENCES FOR PAGES, BUT THESE ISSUES BOIL DOWN TO ONE KEY RESPONSIBILITY OF ANY OFFICER OR CITIZEN WHO WISHES NOT ONLY TO STAY SAFE, BUT TO MAINTAIN THEIR CENTER TO THE POINT WHERE THESE INFLUENCES WILL EITHER NOT IMPACT THEM AT ALL, OR, FAILING THAT, HAVE THE LEAST EFFECT ON HOW THEY CONDUCT THEMSELVES ON A DAY-TO-DAY BASIS.

ALWAYS STAY COOL EVEN WHEN EVERYTHING AROUND YOU IS WHITE HOT!

A FEW WORDS ON MANAGING INFLUENCES

ENCOUNTERS THAT END TRAGICALLY ALMOST ALWAYS HAPPEN **RAPIDLY**, WITH THE USE OF FORCE OCCURRING LESS THAN FIVE (5) SECONDS AFTER THE FIRST OFFICER ARRIVES ON THE SCENE...

CONCLUSION OF INTERNATIONAL CONFERENCE, CHIEFS OF POLICE. "AN INTEGRATED APPROACH TO DE-ESCALATION (2/2012).

ON THE ISSUE – OR, GOAL – OF TRICKING THE SNS, I BELIEVE IT IS A MATTER OF ALTERING THE WAY LAW ENFORCEMENT THINKS ABOUT DEALING WITH HOSTILITY, AGGRESSION AND RESISTANCE IN OUR COMMUNITIES. WE ALL HAVE THESE EMOTIONS, FOLKS. I KNOW I DO. WE ALL HAVE IMPLIED PREJUDICES, EGO, ANGER, FEAR, DEFENSIVENESS. EVEN HATRED. THESE ARE ALL NATURAL EMOTIONS. AND NATURAL EMOTIONS OR FEELINGS ALL INFLUENCE HOW WE (NATURALLY) FEEL.

IF ANYTHING, THE ART OF DEFUSING AGGRESSION AND HOSTILITY (AND THE SEVERELY MENTALLY ILL) ADVOCATES THAT IT DOESN'T MATTER HOW WE FEEL. THE ONLY THING THAT COUNTS IS HOW WE ACT! SURE, WE CAN AND SHOULD RECOGNIZE THAT WE HAVE BEEN TRIGGERED BY AN EVENT, BY WORDS, AND/OR BY THE ACTIONS AND ATTITUDES OF OTHERS, BUT THE KEY IS THAT WE MUST COME TO KNOW OURSELVES, AND KNOWING OURSELVES IS KNOWING THAT WE HAVE BEEN TRIGGERED! THAT WE HAVE HAD ONE OF OUR HOT BUTTONS PUSHED. NOW, KNOWING WHEN AND HOW A TRIGGER HAS BEEN PUSHED IS DIFFERENT FOR EVERYBODY. I KNOW WHEN IT HAPPENS. THE FEELINGS THAT BEGIN TO WASH

218

OVER ME, THE URGE TO DO SOMETHING OR SAY SOMETHING TO THAT PERSON OR THING THAT JUST GOT ME ALL FIRED UP, THE SWIRL OF ADRENALIN THAT IS SHOOTING MOLECULES AND ENERGY UP AND DOWN MY SPINE. THE WAY MY HANDS SHAKE THEN TURN INTO STONE HARD FISTS AND THE WAY MY THROAT GOES DRY. YOU PROBABLY KNOW WHAT I AM TALKING ABOUT. EVERYBODY HAS GONE THROUGH IT.

MY POINT TO LAW ENFORCEMENT AND LAY-CITIZENS IS, WE NEED TO BE AWARE WHEN SOMEONE OR SOMETHING HAS TRIGGERED US. THAT IS POINT NUMBER ONE.

POINT TWO IS, ONCE WE ARE AWARE THAT WE HAVE BEEN TRIGGERED, WE MUST DO SOMETHING TO PREVENT LOSING CONTROL. YOU ALREADY KNOW THAT CONTROLLING OUR EMOTIONS IS NECESSARY FOR US TO BE ABLE TO CONTROL OTHERS. FOR CERTAIN, THIS IS NOT A SIMPLE NOR EASY TASK. A DANGEROUS INDIVIDUAL MAY BE THROWING OFF VIOLENT VIBES, OR DISPLAYING EMOTIONALLY DISTURBED BEHAVIOR. PLUS, MORE LIKELY THAN NOT, THE OFFICER HAS MILLISECONDS TO ACT. TIME, OR THE LACK OF IT, IS A SIGNIFICANT STRESSOR. OUTSIDE NOISE, INCLUDING SIRENS, SCREAMS, CURSES, THREATS, MAYBE GUN SHOTS, BULL-HORNED COMMANDS ECHOING OFF THE SIDES OF BUILDINGS. AND, OF COURSE, THERE ARE THOSE STANDERS-BY AND WITNESSES.

CELL PHONE VIDEOS, CAMERAS CLICKING, CRIES OF SHOCK, FEAR AND AWE. PULSATING, FLASHING RED AND BLUE EMERGENCY LIGHTS...YOU NAME IT.

THEN THERE IS **INSIDE NOISE**. INSIDE NOISE IS INEVITABLE. THESE ARE OUR BELIEFS AND ATTITUDES, WHICH WE TAKE WITH US WHEREVER WE GO. I CALL THESE ATTITUDES, BELIEFS, AND FEELINGS INSIDE NOISE BECAUSE THEY INTERFERE AND SOMETIMES NEGATIVELY AFFECT OUR CONSCIOUS (THOUGHTS) AND ACTIONS. AS I'VE NOTED EARLIER IN THIS BOOK, ATTITUDE IS EVERYTHING. MEANING OUR THOUGHTS AND BELIEFS AFFECT HOW WE ACT TOWARD OTHERS. IF WE ALLOW IT TO, THAT IS.

FOR INSTANCE, OUR **INNER VOICE** IS THE "VOICE" THAT WE OFTEN HEAR ON OUR WAY TO A CONTACT, EVENT OR INTERACTION THAT

SAYS TO US, "AHA, HERE COMES ANOTHER SCUMBAG ASSHOLE!"
THIS VOICE IS TOTALLY INVOLUNTARY, BUT, ALAS, HERE IT IS.

THE TRICK IS TO NEVER, EVER QUOTE THAT INNER VOICE!

WHICH IS WHY I SUGGEST THAT BEFORE ANY ENCOUNTER WITH
THE PUBLIC, WE MUST CLEAR OUR MIND OF ALL INSIDE NOISE. GO
INTO THE CONTACT WITH A **BEGINNER'S MIND. OPEN, FLEXIBLE
AND NIMBLE.**

*SO, IS THERE ANY WAY TO NULLIFY THE NEGATIVE EFFECTS OF
BOTH THE OUTER AND INNER VOICE?*

*THE WAY TO DO THIS IS THE **RTI.** STANDS FOR REASONABLE
TACTICAL INDIFFERENCE. OR, REASONABLE PROFESSIONAL
INDIFFERENCE. SAME THING. RTI HAS BEEN HELPFUL TO MY (AND
OTHERS) BEING ABLE TO CONTROL MY REACTIONS AND EMOTIONS
UNDER ALL CIRCUMSTANCES. IT IS SIMPLE AND EASY AND IT CAN
WORK FOR EVERYONE. RTI CAN MAKE ALL TRIGGERS AND
INFLUENCES EMULSIFY AND VANISH. THINK ABOUT IT. RTI CAN
TOTALLY DISARM VERBAL HOSTILITY. RTI CAN ACT AS A BULKHEAD
AGAINST THE ONSET OF SNS.*

HOW?

*WHEN YOU DIVEST AND DETACH YOURSELF FROM BEING
EMOTIONALLY DEPENDENT UPON COOPERATION AND RESPECT BY
THOSE WHO WOULD RESIST, DISOBEY, AND/OR USE THREATS AND
INTIMIDATION, YOU CAN EASILY DISARM AND DEFLECT FEELING
UPSET OR EMOTIONALLY DISTRESSED ABOUT THE ATTITUDES OF
OTHERS. YOU ARE ABLE TO ACT OUT AND "BECOME" ONE WITH
THE PHILOSOPHY CENTRAL TO WINOLOGY (DE-ESCALATION),
WHICH SAYS:* **ALLOW THE ATTITUDE OF OTHERS TO FLOAT PAST
YOU BY LIKE A BOAT ON A RIVER. INSTEAD, CONCENTRATE ON HIS
ACTIONS!**

*THIS PHILOSOPHY – RTI – CAN DISSOLVE THE MANY INFLUENCES
POLICE OFFICERS ARE UNDER, AND IT CAN ALSO WORK TO
UNDERSTAND AND DEAL WITH THE INFLUENCES THE SUBJECT
MIGHT BE UNDER. IT COULD HELP US TO BE ABLE TO UNDERSTAND*

THE DE-ESCALATION PRECEPT THAT URGES OFFICERS TO UNDERSTAND THAT OFTEN "BAD GUYS," WHO ARE UNDER THE INFLUENCE OF ONE OR MORE OF THE EMOTIONS LISTED ABOVE, ARE BRAIN DAMAGED, AND IT IS OUR JOB TO TRY TO "THINK AND ACT FOR THESE BRAIN-DAMAGED PEOPLE AS IF IT WAS 24-HOURS DOWN THE ROAD AND THEY WERE ABLE TO EXERCISE THEIR POWERS OF REASON AND LOGIC."

TO MY WAY OF THINKING, RTI CAN MINIMIZE THE INFLUENCE OF OUR EGO. ADDITIONALLY, BY EXERCISING RTI, WE ALSO MAKE IT EASIER TO DEPERSONALIZE AS WELL AS TO EASILY AND EFFECTIVELY DEFLECT VERBAL HOSTILITY.

BUT REASONABLE INDIFFERENCE DOES NOT MEAN THAT OFFICERS SHOULD BE BLASÉ AND CAVALIER ABOUT A SUBJECT WHO VERBALLY ATTACKS HIM AND WHO INVADES HIS PSZ (PERSONAL SAFETY ZONE). RTI SIMPLY MEANS THAT A PERSON WHO TRIES TO TRIGGER US BY RESISTING COMMANDS AND CALLING US NAMES DOES NOT CAUSE US EMOTIONAL DISTRESS. WHY? BECAUSE WE ARE NOT PERSONALLY AND EMOTIONALLY INVESTED IN HIS NEGATIVE WORDS AND ACTIONS. WE HAVE FULLY DEPRECIATED ALL HIS VERBAL ICONS AND WE WILL NOW AND FOREVER DO WHATEVER IT IS WE HAVE TO DO TO PROTECT OURSELVES AND THE COMMUNITY.

IN ADDITION TO RTI, THERE IS ONE OTHER STRATEGY I WOULD LIKE OFFICERS TO CONSIDER. THAT IS TACTICAL-INTELLECTUAL-DELAY (TID). TID IS ANOTHER TACTICAL BULWARK DESIGNED TO SLOW US DOWN AND CREATE A MORE DELIBERATE AND STUDIED RESPONSE TO VERBAL AND/OR PHYSICAL AGGRESSION. OF COURSE, TAKING ONE'S TIME – EVEN UNDER TIME PRESSURE – AND EMPLOYING A STUDIED AND DELIBERATE RESPONSE WILL GIVE US THE ABILITY TO KEEP OUR MIND STILL AND CALM, EVEN WHEN UNDER THE DEBILITATING EFFECTS OF SURVIVAL STRESS.

A GREAT BYPRODUCT OF RTI AND TID IS THE FACT THAT WE NOW HAVE THE ABILITY TO MODEL CALM BY THE USE OF PROFESSIONAL AND STUDIED WORDS AND OUR SLOW, DELIBERATE, AND "COOL" MOVEMENTS. WHAT THIS DOES IS TO INFLUENCE THE BAD GUY OR SUSPECT TO SLOW HIS BREATHING. YOU MIGHT FIND IT USEFUL TO KNOW THAT WHEN A PERSON SLOWS HIS RESPIRATION AND HEART

RATE, HIS PURSUANT ACTIONS AND THOUGHTS ARE ALSO SLOW, LEADING TO REDUCED AGGRESSION.

FINALLY, ALLOW ME TO SUGGEST A TACTIC THAT WILL EMPOWER YOU TO AVOID AND DIMINISH THE DEBILITATING EFFECTS OF BEING TRIGGERED. CONSIDER THESE STEPS:

KNOW YOURSELF. I MEAN, REALLY UNDERSTAND YOURSELF. TAKE A REALISTIC INVENTORY.

WHAT ARE MY STRENGTHS & WEAKNESSES? ONCE YOU DO THAT, DO SOME WORK ON MINIMIZING THESE WEAKNESSES. PEOPLE WHO ALMOST ALWAYS PISS YOU OFF? PEOPLE YOU DO NOT LIKE TO WORK WITH?

WHAT ALMOST ALWAYS PISSES ME OFF? WHAT ARE MY TRIGGERS? MAKE YOURSELF A LIST OF THINGS, WORDS, ATTITUDES AND THE TYPE OF PEOPLE WHO MAKE YOU ANGRY ENOUGH TO ACT OUT IN ANGER, MAYBE EVEN LOSE YOUR PROFESSIONALISM OVER.

STUDY YOUR TRIGGER LIST FROM TIME-TO-TIME! REMEMBER, AS SUN TZU ONCE WROTE: "IF YOU CAN DEFINE YOUR ENEMY, YOU WILL OWN HIM!" DEFINING YOUR TRIGGERS, THEN, WILL ALLOW YOU TO EXERCISE RTI AND TID. MEANING, INSTEAD OF THE BAD GUY TRIGGERING YOU, YOU DEFLECT THE ATTACK AND NOW YOU OWN HIM!

PETASIZE YOUR TRIGGERS (VERBAL JUDO): "PET-A-SIZE YOUR TRIGGERS" COMES DOWN TO DEFINING THEM, AND, OVER TIME, MEANS THAT BY DEFINING THEM, YOU WILL OWN THEM! THE EFFECT OF WHICH IS THAT WHEN SOME JOKER TRIES TO GET YOU TO LOSE YOUR COOL, YOU WILL RECOGNIZE THAT TRIGGER(S) HE IS TRYING TO PUSH. THAT TRIGGER HAS BECOME YOUR PET – A PET YOU OWN – AND YOU WILL RECOGNIZE THAT A TRIGGER IS BEING PUSHED AND YOU WILL, IN ESSENCE, SAY TO YOURSELF, "AHH, THAT USED TO BE MY TRIGGER. NOW, LET ME GET DOWN TO BUSINESS WITH THIS GUY…"

In Other Words, You Have Just Attached an Unbreakable Trigger Guard Over Your Triggers Each & Every Time You Interact with Someone!

CHAPTER 12. ON DEFUSING SUICIDE-BY-COP!

STUDIES SHOW THAT SUSPECTS RUN FASTER AND FIGHT HARDER WHEN A POLICE OFFICER USES PROFANITY. THEY FIGHT LIKE MANIACS WHEN A POLICE OFFICER GIVES UP HIS PROFESSIONALISM.

LA STUDY ON WHY THEY RESIST.

YOU MAY RECALL THAT EARLIER I LAMENTED THE LACK OF CREDIBLE DE-ESCALATION TRAININGS FOR LAW ENFORCEMENT. HOWEVER, IN MY OPINION, IT MAY BE EVEN MORE EGREGIOUS THAT, IN VIEW OF RECENT UPTICKS IN THE INCIDENTS OF SUICIDE BY COPS (SBC), ONLY 10% OF OUR NATION'S 15,000 PLUS POLICE DEPARTMENTS OFFER CRISIS INTERVENTION PROGRAMS. SBC IS A REAL ISSUE FACED BY THOSE IN LAW ENFORCEMENT. AS A MATTER OF FACT, FOR BOTH PARTIES INVOLVED, SBC CAN BE FRIGHTENING AND LIFE-CHANGING.

OBVIOUSLY, FOR THE (WILLING) VICTIM, IT IS A TERMINAL TRAGEDY AND A CRISIS FOR HIS FAMILY. BUT FOR THE POLICE OFFICER WHO WAS MANIPULATED BY THE SUICIDAL CITIZEN INTO FIRING THE FATAL BULLET(S), STUDIES REVEAL THAT MANY OF THE OFFICERS FEEL A SENSE OF POWERLESS AND LIVE WITH THE REGRET THAT THEY HAD FAILED TO STOP OR INTERVENE ON THE SUICIDE. MANY OF THESE OFFICERS SUFFER DEFICITS IN MORALE, CONFIDENCE, ARE SEIZED BY FITS OF

DEPRESSIONS, AND END UP LEAVING THE FORCE WITHIN THREE TO FIVE YEARS OF THE SBC INCIDENT.

LAWRENCE MILLER, A PH.D WORKING WITH THE WEST PALM BEACH PD, REPORTS THAT THERE ARE OVER 600 SBC SHOOTINGS A YEAR, THE GREATEST NUMBER OCCURRING IN CONTEXT OF A RESPONSE TO AN ARMED ROBBERY. THE NEXT MOST COMMON IS DOMESTIC DISTURBANCE CALLS. DR. MILLER AND OTHER EXPERTS POINT OUT SEVERAL CHARACTERISTIC FEATURES OF THOSE WHO COMMIT SUICIDE BY COP.

COMMON CHARACTERISTICS OF SBC "VICTIMS."

ALMOST ALL SBC EPISODES ARE PRECEDED BY THE RUPTURE OR DISRUPTION OF AN IMPORTANT RELATIONSHIP WITH ONE OF THE SUBJECT'S SOCIAL SUPPORT SYSTEM, SUCH AS HIS FAMILY AND/OR EMPLOYMENT. A KEY FEATURE OF A PERSON PUTTING HIMSELF IN POSITION – WILLINGLY AND EVEN ENTHUSIASTICALLY – TO BE SHOT AND KILLED BY AN OFFICER IS HOPELESSNESS.

- *ALL RESISTED ARREST AND/OR COMMANDS TO SURRENDER THEIR FIREARM(S).*
- *OVER 60% SUFFERED FROM PSYCHOLOGICAL DISORDERS (DIAGNOSED).*
- *OVER 2/3 OF SBC SUSPECTS (1998 STUDY BY WILSON) TOOK HOSTAGES.*
- *A MAJORITY OF SBC ATTEMPTS (2000 LORD STUDY) BEGAN AS SELF-SUICIDE, BUT WHEN LAW ENFORCEMENT ARRIVED, THE PERSON DECIDED TO FORCE THE OFFICERS TO DO THE JOB.*
- *OVER 90% OF ALL SBC "VICTIMS" ARE WHITE AND IN THEIR MID-20'S.*
- *MOST OF SBC "VICTIMS" CARRY WEAPONS, SUCH AS GUNS, BUT ONLY ABOUT 50% OF THOSE ARE LOADED.*

- *SEVENTEEN PER CENT OF SBC VICTIMS BRING FAKE WEAPONS INTO THEIR FATAL INTERACTION WITH POLICE.*
- *ABOUT 17% OF SBC "VICTIMS" ARE MOTIVATED BY ISSUES INVOLVING CHILDREN.*
- *GREAT MAJORITY HAVE A HISTORY OF SUBSTANCE ABUSE, DOMESTIC VIOLENCE AND HAD ATTEMPTED SUICIDE BEFORE THE SBC INCIDENT.*
- *ALMOST HALF OF THE SBC INITIATORS HAVE ATTEMPTED SUICIDE PRIOR TO SBC INCIDENT.*
- *A GREAT MAJORITY HAVE HAD PREVIOUS CONTACT WITH LAW ENFORCEMENT FOR MINOR OFFENSES.*
- *PSYCHOLOGICAL HISTORY IS COMMON, USUALLY SCHIZOPHRENIA OR BIPOLAR DISORDER.*

FORECASTING AN SBC EVENT – CUES AND SIGNS

❖ *BE CAUTIOUS WHEN DISPATCHED TO ANY DISTRESSED PERSON SITUATION.*

❖ *MOST COMMON SBC SCENARIOS STEM FROM A ROBBERY IN PROGRESS OR DOMESTIC DISTURBANCE INTERACTION.*

❖ *BE ESPECIALLY VIGILANT WHEN DISPATCHED TO A NWAG (NUT WITH A GUN) INCIDENT.*

❖ *VERBAL CUES.*

1) EXPLICIT DEMANDS OR CHALLENGES, SUCH AS "COME ON, PIGS, KILL ME! WHAT ARE YOU WAITING FOR?."

2) GIVING UP. "OKAY, YOU WANT ME SO BAD? COME AND GET ME."

3) SETTING DEADLINES. "LISTEN, COPPERS, I'M GIVING YOU 10 MINUTES TO CLEAR OUT OF HERE. THEN I'M COMING OUT BLAZING!"

4) **THREATS TO OTHERS.** "LISTEN, DICKHEAD, EITHER YOU GET OUT NOW OR THE BITCH GETS IT!"
5) **BLAZE OF GLORY.** "TELLING YOU HERE AND NOW. NO WAY I'M GOING BACK TO PRISON. YOU AIN'T TAKING ME ALIVE!"
6) **NOBLE LOSER.** "OFFICERS, HERE'S YOUR CHANCE TO GET ME!"
7) **VERBAL WILL – FINAL PLANS.** "SIR, PLEASE TELL MY SON I AM SORRY FOR EVERYTHING..."
8) **RELIGIOUS REFERENCES.** "MY FINAL WORDS WILL RESONATE FROM HEAVEN..."
9) **FINAL COUNTDOWN.** "YOU READY, OFFICERS? THIS IS IT. 10-9-8-7-6..."

SBC BEHAVIOUR CUES.

✓ **THE SBC INITIATOR CALLS IN THE CRIME HIMSELF.**

✓ **HE MAKES NO SUBSTANTIVE DEMANDS.**

✓ **INTOXICATION. D/A INTOXICATION ALWAYS A BAD SIGN.** *INCREASES INSTABILITY AND IMPULSIVENESS, BUT, IF YOU CAN WAIT HIM OUT, HE MAY FALL ASLEEP, HE MAY MELLOW OUT OR EVEN FALL ASLEEP.*

✓ **ADVANCES THE LINE.** *SBC INITIATOR DECIDES TO MOVE TOWARD POLICE AND IGNORES ORDERS TO STOP.*

✓ **WIELDS A WEAPON AND/OR AN "UNREAL WEAPON:" THE** GREAT MAJORITY OF SBC INCIDENTS INVOLVES A SUBJECT WIELDING A WEAPON, USUALLY *A GUN. HOWEVER, IN SOMETHING* LIKE 72% OF INCIDENTS, THE GUN IS EITHER UNLOADED OR A TOY GUN OR OTHER HARMLESS OBJECT. SOME SUBJECTS MAY

PANTOMIME REACHING FOR AND/OR FIRING AN
IMAGINARY WEAPON.

✓ *DEPRESSION NUMBER 1 CAUSE OF SUICIDE.*

PREVENTING OR STOPPING AN SBC INCIDENT.

I AM CONFIDENT THAT BY USING THE DE-ESCALATION TACTICS I HAVE DETAILED IN THIS BOOK, ESPECIALLY THE SERIES OF TECHNIQUES SUGGESTED FOR DEFUSING THE MENTALLY ILL AND THE EMOTIONALLY DISTURBED, PLUS SOME COMMON SENSE, YOU CAN MANAGE MANY OF THESE SCENARIOS. MIND YOU, A DETERMINED SBC INITIATOR WILL ACT QUICKLY AND WITH DEADLY DETERMINATION, SO, THERE IS LITTLE AN OFFICER CAN DO BY WAY OF DISSUADING HIM FROM HIS PROVOCATIVE ACTIONS, BUT, BY READING THE SIGNS, OFFICERS MAY BE ABLE TO ACT TO KEEP FROM FIRING THAT FATAL BULLET.

FIRST OF ALL, IT DOESN'T TAKE AN EXPERT TO STUDY SOME OF THE SNS SCENARIOS WHICH ENDED CATASTROPHICALLY AND FIGURE OUT WHAT WENT WRONG. LET'S START WITH AN OFFICER RESPONDING TO A DISTRESSED PERSON CALL AND APPROACHING THE DISTURBED PERSON WITH A SWAGGER OR EVEN A "GORILLA WALK." OR, AN OFFICER WHO APPROACHES WITH A CONFIDENT AND CALM DEMEANOR, BUT ASSUMES A TYPICAL POLICE POSE. YOU KNOW, FEET SPREAD, FIRMLY PLANTED, STRONG FOOT BACK, HAND ON GUN. DOESN'T EXACTLY SAY, I'M HERE TO HELP YOU, DOES IT? HOW SHOULD AN OFFICER APPROACH?

SO, EXACTLY HOW SHOULD WE APPROACH? I DON'T BELIEVE THERE IS AN "EXACT" WAY WE SHOULD APPROACH – BE IT IN A CRUISER OR ON FOOT – BUT HERE ARE A FEW SAGE SUGGESTIONS:

- ✓ **APPROACH WITH CAUTION USING PATIENT LANGUAGE. "HOW ARE YOU DOING TODAY, SIR? IT LOOKS LIKE MAYBE YOU'RE HAVING YOURSELF A BAD DAY TODAY. WOULD YOU CARE TO CHAT ABOUT IT, SIR?**

- ✓ ***TIME AND DISTANCE CAN BE YOUR ALLIES.*** *THIS IS REVOLUTIONARY TO SOME COPS WHO ARE USED TO DEMANDING AND RECEIVING IMMEDIATE ANSWERS. DR. LAWRENCE MILLER, FLORIDA POLICE PSYCHOLOGIST, STATES THAT* "AN OFFICER'S MOST IMPORTANT WEAPONS ARE HIS BRAIN AND MOUTH. OVER 90% OF POTENTIALLY LETHAL SITUATIONS CAN BE TALKED DOWN THROUGH NEGOTIATIONS.

BE PATIENT AND USE YOUR BRAIN AND
COMMON SENSE..."

✓ **ASSESS THE SITUATION.** *EXPERTS
LIKE DR. MILLER AND GLEN NASH, HEAD OF THE
OKLAHOMA POLICE DEPT. CRISIS INTERVENTION
TEAM, SUGGEST TAKING EVERY CALL SERIOUSLY.
EVEN IF THIS IS THE UMPTEENTH "EMERGENCY"
WITH A LOCAL TROUBLEMAKER. YOU NEVER KNOW
WHICH WILL BE THE "FATAL CRISIS." OBTAIN AS
MUCH BACKGROUND INTELLIGENCE ABOUT THE
SUBJECT. FACTS ARE CRUCIAL. BY UNDERSTANDING
WHAT IS GOING ON NOW, WHAT IS HIS BACK STORY,
AND BY EXAMINING SOME OF HIS "INFLUENCES,"
YOU MAY BE ABLE TO PREVENT AN SBC
CATASTROPHE.*

✓ **EVALUATE SUICIDE RISK.**

✓ **ESTABLISH CONTACT &
DETERMINE THE MAIN
PROBLEM.**

1) *INTRODUCE YOURSELF BY NAME, TITLE AND
DEPARTMENT.*
2) *"WE ARE HERE TO HELP YOU."*
3) *TRY TO ESTABLISH RAPPORT WITH THE SUBJECT.*
4) *DETERMINE THE MAIN PROBLEM OR ISSUES: "*
LOOK, ARTIE, IT DOESN'T LOOK LIKE WE'RE
GOING ANYWHERE FOR A SPELL, SO HOW ABOUT
WE CHAT FOR A WHILE SO YOU CAN TELL ME
WHAT'S ON YOUR MIND?"

5) COMPLY WITH ANY REASONABLE REQUESTS. "WELL, ARTIE, I'M NOT ALLOWED TO BRING YOUR BOSS IN HERE, BUT I PROMISE I'LL GIVE HIM THE NOTE YOU TOSSED OUT IF YOU DROP THE GUN AND COME ON OUT."

6) IF THERE ARE NO DEMANDS, ASK HIM ABOUT HIS IMMEDIATE NEEDS.

7) OFFER ALTERNATIVES USING REALISTIC OPTIMISM. "LARRY, YOU KNOW WE CANNOT FORCE YOUR WIFE TO FLY IN HERE FROM KENTUCKY, BUT LET ME ASSURE YOU, WE ARE WORKING ON IT."

8) CONSIDER NON-LETHAL CONTAINMENT. CAN YOU OBLIGE THE SUICIDAL PERSON BY SHOOTING HIM, BUT INSTEAD OF BULLETS, USE A NON-LETHAL WEAPON? CONSIDER TASING.

9) UTILIZE APPROPRIATE FOLLOW-UP. I BELIEVE IT IS IMPORTANT NOT TO NEGLECT THE SUBJECT AFTER A CRISIS RESOLUTION. AFTER ALL, ESPECIALLY IF YOU WORK IN A SMALL COMMUNITY, YOU MAY CROSS HIS PATH AGAIN. APPROPRIATE FOLLOW-UP ASSURES THAT THE PERSON WILL HAVE A POSITIVE MEMORY OF YOU, YOUR DEPARTMENT AND YOUR EFFORTS. SPEND A FEW MOMENTS WITH THE PERSON, COMMEND HIM FOR HIS COURAGE IN DOING THE RIGHT THING, REPEAT YOUR REASSURANCE AND YOUR CONFIDENCE IN HIS ABILITY TO GET HIS LIFE IN ORDER. ALSO, YOU MIGHT BACK UP ANY OFFERS – WITHIN REASON – THAT YOU MADE DURING THE CRISIS. BY DOING SO, YOU ARE REDUCING THE POSSIBILITY OF A REPEAT EPISODE.

A TRUE SUICIDE-BY-COP EPISODE

DE-ESCALATION TECHNIQUES ARE INHERENTLY ABNORMAL.
THESE TACTICS GOVERN OUR NATURAL FIGHT OR FLIGHT
REFLEXES. THESE ARE CALM-CENTERED, PROFESSIONALLY-
DETACHED TECHNIQUES AND TACTICS THAT REQUIRE
PRACTICE.
COMMUNITY COLLEGE OF RHODE ISLAND POWER
POINT ON DE-ESCALATION.

AND

"WHEN WE MISUSE OUR WORDS AND ACTIONS,
WE BUILD GROUND FOR THE BAD GUY
TO FIGHT ON AND WIN ON!"

TIMELESS ADVANCED DE-ESCALATION/WINOLOGY
TRUISM.

SETH BOYER SUFFERED FROM DEPRESSION. HE FOUGHT IT DAY AND NIGHT, BUT ITS DARKNESS WOULD GRAB HIM AND SHAKE HIM LIKE A BIG BEAR AND THERE WAS NOTHING HE COULD DO TO ESCAPE THE CLAWS OF WHAT HE CALLED THE BEAST. AFTER TWO OR THREE YEARS OF THIS, SETH DECIDED THAT SUICIDE WAS HIS ONLY SALVATION. FOR MONTHS, ALL HE COULD THINK OF WAS HOW TO DO IT. HE BECAME OBSESSED, AND HIS STUDIES SUFFERED AND HIS APPEARANCE ALSO DEGRADED. ONE DAY, ON THE WAY TO HIS COLLEGE CLASSES, HE SAW A POLICE OFFICER STRIDING BY, A BIG CONFIDENT GRIN ON HIS FACE. BUT IT WASN'T THE OFFICER'S FACE THAT DREW SETH'S ATTENTION. IT WAS THE OFFICER'S BIG RIGHT HAND WHICH RESTED ON THE GRIP OF HIS HOLSTERED GUN. I WILL SHOOT MYSELF, THAT'S IT, HE DECIDED, AND, FOR THE FIRST TIME IN MONTHS HE FELT RELAXED AND AT PEACE.

BUT AFTER A FEW DAYS, SETH FOUND HIMSELF GRAPPLING WITH ANOTHER PROBLEM. HE WAS DETERMINED AND COMMITTED TO KILLING HIMSELF. HE COULD NOT LIVE WITH THE "BEAST" ANY LONGER, BUT, THE FACT WAS, HE DIDN'T HAVE A GUN, NOR DID HE KNOW HOW TO GET ONE.

HE WAS ALONE IN HIS BEDROOM, DEPRESSION AND HOPELESSNESS TORTURING HIM AGAIN, WHEN HE CAME UP WITH A SIMPLE BUT ELEGANT PLAN.

I'LL JUST GET IN MY CAR AND DRIVE LIKE CRAZY. EVENTUALLY, A COP HAS TO PULL ME OVER, AND, BANG, SOMEHOW, I WILL PROVOKE
THAT COP INTO SHOOTING ME DEAD. PERFECT!

SO, ON THE NIGHT OF MARCH 22, 1997, SETH DROPPED HIS GIRL-FRIEND OFF AFTER A COLLEGE FORMAL, POPPED THE BOTTLE OF CHEAP CHAMPAGNE THAT HAD BEEN ROLLING AROUND ON THE BACK SEAT AND STARTED DRIVING: FAST. HE TORE THROUGH NEW JERSEY AND INTO HIS HOME STATE OF CONNECTICUT. IT WAS 3 A.M. NOW, AND, STILL, HE HAD ENCOUNTERED NO COP. NO STATE TROOPERS, NOTHING. "DAMN!"

DESPERATE TIMES CALLS FOR A BACKUP PLAN.
SO, HE DROVE INTO THE PARKING LOT OF THE WALLINGFORD POLICE DEPT. AND LEANED ON HIS HORN TRYING TO DRAW THE ATTENTION OF THE POLICE. IT WORKED. A CHASE ENSUED WITH SQUAD CARS FROM SEVERAL CITIES, EITHER FOLLOWING HIM OR TRYING TO CUT HIM OFF.

FINALLY, SETH PURPOSELY RAMMED INTO A POLICE CRUISER BELONGING TO AN OFFICER POISSON, WHO HAD

233

BEEN CHASING HIM. POISSON SCREECHED TO A HALT AND PREPARED TO CHASE SETH ON FOOT, BUT INSTEAD OF RUNNING AWAY, SETH RAN TOWARD POISSON, BRANDISHING THE CHAMPAGNE BOTTLE AS A WEAPON.

"I'M GOING TO KILL YOU. YOU'D BETTER SHOOT ME, OR I'LL KILL YOU!" SETH SCREAMED.

POISSON, ONE OF TWO OFFICERS ON THE SCENE, DREW HIS GUN AND BACKED AWAY. SETH KEPT COMING, STILL SCREAMING. "I'LL KILL YOU IF YOU DON'T SHOOT ME!"

POISSON FOUND HIMSELF BACKING INTO THE MIDDLE OF A HIGHWAY, WHERE ANY CAR MIGHT WIPE HIM OUT. HE SHOT SETH ONCE AND SETH FELL TO THE GROUND. POISSON CUFFED SETH AND TURNED HIM OVER AND KNELT BESIDE THE BLEEDING BOY, WHO LOOKED UP AT HIM AND SAID, "PLEASE, SHOOT ME IN THE HEAD."

LEARNING FROM THE SETH BOYER STORY

IF YOU WERE IN MY CLASS, THIS IS WHEN I WOULD SAY SOMETHING LIKE, "SO, WHAT DO YOU THINK? WOULD YOU HAVE DONE ANYTHING DIFFERENTLY THAN OFFICER POISSON?" AND, ON AND ON WE GO. FOR THE NEXT HALF-HOUR OR SO, WE WOULD PLAY MONDAY MORNING QUARTERBACKS AND, IN THE COMFORT OF OUR CLASSROOM, WITH ALMOST ALL THE TIME IN THE WORLD TO MAKE OUR DECISION(S), AND WITH NO SUICIDAL KAMIKAZE-KID COMING HEAD-FIRST TOWARD US WITH LORD-KNOWS-WHAT IN HIS HANDS, WE DISSECT THE SCENARIO, PIECE BY PIECE, AND, PROBABLY IN THE END

DECIDE THAT WE COULD HAVE AND WOULD HAVE ACTED DIFFERENTLY THAN THE OFFICER.

BUT, THIS IS NOT AN ANTISEPTIC CLASSROOM EXERCISE. THIS IS THE REAL SHIT. I AM WRITING THIS IN HOPES WE CAN EXTRACT SOME REAL LIFE PRESERVING LESSONS FROM THE ABOVE SBC EPISODE. PERHAPS A BETTER UNDERSTANDING OF HOW TO PREDICT, PREVENT, AND, LORD HELP US, MAYBE EVEN STOP AN SBC EVENT, IF IT EVER COMES YOUR WAY, LET'S EXAMINE THIS TRUE SCENARIO AND BREAK IT DOWN A BIT.

SBC PREDICTION & THE STORY

IF LT. POISSON WOULD HAVE HAD THE BENEFIT OF THE INFORMATION WE NOW HAVE ABOUT THE TYPICAL SBC "VICTIM," HE PROBABLY WOULD HAVE ACTED AND REACTED FAR DIFFERENTLY THAN HE DID BACK ON THE FATEFUL NIGHT. AS A MATTER OF FACT, WE HAVE THIS QUOTE FROM THE NOW LT. POISSON GIVEN EARLIER LAST YEAR ABOUT THE INCIDENT:

"IF I HAD THOUGHT HE MIGHT BE TRYING TO USE ME TO COMMIT SUICIDE, I WOULD HAVE PULLED UP MUCH FURTHER AWAY FROM HIM, SO I COULD KEEP MY DISTANCE AND NOT HAVE TO MAKE THE DECISION TO SHOOT."

LT. POISSON IS ONTO SOMETHING THERE. CAPTAIN CLEVE NASH, WHO RUNS THE OKLAHOMA CITY POLICE DEPT. CRISIS INTERVENTION PROGRAM, PROPOUNDS THAT "TIME AND DISTANCE ARE OUR ALLIES IN THIS KIND OF CRISIS," WHILE DR. LAWRENCE MILLER NOTES THAT AN OFFICER'S MOST IMPORTANT WEAPONS IN A SBC CRISIS, OR ANY OTHER CRISIS FOR THAT MATTER, ARE HIS BRAIN AND HIS MOUTH. "OVER NINETY-PER CENT OF POTENTIALLY LETHAL SITUATIONS CAN BE TALKED DOWN."

PROFILING THE SBC "VICTIM."

TYPICAL SBC THAT MATCH THE SETH BOYER STORY _

1. SETH WAS A WHITE MALE IN HIS MID-20'S. WHICH MATCHES THE PROFILE TO A TEE!
2. PSYCHIATRIC HISTORY IS TYPICAL. BOYER HAD A HISTORY.
3. PREVIOUS SUICIDE ATTEMPTS IS ALSO TYPICAL.
4. DEPRESSION IS A KEY FACTOR IN SUICIDAL IDEATION. RIGHT ON TARGET AGAIN WITH SETH.

VERBAL CUES THAT A SBC IS COMING.

➤ THE NUMBER 1 VERBAL CUE IS AN EXPLICIT DEMAND OR CHALLENGE, WHICH IS EXACTLY WHAT SETH DID. "I'M GONNA KILL YOU! YOU'D BETTER SHOOT ME!"

BEHAVIOR CUE THAT SBC IS COMING.

➤ CALL IN THE CRIME HIMSELF. MANY SUICIDAL PEOPLE CALL IN POLICE ON THEMSELVES. REPORT A CRIME, ETC. IN THIS CASE, SETH LEANED ON HIS HORN IN A PD PARKING LOT, INITIATING THE POLICE CHASE AND HIS EVENTUAL WOUNDING.

➤ INTOXICATION IS ANOTHER BEHAVIORAL CLUE THAT SBC IS UPON YOU. SETH POPPED A BOTTLE OF CHAMPAGNE AND I ASSUME HE DRANK FROM THE MAGNUM, PROBABLY FINISHING OFF THE BOTTLE.

➤ NO SUBSTANTIVE DEMANDS. ANOTHER TIPOFF. SETH SPOKE NO WORDS OR MADE NO DEMANDS. ONLY ISSUED DEADLY THREATS AND ASKED THE OFFICER TO SHOOT HIM IN THE HEAD.

➤ "ADVANCES THE LINE." THIS TERM IS USED TO DESCRIBE ONE OF THE TYPICAL SBC (FINAL) TACTICS. THE VICTIM MOVES TOWARD THE POLICE, IGNORING ORDERS TO STOP. EXACTLY WHAT SETH DID THAT FATEFUL NIGHT!

➤ USES WEAPONS. ANOTHER TYPICAL SBC BEHAVIORAL CUE. IN THIS INSTANCE, SETH BRANDISHED THE MAGNUM AS IF IT WERE A WEAPON.

> ➤ **NOT A REAL WEAPON.** ALSO, TYPICAL SBC CUE. INSTEAD OF A REAL GUN, THIS TYPE OF "ATTACKER" WILL WIELD EITHER AN UNLOADED GUN, A TOY GUN, OR MAY EVEN PANTOMIME USING A REAL WEAPON. SETH'S CHAMPAGNE BOTTLE "WEAPON," AGAIN, IS TYPICAL AND A GREAT SBC CUE!

STRAIGHT OFF, I AM SAYING THAT I ADMIRE LT. POISSON AND EMPATHIZE WITH THE DILEMMA THIS SBC "ATTACK" PUT HIM IN. FROM WHAT I CAN GATHER FROM RESEARCH, I BELIEVE THAT IN THE MANY YEARS THAT HAVE PASSED SINCE THIS INCIDENT, HE HAS SUFFERED PLENTY IN THE WAY OF REGRET. MAYBE EVEN SOME SOUL SEARCHING AND GENUINE DEPRESSION. THIS, BY THE WAY, IS TYPICAL OF ANY COP THAT HAD GONE THROUGH WHAT HE DID.

HOWEVER, WITH THE BENEFIT OF TIME, EXPERIENCE, AND BEING ABLE TO THINK USING MY NEO CORTEX, OR INTELLIGENT BRAIN – AN ADVANTAGE THAT POISSON DID NOT HAVE AT THE TIME (MORE ON THAT DOWN THE LINE). THERE IS NO DOUBT IN MY MIND, BASED UPON THE CIRCUMSTANCES IN THIS STORY, THE OFFICER WAS A VICTIM OF **SNS ACTIVATION** THE SECOND HIS PLAN TO GIVE CHASE TO SETH CHANGED WHEN SETH CAME CHARGING AT HIM. SETH'S CHARGE, PLUS HIS CHALLENGING WORDS WARNING POISSON THAT HE WAS GOING TO KILL HIM AND CHALLENGING HIM OVER AND OVER TO SHOOT HIM (SETH) TO DEATH, CREATED DEBILITATING SURVIVAL STRESS WHICH IMMEDIATELY FLOODED HIS BODY AND MIND WITH STRESS HORMONES.

SNS ACTIVATION, DESIGNED FOR FIGHT OR FLIGHT, BYPASSED POISSON'S SMART BRAIN, MAKING HIM STRONGER AND FASTER, BUT, IN THIS CASE AT LEAST, MORE EMOTIONAL AND MUCH LESS INTELLIGENT, SINCE HE

WAS FORCED TO RELY ON HIS PRIMITIVE OR LIZARD BRAIN!. ERGO:

➢ HIS VISION WAS IMPACTED, CREATING AN INABILITY TO USE HIS NIGHT VISION (IT WAS 0300), MAKING IT NEAR IMPOSSIBLE FOR HIM TO RECOGNIZE THAT SETH'S WEAPON WAS ONLY A CHAMPAGNE BOTTLE.

➢ IF HE WOULD HAVE DETERMINED THAT SETH DID NOT HAVE A LETHAL WEAPON, CHANCES ARE HE WOULD HAVE USED HIS IMPACT WEAPON – IF THAT – INSTEAD OF HIS GUN!

➢ THE ONLY CHANCE POISSON HAD – AND I HAVE NO IDEA IF THIS WAS PRACTICABLE – WAS TO RECOGNIZE THE SIGNS, THAT SHOULD HAVE BEEN PLAIN, AND TO BUY HIMSELF SOME **TIME AND DISTANCE,** WHICH WE KNOW TO BE CRUCIAL IN THIS TYPE OF CRISIS, BY PLACING HIS SQUAD CAR BETWEEN HIM AND THE CHARGING SUICIDAL MANIAC. ONCE HE COULD CAUSE SETH TO SLOW DOWN OR EVEN STOP FOR A MINUTE, HE MAY HAVE BEEN ABLE TO START THE PROCESS OF TALKING HIM DOWN.

➢ LT. POISSON, I CAN ONLY ASSUME, HAD NO CRISIS INTERVENTION NOR SBC-RELATED TRAINING. IF HE HAD – AND I FIND THIS A LITTLE SAD – HE WOULD HAVE SURELY RECOGNIZED HE HAD A SBC-INITIATOR ON HIS HANDS BASED UPON ALL THE COMMON SBC CHARACTERISTICS SETH OWNED, PLUS THE FACT THAT HE HAD INITIATED THE EPISODE BY BLOWING HIS HORN OVER AND OVER

OVER IN THE POLICE DEPT. PARKING LOT UNTIL HE DREW THE POLICE'S ATTENTION AND THEN WAITED UNTIL THE POLICE SCRAMBLED INTO THEIR SQUAD CARS BEFORE TAKING OFF AND LEADING THEM ON A HIGH-SPEED CHASE.

COME ON. SERIOUSLY. WHAT ELSE – WHEN YOU HAVE THE TIME TO THINK ABOUT IT – COULD HE HAVE BEEN DOING?

> A FINAL CONCLUSION. THERE IS LITTLE DOUBT IN MY MIND THAT, DURING THIS INCIDENT. FROM THE BLASTING OF SETH'S HORN, TO THE SCRAMBLE TO HIS SQUAD CAR, TO THE ADRENALIN-RUSH OF THE CAR CHASE, TO SETH RAMMING OF A POLICE CRUISER, AND, THEN TO EMERGING FROM HIS VEHICLE AND HAVING THE CRAZED DRIVER CHARGING HIM WITH A "WEAPON" AND THREATENING TO KILL HIM, THAT **LT. POISSON WAS BRAIN-DAMAGED!** I HAVE LITTLE DOUBT ABOUT IT. SNS DOES THAT. PUTS YOU **UNDER THE INFLUENCE OF SO MANY PERSONAL AND NATURAL EMOTIONS: FEAR, CONFUSION, ANGER, RAGE, HUMILIATION. YOU NAME IT.**

AND, I AM SURE, BY NOW, YOU GET IT. I DON'T WANT TO BE PRESUMPTIVE. MAYBE YOU GOT IT ALL ALONG. MAYBE EVEN LONG BEFORE I WROTE THIS BOOK. BUT, EITHER WAY, I HOPE THE MESSAGE THAT WAS IMPLANTED A COUPLE HUNDRED PAGES AGO, THAT IF WE WANT TO CONTINUE OUR CAREERS IN LAW ENFORCEMENT, SECURITY, CORRECTIONS, AS WELL AS THE MANY CIVILIAN OCCUPATIONS WHICH DEAL WITH THE CONTINUUM OF PEOPLE, RANGING FROM THE DIFFICULT ALL THE WAY ACROSS TO THE HOSTILE AND AGGRESSIVE PERSON, WE NEED TO THINK AND ACT AS MUCH AS POSSIBLE FROM OUR INTELLIGENT BRAIN. WE NEED TO EXERCISE PROFESSIONAL FACE AND EXCISE PERSONAL FACE.

AFTER ALL, THE WORLD WITHIN WHICH WE WORK AND LIVE IS A DANGEROUS ONE. GETTING MORE TOXIC EVERY DAY.

TO SURVIVE – NO – TO PREVAIL, WE MUST TRICK THE SNS!

THIS WONDERFUL COP

THAT SAME WONDERFUL POLICE OFFICER I INTRODUCED AT THE BEGINNING OF THIS BOOK ANSWERED THE DISPATCHER'S URGENT CALL FOR A DOMESTIC DISTURBANCE. HE WAS ACCOMPANIED BY NONE OTHER THAN GEORGE THOMPSON. THEN A POLICE OFFICER. BOTH OFFICERS ARRIVED ON THE SCENE AROUND TWO A.M. AND FOUND THE FRONT DOOR WIDE OPEN. BOTH HEARD THE MAN AND WOMAN SCREAMING THREATS AND DAMNATION AT EACH OTHER.

WHEN THE TWO OFFICERS HAD APPROACHED. THEY FOUND ARTICLES AND ITEMS THAT NORMALLY ARE TO BE FOUND INSIDE A HOME. LAYING ON THE SIDEWALK. TWO OF THE WINDOWS WERE SMASHED AND NEIGHBORS STOOD ABOUT. SOME WITH THEIR HANDS OVER THEIR MOUTHS.

RON. THE LEAD OFFICER. ENTERED FIRST. SCANNED ABOUT. THOMPSON HAD ALREADY INDEXED HIS FIREARM. THE SCENE SEEMED THAT VOLATILE. BUT RON SHOOK HIS HEAD SLOWLY AND HELD OUT A HAND. AS IF TO SIGNAL TO THOMPSON. "NOT YET. GEORGE."

AND, THEN, RON SAID, "TRUST ME, PAL," TO THOMPSON AND THEN WALKED PAST THE FIGHTING COUPLE AND PICKED UP A RIPPED-UP NEWSPAPER FROM THE FLOOR. THOMPSON REMAINED NEAR THE DOORWAY, NOT KNOWING EXACTLY WHAT TO DO NEXT. MEANWHILE, OFFICER RON LEANED AGAINST A WALL, SEEMINGLY IGNORING THE COUPLE, STILL FIGHTING IN THE MIDDLE OF THE LIVING ROOM.

"YO, GEORGE," OFFICER RON SAID, LOUD ENOUGH SO THAT HIS VOICE ROSE ABOVE THE ARGUMENT. "THAT RED CONVERTIBLE IS STILL FOR SALE. CAN YOU BELIEVE IT?"

THOMPSON COULDN'T BELIEVE IT. ESPECIALLY SINCE HE HAD NO IDEA WHAT RED CONVERTIBLE RON WAS TALKING ABOUT. "BEAUTIFUL," THOMPSON REPLIED.

OFFICER RON WALKED CLOSER TO THE COUPLE, WHO HAD NOW STOPPED FIGHTING AND WERE GAWKING AT THE STRANGE POLICE OFFICER. "EXCUSE ME, MA'M, SIR, WOULD YOU GUYS MIND IF I USED YOUR PHONE SO I CAN CALL THIS GUY ABOUT THIS FANTASTIC RED CONVERTIBLE?"

THE MAN AND WOMAN EXCHANGED LOOKS, AND FINALLY, THE WOMAN SHRUGGED HER SHOULDERS, RAN A HAND THROUGH HER MUSSED-UP HEAD OF HAIR, AND SAID, "SURE, I GUESS."

"THANK YOU, MA'M," OFFICER RON RESPONDED WITH A MOCK SALUTE, THEN TOOK THEIR LAND LINE AND PROCEEDED TO TAKE PART IN A FAKE CONVERSATION WITH A TOTALLY FABRICATED AND NON-EXISTENT CAR DEALER WHO HAPPENED TO BE OPEN AT THREE-SOMETHING IN THE MORNING.

"I CANNOT BELIEVE MY LUCK," HE SAID, FINALLY, TO NOBODY IN PARTICULAR. "THE CAR IS STILL AVAILABLE AND I CAN COME BY ANYTIME TOMORROW AND PICK HER UP."

BY THEN THE MAN AND WOMAN HAD PROBABLY TOTALLY FORGOTTEN WHATEVER IT WAS THEY WERE FIGHTING ABOUT. THEY EVEN SEEMED CALM AS THEY STOOD THERE IN THE MIDDLE OF THE ROOM, THEIR ARMS CROSSED ON THEIR CHESTS.

"WELL," RON SAID, BEAMING HIS BEST SMILE, "LOOKS LIKE I HAVE PLENTY OF TIME BEFORE I HAVE TO PICK UP MY CAR. THANK YOU FOR LETTING ME USE YOUR PHONE." RON SALUTED THE COUPLE ONCE AGAIN AND THEN TURNED TOWARD HIS PARTNER, WHO WAS STILL POISED IN THE DOORWAY, HIS RIGHT HAND STILL INDEXING HIS SMITH. "YO, GEORGE, DO YOU HAVE ANYTHING TO SAY BEFORE WE TAKE OFF?"

"NOT REALLY, EXCEPT I'D REALLY LIKE TO KNOW WHAT WAS THE PROBLEM THAT MADE THESE NICE PEOPLE HERE BE FIGHTING LIKE THEY WERE," GEORGE SAID.

THE COUPLE LOOKED AT EACH OTHER AND THEN BACK AT THOMPSON.

"I HAVE AN IDEA," GEORGE THOMPSON SAID. "WHY DON'T OFFICER RON OVER THERE AND THE THREE OF US SIT DOWN AND HAVE OURSELVES A LITTLE CHAT ABOUT WHAT HAPPENED AND MAYBE WHAT WE CAN DO TO MAKE SURE EVERYTHING IS GOING TO BE OKAY HERE. I DON'T THINK WE'RE ALLOWED TO LEAVE HERE UNTIL THINGS SETTLE DOWN. WHAT DO YOU GUYS THINK?"

THERE ARE NUMEROUS WAYS TO BRING CALM TO SEEMINGLY UNCALMABLE SCENARIOS. ALL OF THEM HAVE MERIT, BUT NOT ALL OF THEM WILL WORK IN EVERY SITUATION WITH DIFFERENT TYPE OF PEOPLE. IN THE CASE OF A DOMESTIC VIOLENCE CALL – ALONG WITH TRAFFIC STOPS, THE MOST UNPREDICTABLE AND DANGEROUS OF ALL CALLS – THIS TYPE OF CREATIVE APPEAL IS NOT ALWAYS THE BEST APPROACH. THIS TYPE OF (CREATIVE) TACTIC, LIKE HUMOR, WILL OFTEN WORK, BUT SOMETIMES IT CAN BACKFIRE.

IT ALL COMES DOWN TO WHAT YOU BELIEVE BEST FITS YOUR PERSONAL STYLE. IN THE ABOVE SCENARIO, SEEMINGLY IGNORING THE BATTLE AND BUSYING HIMSELF WITH READING A NEWSPAPER, DREW THE CURIOSITY OF THE TWO PEOPLE AND CREATED AN EFFECTIVE **DISTRACTION, AND DISTRACTIONS,** AS YOU PROBABLY KNOW, WEAKENS MOTOR ACTIONS BY CHANGING THE PERSON'S THOUGHT PROCESS.

NEVER UNDERESTIMATE THE CALMING EFFECT OF USING TIME AND SPACE TO EASE AGGRESSION AND HOSTILITY. WE SEE SOME OF THAT IN THE ABOVE DOMESTIC DISTURBANCE SCENARIO. I HAVE NO IDEA, AND UNFORTUNATELY, DR. THOMPSON IS NO LONGER AROUND FOR ME TO ASK, IF OFFICER RON KNEW THE INTRICACIES OF TIME AND SPACE AND HOW TO USE THEM TO BRING CALM, BUT THE FACT IS THAT HUMANS ARE ONLY CAPABLE OF A CERTAIN AMOUNT OF MAXIMUM ENERGY WHEN IN A STATE OF RAGE.

BY THIS I MEAN THAT WE ALL HAVE THREE ENERGY SYSTEMS. WE ARE CAPABLE OF FIGHTING AT 100% MAXIMUM OUTPUT FOR NO

*MORE THAN 10 TO 15 SECONDS WHEN WE ARE IN OUR INITIAL SYSTEM, **ATP/PC** (ADENOSINE TRIPHOSPHATE), WHICH CONSISTS OF SMALL ENERGY BUNDLES LOCATED IN OUR MUSCLES. THE ATP/PC HELPS OFFICERS FIGHT AT THEIR MAXIMUM PHYSICAL OUTPUT AND PERFORM OTHER HEAVY DUTY SURVIVAL TASKS. WELL, THIS ATP SYSTEM WORKS FOR OTHER PEOPLE, ALSO, SO, OFTEN I TEACH OFFICERS, TEACHERS, HEALTH CARE WORKERS, SECURITY AND OTHERS WHO WORK WITH TROUBLED AND ANTI-SOCIAL PEOPLE THAT WHEN THEY CONFRONT FIGHTING PEOPLE – AS LONG AS IT IS SAFE TO DO SO – TO SIMPLY SECURE THE SCENE AND ALLOW THE FIGHTING PEOPLE TO USE UP THEIR ATP/PC SYSTEM UNTIL THE FIGHTERS LAPSE INTO THEIR **LACTIC ACID ENERGY SYSTEM**, WHERE THE FIGHTERS' ABILITY TO FIGHT AT THEIR MAXIMUM OUTPUT HAS BEEN REDUCED FROM 100% TO 55 TO 45% MAXIMUM OUTPUT OR LOWER.*

SO, WITH A LITTLE ASSISTANCE TO OFFICER RON'S CREATIVE DISTRACTION ACT, WHAT HAPPENED IN THIS SCENARIO IS WHAT I TEACH CIVILIANS AND OFFICERS TO CONSIDER WHEN FACING FIGHTING PEOPLE. SECURE THE SCENE – THOMPSON WAS ALERT AT THE DOORWAY AND I AM SURE OFFICER RON WAS READY TO INTERVENE PHYSICALLY IF HE HAD TO. SECURE THE SCENE, CONSTANTLY ASSESS, AND ALLOW TIME AND OUR NATURAL ENERGY SYSTEMS TO DO THEIR THING.

CHAPTER 13. SOME SALIENT FINAL THOUGHTS AND QUOTATIONS

"WE TREAT PEOPLE LIKE LADIES AND GENTLEMEN, NOT NECESSARILY BECAUSE THEY ARE, BUT BECAUSE WE ARE."

NORTH DAKOTA HIGHWAY PATROL QUOTATION.

THIS IS THE FINAL CHAPTER, BUT, PLEASE, DO NOT MINIMIZE THE WORDS, THOUGHTS AND PRINCIPLES WITHIN THESE LAST FEW PAGES. WITHIN THESE PAGES ARE SOME SALIENT "UNIVERSAL TRUTHS" ABOUT "DISARMING" DANGEROUS PEOPLE. SOME MEANINGFUL WORDS AND PHRASES THAT JUST MIGHT KEEP YOU LEGALLY, TACTICALLY, AND MEDICALLY IN GOOD STEAD THROUGHOUT YOUR CAREER.

DE-ESCALATION IS THE MASTERY OF COMMUNICATIONS BY REDIRECTING BEHAVIOR WITH WORDS.

THE UNPROFESSIONAL USE OF LANGUAGE TO EXPRESS ONE'S PERSONAL FEELINGS ARE

WHAT I CONSIDER WAR WORDS! YOU CAN BET YOUR LIFE THAT AT LEAST 98% OF THE TIME, THESE WORDS WILL ESCALATE EMOTIONS. OR, MAYBE ANOTHER WAY OF PUTTING THIS: NEVER UTTER WORDS WHICH RISE NATURALLY TO YOUR LIPS!

COMMAND OR PROFESSIONAL PRESENCE IS ACHIEVED NOT BY WHAT YOU SAY, BUT HOW YOU SAY IT.

ALWAYS EMPLOY TACTICAL EMPATHY. TACTICAL EMPATHY IS SEEING SITUATIONS THROUGH THE EYES OF THE OTHER PERSON TO MAINTAIN A TACTICAL ADVANTAGE.

CONSIDER EVERY ENCOUNTER UNIQUE AND ALWAYS REMEMBER EVERYBODY HAS A "GOOD REASON" FOR WHAT THEY DO. NO MATTER HOW "UNNATURAL" AND DISTURBING THAT PERSON'S ACTIONS ARE TO YOU, THE OTHER PERSON FEELS HE IS JUSTIFIED IN THOSE ACTION(S).

IF YOU CANNOT CONTROL YOURSELF, YOU CAN NEVER CONTROL THE STREETS.

WE DEFLECT VERBAL ABUSE FOR A LIVING.

"WHENEVER ANGRY, IF YOU SAY THE FIRST THING THAT COMES TO MIND, YOU WILL CREATE THE GREATEST SPEECH YOU WILL EVER LIVE TO REGRET."

HERE IS THE WAY I SEE DE-ESCALATING AGGRESSION: IT IS LIKE MUHAMMED ALI AND HIS ROPE-A-DOPE. WE JUST BOP ALONG THE ROPES, OUR ARMS HANGING LOOSE, A BIG SMILE ON OUR FACES, AND WE LET THE BAD GUY THROW HIS BEST SHOTS AT US, AND THERE WE ARE, STILL BOPPING ALONG THE ROPES, UNTIL AT LONG LAST THE BAD GUYS IS EXHAUSTED. FINISHED. AND, THEN, WITH NO MALICE AND WITH MINIMAL HOOPLA, WE DO WHAT WE CAME TO DO & EVERYONE IS SAFE...

*THERE ARE **FOUR C'S OF MENTAL STRENGTH.** MENTAL STRENGTH IS THE CAPACITY TO DEAL EFFECTIVELY WITH STRESSORS, PRESSURES AND CHALLENGES TO THE BEST OF AN OFFICER'S ABILITIES, IRRESPECTIVE OF THE CIRCUMSTANCES IN WHICH HE FINDS HIMSELF. THERE IS A*

STRONG LINK BETWEEN MENTAL STRENGTH AND PEAK PERFORMANCE, STRESS MANAGEMENT, AND THE ABILITY TO DE-ESCALATE. THE FOUR ARE *CONTROL, CONFIDENCE, CHALLENGE* AND *COMMITMENT.*

BRIEFLY, "WINNERS" BELIEVE THEY ARE GOING TO WIN – THEY TAKE ON CHALLENGES MENTALLY! THIS IS WHAT LEADS ME TO SUGGEST THAT OFFICERS DEVELOP MENTAL STRENGTH (OR, MULTIPLY THE STRENGTH THEY ALREADY POSSESS) AND THAT THEY GO INTO TOUGH CONFRONTATIONAL SITUATIONS <u>BELIEVING THEY CAN DE-ESCALATE ANYONE, ANYTIME!</u>

ON DEALING WITH THE MENTALLY DISTURBED WHO ARE HALLUCINATING OR EXPERIENCING DELUSION. BE AWARE THAT THIS IS THIS PERSON'S REALITY. UNDERSTAND THAT YOU CANNOT TALK THIS PERSON OUT OF HIS REALITY OR CONVINCE HIM HE IS NOT HEARING WHAT HE IS HEARING OR SEEING WHAT HE IS SEEING. REALIZE THIS PERSON IS MOTIVATED BY HIS HALLUCINATION OR

DELUSIONS. INSTEAD, COMMUNICATE THAT YOU UNDERSTAND THAT THEY ARE EXPERIENCING THESE EVENTS. NEVER PRETEND YOU ARE EXPERIENCING THEM ALSO. DAVID BERGER, ONE FINE OFFICER WHOM I HAD THE HONOR OF TRAINING, TOLD ME THAT HE HAD JUST "DEALT" WITH A MENTALLY DISTURBED PERSON WHO LOOKED LIKE HE WAS SEEING THINGS. HE INTIMATED THAT HE COMMUNICATED WITH THE MAN "HONESTLY" BY ASKING HIM WHAT HE WAS SEEING. THE PATIENT THEN COMMUNICATED EXACTLY WHAT HIS HALLUCINATION WAS ("TELL ME, SIR, WHAT YOU ARE SEEING?"), WHAT THAT DELUSION REPRESENTED, AND HOW HE FELT ABOUT IT ("I'M SO SCARED, MR. DAVE...").

SUBJECTS WHO ARE PARANOID ARE OFTEN FRIGHTENED. BE AWARE THEY MAY NEED MORE SPACE!

DO NOT PASS AN EDP OR MENTALLY ILL PERSON OFF TO ANOTHER OFFICER OR WORKER LIKE A "HOT POTATO."

THEY WILL OFTEN REACT WITH ANGER. INSTEAD, LISTEN AND TRY TO UNDERSTAND WHAT REALITY-BASED NEEDS YOU CAN MEET.

WITH EVERYBODY, INCLUDING THE SEVERELY MENTALLY ILL, ALWAYS SET LIMITS. IN SOME CASES, IT MIGHT BE SOMETHING LIKE, "IF YOU USE PROFANITY OR THREATEN ME, I CANNOT HELP YOU, SIR." OR, MAYBE, "SIR, IF YOU KEEP SCREAMING AT ME LIKE THIS, I WILL NOT BE ABLE TO TALK TO YOU." OR, MAYBE, "SIR, I AM GOOD WITH YOU VENTING YOUR FEELINGS, BUT, IF YOU KICK THE FURNITURE AGAIN, THIS SESSION IS OVER."

AGAIN, WHEN DEALING WITH THE MENTALLY ILL, MAKE THEIR BEHAVIOR A CONDITION OF YOUR HELP. "I CAN HELP YOU, SIR, BUT ONLY IF YOU STOP THROWING THINGS."

USE WHAT I CALL "BOOMERANG LINES" TO KEEP THE OTHER PERSON FOCUSED ON THE ISSUE AT HAND. BOOMERANG LINES ARE PRE-DESIGNED STATEMENTS THAT YOU CAN

ALWAYS USE FOLLOWING PREDICTABLE COMPLAINTS, VERBAL ATTACKS, ETC. FOR INSTANCE, I HAVE USED SOME OF THESE LINES:

"LARRY, YOU ARE GETTING ANGRY AGAIN, AND I AM DOING EVERYTHING I CAN TO HELP YOU."

"I KNOW YOU ARE UPSET, JANE, BUT TELL ME THIS: WHAT WOULD YOU DO IF YOU WERE IN MY PLACE?"

"JERRY, I HEAR YOU. BUT WE ARE PAST THAT, SO LET'S FOCUS ON WHERE WE CAN GO FROM HERE."

THE THING WITH BOOMERANG LINES AND OTHER DE-ESCALATION TACTICS IS TO KEEP ALL CONVERSATIONS <u>FUTURE FOCUSED.</u> *ONCE YOU GET TO THE GIST, FOCUS ON WHAT WE CAN DO FROM HERE?*

USE DELAYING TACTICS. *GIVE THE SUBJECT SOME TIME TO CALM. MAYBE YOU CAN OFFER HIM A DRINK OF WATER, A STICK OF GUM, SOMETHING...*

USE SILENCE AND A CALM DEMEANOR TO ENHANCE THE DELAY.

A GREAT VERBAL JUDO PHILOSOPHY THAT YOU MIGHT LIKE. **MIZU NO KIKORO** *IS A JAPANESE TERM LITERALLY MEANING, "MAKE YOUR MIND LIKE CLEAR WATER." WHAT THIS MEANS IS, IF YOUR MIND IS RUFFLED BY THE HIGH WINDS OF BIAS AND PREJUDICE, THE "WATER'S" SURFACE WILL BECOME CHOPPY AND UNCLEAR. MIZU NO KIKORO ADMONISHES OFFICERS TO MAKE THEIR MIND FLAT, CALM AND SMOOTH LIKE THE CLEAR SURFACE OF WATER. "ONCE WE ALLOW THE EMOTIONS OF OUR NATURAL FEELINGS TO DISTURB OUR WATERS, WE CANNOT SEE OUTSIDE. WE CAN ONLY SEE INSIDE (EGO)..."*

VERBAL JUDO SAYS TO THE BAD GUY: "SAY WHAT YOU WANT. DO WHAT I SAY!" AND, "YOU HAVE THE LAST WORD. I HAVE THE LAST ACT."

"COPS ARE LIKE STEEL. WHEN THEY LOSE THEIR TEMPER, THEY ARE USELESS."

"DON'T TAKE IT PERSONALLY, TAKE IT SERIOUSLY."

"USE POSITIVE FEEDBACK WHEN YOU LEAST WANT TO."

"USE SELF-TALK TO MAINTAIN CONTROL."

"REDIRECT RATHER THAN RESIST."

"DO NOT TAKE THE BAIT! RELEASE YOUR EGO AND LET GO OF YOUR NEED TO CONTROL THE OTHER PERSON(S). ESCALATION IS A CHOICE.

IF YOU STAY DEFUSED AND UNDER CONTROL, CHANCES ARE, SO WILL THE DISTURBED PERSON."

BE TENTATIVE. *IT IS IMPORTANT THAT YOU ACT AND SPEAK IN A WAY THAT INDICATES OPENNESS TO OTHER THOUGHTS, IDEAS, ARGUMENTS.*

"IF IT (YOUR WORDS) MAKES YOU FEEL GOOD – LIKE "YOU ASSHOLE!", IT IS NO GOOD!"

"NEVER INFLATE PEOPLE WITH ADRENALIN!"

SHAWN WILLOUGHBY, VICE PRESIDENT OF THE ALBUQUERQUE POLICE ASSOCIATION, STATES THAT DE-ESCALATION TECHNIQUES TRAINING IS NOW A MANDATORY PART OF BOTH RECRUIT AND REGULAR OFFICER TRAINING. WILLOUGHBY AVERS THAT THIS IS A POSITIVE STEP FORWARD IN POLICING, BUT CONCEDES THAT THE "REALITY OF THE STREETS IS MUCH MORE COMPLICATED AND CHALLENGING..." HE ALSO NOTED THAT THE ALBUQUERQUE POLICE HAVE A VERY WELL DRAFTED AND VERY WELL THOUGHT-OUT SET OF PROCEDURES FOR DEALING WITH THE MENTALLY ILL, BUT CONCEDED THAT THE STREET OFFICERS DON'T OFTEN FOLLOW THE PROCEDURES."

WHAT DOES WILLOUGHBY'S OBSERVATION MEAN TO US? I THINK POLICE ADMINISTRATIONS AND OUR OFFICERS NEED TO ARRIVE AT A TRAINING SYSTEM THAT RESONATES WITH STREET OFFICERS. HOWEVER, LET'S NOT REMOVE THE ONUS FROM THE STREET OFFICERS, WHO ARE THE ONES CHARGED WITH KEEPING THE PEACE. WE (STREETS OFFICERS) NEED TO MEET THE ADMINISTRATORS AND THE INSTRUCTORS AT LEAST HALFWAY. WE MUST DISMISS OUR NEED FOR IMMEDIATE RESOLUTION TO ALL KINDS OF

RESISTANCE. WE NEED TO FORCE OURSELVES TO BE PATIENT. WE NEED TO GIVE OUR CITIZENS UNDERGOING CRISIS AND THE COMMUNITIES WITHIN WHICH THEY FUNCTION A CHANCE TO COMMUNICATE THEIR NEEDS. NOT THAT THIS WILL BE EASY, BY ANY MEANS. HELL, NO. IT IS JUST THAT I DON'T THINK WE CAN GO ON THIS WAY MUCH LONGER...

INCIDENTALLY, RESEARCH SHOWS THAT, SINCE 2011, OVER 75% OF CITIZENS SHOT WERE SUFFERING FROM A MENTAL ILLNESS.

OUR COURTS HAVE LEFT POLICE HOLDING THE BAG. WHILE GIVING POLICE VERY LITTLE DIRECTION OVER THE LAST 15-YEARS ON HOW TO HANDLE THE FLOOD OF MENTALLY ILL CITIZENS WITHOUT TREATMENT OR MEDICATION, THEY HAVE, AT THE SAME TIME, GIVEN POLICE AN ELEVATED STANDARD REGARDING INTERACTING WITH THE SEVERELY MENTALLY ILL. WORSE, THE COURTS HAVE GIVEN POLICE NO GUIDELINES ON HOW THOSE STANDARDS ARE TO BE MET.

OFFICERS AND OTHERS MIGHT CONSIDER USING LEAPS FOR A FORMULA TO DEFUSE AGGRESSION. LEAPS STANDS FOR:

- *LISTEN.*
- *EMPATHIZE.*
- *ASK (QUESTIONS).*
- *PARAPHRASE.*
- *SUMMARIZE (TO THE SUBJECT).*

ADVANCED DE-ESCALATION USES TACTICS AND STRATEGIES THAT ADHERE TO THE PRINCIPLES OF ME TRIPLED. MEANING THE TACTICS ARE DESIGNED TO

WORK WITH *MAXIMUM EFFECTIVENESS AND MAXIMUM EFFICIENCY USING MINIMUM ENERGY!*

USE PACE TO DIAGNOSE A VERBAL ENCOUNTER. PACE STANDS FOR:

- **PROBLEM** – *HOW DOES THE SUBJECT SEE HIS PROBLEM AND HOW DO YOU SEE THE PROBLEM?*

- **AUDIENCE** – *WHAT IS YOUR RELATIONSHIP WITH THE SUBJECT LIKE? ARE YOU SHOWING RESPECT? ARE YOU ACTIVELY LISTENING?*

- **CONSTRAINTS** – *WHAT IS/ARE THE OBSTACLE(S) TO COMMUNICATIONS? CAN YOU BYPASS THOSE CONSTRAINTS, OR CAN YOU USE THOSE CONSTRAINTS TO SOLVE THE PROBLEM? REMEMBER, YOU CAN ALWAYS FIND THE SOLUTION IN HIS OWN WORDS. HOWEVER, YOU CANNOT ACCOMPLISH THAT UNLESS YOU FIND OUT THE FACTS BY ASKING QUESTIONS, LISTENING, AND BEING OPEN & FLEXIBLE.*

- **ETHICAL PRESENCE** – *HOW ARE YOU PRESENTING YOURSELF? EMPATHIZING? ETHICAL PRESENCE IS THE MOST IMPORTANT "PRESENCE." IT IS HOW YOU DEPORT YOURSELF; IT IS HOW YOU **REPRESENT (THE ART OF REPRESENTATION)** YOUR DEPARTMENT OR AGENCY; HOW YOU REPRESENT ALL LAW ENFORCEMENT ENTITIES AND HOW YOU REPRESENT THE CONSTITUTION OF THE UNITED STATES!*

STUDIES SHOW THAT THE IMPRESSION YOU LEAVE WITH AN INDIVIDUAL, HIS FAMILY, AND OTHER IN THE COMMUNITY CAN LAST A LIFETIME. FOR INSTANCE, ONE STUDY I TOOK PART IN REVEALED THAT PEOPLE WILL ALWAYS REMEMBER AND NEVER FORGET AN OFFICER, OR ANOTHER AUTHORITY

FIGURE, WHO MISTREATS, ABUSES, DISRESPECTS OR USES UNNECESSARY FORCE ON THEM WHEN THEY INTERSECT WITH LAW ENFORCEMENT WHEN THEY ARE FEELING DOWN, DEPRESSED OF IN SOME OTHER WAY, IN TROUBLE.

REMEMBER: *IF A PERSON DOESN'T GET RESPECT, HE WILL GET REVENGE!*

IMPORTANTLY, NEITHER WILL PEOPLE WHO ENCOUNTER POLICE WHEN THEY ARE UNDER STRESS OR ARE FEELING VULNERABLE. THEY WILL REMEMBER THAT OFFICER'S KINDNESS FOR THE REST OF THEIR LIVES AND WILL TELL OTHERS ABOUT THAT KINDNESS THEY RECEIVED!

*UNFORTUNATELY, PEOPLE WILL REMEMBER THE BAD THINGS OFFICERS DO – THE ABUSE – MUCH LONGER THAN THE GOOD THINGS. OFFICER CAN GO FROM **HERO-TO-ZERO** IN A MILLISECOND!*

WHEN IT COMES TO DEFUSING HOSTILITY AND ANGER, ALWAYS REMEMBER THAT "THE ANGRIER THE OTHER PERSON, THE MORE IMPORTANT IT IS TO ACKNOWLEDGE HIS ANGER, TO USE EMPATHIC STATEMENTS, AND TO LISTEN.

SPEAKING OF LISTENING: MAKE NO MISTAKE. LISTENING IS A VERY POWERFUL DE-ESCALATION TOOL. THE FACT IS, WHEN OTHERS BELIEVE THAT YOU ARE NOT LISTENING TO THEIR CONCERNS, THEY ALMOST INVARIABLY CONSIDER YOU A THREAT. THIS MAY BE CRUCIAL, BECAUSE TO REVERSE THE COURSE OF AN ESCALATING CONFLICT, IT IS INCUMBENT UPON YOU TO MAKE YOURSELF AS UNTHREATENING AS POSSIBLE!

IT IS SAID THAT VERY FEW CONFLICTS ARE THE FAULT OR RESPONSIBILITY OF ONLY ONE PERSON. DO SOME SELF-EVALUATION ON THE SPOT AND SEE IF SOMETHING YOU SAID OR DID CONTRIBUTED TO THE ESCALATION OR CONFLICT. YOU MAY BE ABLE TO QUICKLY DEFUSE RISING EMOTIONS BY ACCEPTING RESPONSIBILITY AND APOLOGIZING.

MANY OFFICERS CONSIDER APOLOGIZING AN ACT OF WEAKNESS. STUDIES AND "HISTORY" SHOW THAT APOLOGIZING FOR A "WRONG." EVEN ONLY A WRONG PERCEIVED BY THE BAD GUY AND NOT THE OFFICER, CAN BRING CALM TO EVEN THE MOST VOLATILE OF INTERACTIONS!

HERE IS SOMETHING TO CONSIDER. IF IT IS SAFE AND/OR PRACTICABLE TO DO SO, CONSIDER TEMPORARILY DISENGAGING TO ALLOW THE OTHER PERSON, WHO IS ARGUMENTATIVE, TO CALM. "SIR, LOOK, YOU MIGHT BE RIGHT, I DON'T KNOW. HOW ABOUT GIVING ME A MINUTE TO CHECK WITH MY PARTNER (OR, MY SUPERVISOR). I'LL BE RIGHT BACK, OKAY?"

IN THE MINUTE OR TWO THAT YOU ARE GONE, THE SUBJECT WILL HAVE TIME TO THINK ABOUT HIS WORDS AND ACTIONS. BY DISENGAGING, YOU GIVE HIM THE CHANCE TO COMPLY WITH YOUR REQUEST(S) OR DIRECTION WITHOUT LOSING FACE (HE CAN DO THIS BECAUSE YOU ARE NOT STANDING IN FRONT OF HIM, WAITING FOR HIM TO DO WHAT YOU DIRECTED HIM TO). THE (INTELLECTUAL) DELAY ALSO WILL ALLOW HIM TO BEGIN THE PROCESS OF SELF-EVALUATION AND COME TO THE CONCLUSION OF – *MAYBE, JUST MAYBE, I WAS WRONG AND THE OFFICER WAS RIGHT...*

DISENGAGING WORKS WONDERS IN SITUATIONS WHERE YOU MIGHT BE ALONE AND OUTNUMBERED. YOU ARE NOT BACKING DOWN. YOU ARE INFORMING HIM THAT *"SIR, WHEN I RETURN, I WILL RETURN WITH BACK-UP AND, IF YOU ARE STILL DRINKING HERE (I AM CITING THIS EXAMPLE OF TWO DRUNKS DRINKING BEER IN A "NO-ALCOHOL" SECTION OF A STADIUM BEING ADDRESSED BY A LONE SECURITY OFFICER), WE WILL HAVE NO CHOICE BUT TO ESCORT YOU OUT OF THE STADIUM AND YOU WILL NOT BE ALLOWED TO RETURN FOR THE REST OF THE SEASON. LET ME ASK YOU, DO YOU GUYS REALLY NEED THAT KIND OF PROBLEM TODAY?"*

I ASK YOU TO CONSIDER THIS TACT WHEN IT COMES TO REVERSING THE TIDE OF ESCALATING EMOTIONS. THE TACTIC IS NOT TO GET HUNG-UP IN THE PAST. DWELLING ON PAST ISSUES IS A SURE-FIRE WAY OF MAKING CONFLICTS WORSE! INSTEAD, SHIFT THE CONVERSATION OR INTERACTION TO THE FUTURE. THIS IS A GREAT TACTIC FOR ENGAGING BOTH OF YOU IN A PROBLEM-SOLVING ACTIVITY RATHER THAN A FAULT-FINDING EXPEDITION. THE DESIGNED GOAL: CREATE HOPE AND MAKE YOURSELF LESS OF A THREAT.

MORE ON DEFUSING HOSTILE PEOPLE.

DEAL WITH FEELINGS FIRST.

BEGIN TO DE-ESCALATE EARLY! A GOOD IDEA IS TO PRE-EMPT THE ATTACK BY BEGINNING THE DEFUSING PROCESS BEFORE THE OTHER PERSON EXPLODES INTO A

RANT. YOU MIGHT OBSERVE THE SUBJECT'S BODY LANGUAGE AND YOUR GUT FEELINGS ARE TELLING YOU THAT HE IS ABOUT TO LAUNCH SOME VERBAL ABUSE YOUR WAY. "YO, PETE, LOOKS LIKE YOU'RE UPSET ABOUT SOMETHING. WHAT'S UP?" SOME EXPERTS SAY THIS SETS A RESPECTFUL TONE FOR THE INTERACTION.

BE ASSERTIVE. *DON'T BE HESITANT TO HOLD THE OTHER PERSON ACCOUNTABLE WHEN HE CROSSES THE LINE WITH HIS COMMENTS OR ACTIONS. AS I POINTED OUT THROUGHOUT THIS BOOK, THERE ARE SCORES OF CLEVER WAYS TO PLAY WITH HIS HEAD AND TO GET HIM TO DO WHAT YOU WANT, BUT, CERTAINLY, IF HE CROSSES THAT LINE, LET HIM KNOW THIS CRITICAL MESSAGE: **"THAT CRAP IS NOT GOING TO WORK WITH ME!"***

IMPOSING CONSEQUENCES, AS I STATED IN AN EARLIER CHAPTER(S), IS IMPORTANT. AS A MATTER OF FACT, IF YOU DON'T SPEAK UP, MOST SUBJECTS WILL VIEW YOU AS A VICTIM AND HE WILL CONTINUE BULLYING YOU UNTIL YOU SAY OR DO SOMETHING TO COMPEL HIM TO STOP.

"PETE, LOOK, I WILL HELP YOU RESOLVE THIS PROBLEM, BUT, IF YOU RAISE YOUR VOICE AGAIN, THIS INTERVIEW IS OVER AND YOU WILL HAVE TO COME BACK SOME OTHER TIME, THIS TIME WITH MY SUPERVISOR. WHAT WILL IT BE?"

THE 5 TIMES WORDS FAIL (FROM VERBAL JUDO).

THE FOLLOWING SITUATIONS ARE CIRCUMSTANCES WHERE OFFICERS MIGHT CONSIDER TRANSITIONING FROM "WORDS" TO EITHER DISENGAGING OR THE DIRECT USE OF FORCE.

1. **SECURITY.** "SECURITY" REFERS TO ANY SITUATION WHEN OTHERS UNDER OUR CONTROL ARE THREATENED OR UNDER IMMINENT JEOPARDY. SECURITY ALSO APPLIES WHEN PROPERTY UNDER OUR CONTROL IS BEING DESTROYED. "PROPERTY" BEING THREATENED OR DESTROYED COULD INCLUDE EVIDENCE BEING FLUSHED.

2. **ATTACK.** "ATTACK" REFERS TO ANY SITUATION WHEN **YOU** ARE UNDER ATTACK. THE OTHER PERSON'S WORDS AND/OR ACTIONS CREATE A DIRECT THREAT TO YOUR LIFE OR SAFETY. THIS WILL INCLUDE SITUATIONS WHEN THAT PERSON INVADES YOUR PERSONAL SPACE, ESPECIALLY AFTER YOU HAVE ORDERED OR REQUESTED THE SUBJECT TO STAY BACK.

3. **FLIGHT.** IN "FLIGHT," WORDS FAIL BECAUSE THE OTHER PERSON HAS TAKEN FLIGHT.

4. **EXCESSIVE REPETITION.** YOU APPEAR WEAK AND A LITTLE BUMBLING WHEN YOU REPEAT A REQUEST OR A COMMAND MORE THAN TWICE. I SAY "TWICE" ONLY BECAUSE

THERE IS ALWAYS THE CHANCE THAT THE PERSON – BECAUSE OF AUDITORY EXCLUSION, A BYPRODUCT OF SNS – DID NOT HEAR YOU. IN SOME CASES, GIVE THE COMMAND ONLY ONCE AND THAT IS IT. BASICALLY, "EXCESSIVE REPETITION" MEANS THAT NO VOLUNTARY COMPLIANCE IS FORTHCOMING AND ALL VIABLE OPTIONS HAVE BEEN USED UP. ONE SUGGESTION IN A SITUATION LIKE THIS IS TO *SET THE CONTEXT – AS IN THE FIVE-STEP -* BY ASKING THE *CONFIRMATION QUESTION,* SO THAT YOU CAN SHOW IN COURT THAT YOU USED UP ALL OPTIONS, MEANING YOU HAVE ESTABLISHED *PRECLUSION.*

5. **REVISED PRIORITIES.** WHAT THIS MEANS IS THAT WE SHOULD STOP UTTERING WORDS WHEN AN EMERGENCY OCCURS ELSEWHERE. FOR INSTANCE, YOU ARE INTERVIEWING A FAMILY MEMBER TRYING TO ASCERTAIN THE WHEREABOUTS OF A FUGITIVE WHEN YOU HEAR A PARTNER YELL OUT, GUN!" FROM ANOTHER PART OF THE RESIDENCE. REVISED PRIORITIES REQUIRES YOU TO STOP THAT INTERVIEW AND PROCEED IMMEDIATELY TO THE EMERGENCY ELSEWHERE.

MORE DE-ESCALATION GEMS....

IN A "PERFECT WORLD," WHAT EVERY POLICE OFFICER THINKS AND BELIEVES IS THAT "EVERYBODY IN MY COMMUNITY IS SAFER BECAUSE OF MY PRESENCE."

ANOTHER VALUE OF "MUSHIN," AND "MIZU NO KIKORO (MIND LIKE CALM, STILL WATER)" IS THAT, WHEN YOUR MIND IS STILL AND CALM, YOU ARE SAFER

BECAUSE IT IS EASY TO READ YOUR "AUDIENCE." HOWEVER, IF YOUR EGO IS PART OF YOUR REPERTOIRE DURING A CONTACT, YOUR "WATERS" ARE CHOPPED UP AND UNCLEAR. YOU CANNOT READ YOUR AUDIENCE. YOU ARE VIRTUALLY "BLIND" IN A DANGEROUS WORLD!

ONCE WE PERMIT THE EMOTIONS OF YOUR <u>NATURAL FEELINGS</u> TO DISTURB YOUR "WATERS," YOU WILL FIND IT ALMOST IMPOSSIBLE. WE CANNOT SEE OUTSIDE FACTORS AND DANGERS. THIS IS WHAT I CALL "BRAIN-DAMAGED" BECAUSE WE CAN ONLY SEE INSIDE WHERE OUR NATURAL EMOTIONS ARE HOUSED.

EGO MAKES US BLIND WITH RAGE. WE LOSE OUR CENTER AND BALANCE. EGO MANIFESTS ON THE STREETS AS REACTING DEFENSIVELY TO QUESTIONS; TO PERSONAL RAGE OVER "BAD ATTITUDES" TO IMMEDIATE USE OF FORCE AND/OR ARRESTING PEOPLE BECAUSE OF PERSONAL INSULTS, ETC.

PEOPLE — EVEN EVIL MOTOR SCOOTERS — CARE ABOUT KNOWING; HENCE, SET CONTEXT. "SIR, THE REASON I AM ASKING YOU TO——IS——"

"CHECK YOUR ASSUMPTIONS: BEWARE OF BRAIN DAMAGE (VERBAL JUDO, INC.)!"

RESPOND TO PEOPLE. DO NOT REACT.

FLEXIBILITY IS STRENGTH. RIGIDITY IS WEAKNESS. PEOPLE ARE FLAWED, NOT EVIL.

REMEMBER: UP TO 93% OF COMMUNICATIONS IS DELIVERY AND PRESENTATION STYLE.

Use Self-Talk to maintain control; use LEAPS and PACE.

Redirect rather than resist.

More Peace Phrases You Can Use:

➢ "Excuse me, sir, can I talk with you?"
➢ "Miss, would you assist me...?
➢ "Can you work with me today?"
➢ "Can you go along with me on this...?"
➢ "Sir, I don't think you need this kind of trouble today. Do you?"
➢ "Wuz the matter?
➢ "I think we both need to relax, sir, why don't we both have a seat?"
➢ "How you doing today, sir?"
➢ "Sir, you are much too smart to do something like that..."
➢ "I would probably have done the same thing, miss..."

The Foundation for Success forms around "Officer Presence," which consists of our appearance, our use of language, knowledge and our skills. Officer Presence also involves how officers on the scene manage "Contact and Cover," assigning and carrying out individual and team roles, et al.

Relative to the Tactical-10 Car Stop, here is how one outstanding officer responded to hesitation by a motorist after the officer asked

HIM FOR HIS LICENSE AND REGISTRATION (REMEMBER, HESITATION IN ANSWERING IS A SIGNATURE OF DANGER):

"SIR, I HAVE GIVEN YOU A LEGAL, LAWFUL REASON FOR THIS CAR STOP. YOU HAVE A LEGAL OBLIGATION, THEREFORE, TO COOPERATE. I THINK YOU KNOW THAT. NOW, SIR, WOULD YOU SHOW ME YOUR LICENSE? I'LL GET YOU ON YOUR WAY, PRETTY DARN QUICK."

A FEW PARAGRAPHS AGO, I "SPOKE" ABOUT DOING SOME SELF-EVALUATION DURING OR AFTER A CONTACT OR INTERACTION GOES BAD. I NOTED THAT IT IS RARE WHEN ONLY ONE PERSON IS TOTALLY AT FAULT WHEN AN INTERACTION IMPLODES. SO, EVEN THOUGH I KNOW HUNDREDS OF PEOPLE — NOT JUST POLICE OFFICERS — WHO BELIEVE IN THE ADAGE "NEVER APOLOGIZE," I AM ASKING YOU, IF YOU HAPPEN TO BE AMONG THAT GROUP OF PEOPLE, TO SUSPEND DISBELIEF FOR A MINUTE.

LET ME REMIND YOU THAT THE MAIN THEME OF THIS BOOK IS DE-ESCALATING AGGRESSIVE AND HOSTILE PEOPLE. WITH THAT IN MIND, I THINK IT WOULD BE PRUDENT FOR OFFICERS TO RECONSIDER THE ACT OF APOLOGIZING WHEN YOU HAPPEN TO HAVE SOME RESPONSIBILITY FOR A CITIZEN GETTING AGGRESSIVE OR DISRESPECTFUL.

IF YOU NEED CONVINCING, MAYBE THIS LITTLE FACTOID WILL PUSH YOU IN THE RIGHT DIRECTION.

MAYBE YOU REMEMBER THE RODNEY KING INCIDENT WHERE A PLATOON OF LAS ANGELES POLICE OFFICERS WERE VIDEOTAPED QUADRUPLE-TAPPING KING FOR

LONG, SEEMINGLY INTERMINABLE MINUTES WITH IMPACT WEAPONS. THEY ALSO HIT HIM WITH OTHER INTERMEDIATE WEAPONS. IF YOU RECALL THAT, *YOU HAVE TO REMEMBER THAT THE CHIEF-OF-POLICE WAS FIRED,* SEVERAL

OFFICERS WENT ON TRIAL, AND THE CITY WAS NEARLY BURNED TO THE GROUND IN ENSUING RIOTS AND OTHER DISTURBANCES.

AND, OF COURSE, THEN CAME THE PREDICTABLE MULTI-MILLION DOLLAR LAW SUIT THAT COST THE LAPD AND THE CITY DEARLY.

ALL OF WHICH, ACCORDING TO KING, COULD HAVE BEEN AVOIDED, OR AT LEAST MINIMIZED IF:

"IF THOSE OFFICERS — MAYBE EVEN ONE OF THEM — WOULD HAVE COME TO ME WHILE I WAS IN THE HOSPITAL AND WERE HUMAN ENOUGH TO HAVE APOLOGIZED FOR THE BEATING, I WOULD HAVE BEEN SATISFIED, AND THERE WOULD HAVE BEEN NO (LAW) SUIT, MAYBE NO RIOT."

COPS AND COMMUNICATIONS

VERY IMPORTANT STUFF

DE-ESCALATION IS NOT JUST VALUABLE FOR MANAGING HOSTILE AND VIOLENT PEOPLE. ITS CENTER IS WRAPPED AROUND THE ART OF COMMUNICATIONS, OR TACT COM. THE SALIENT FACT IS, ALL PEOPLE, FROM THE GOOD CITIZEN TO THE POTENTIAL KILLER, WILL REMEMBER A COP WHO ACTS LIKE A JERK **FOREVER!** JUST ASK THE MOTORIST WHO ASKS A TRAFFIC COP FOR DIRECTIONS AND GETS A COLD LOOK AND A THUMB POINTING "THAT-A-WAY." **WHAT A JERK**, HE OR SHE WILL MUTTER DRIVING OFF.

IT TAKES ONLY A FEW SECONDS LONGER TO SMILE AND SAY, "JUST KEEP HEADING THE WAY YOU ARE GOING, SIR. YOU'LL SEE IT RIGHT ACROSS FROM THE STADIUM. I'LL BE HERE ALL DAY, IF YOU GET LOST." THAT MOTORIST WILL DRIVE OFF WITH A GREAT FEELING AND WILL TELL 10 OR 20 PEOPLE ABOUT THE "GREAT COP."

NYC COP AND INSTRUCTOR, KEVIN DILLON, STATES THAT CITIZENS AND BAD GUYS — STUDIES REVEAL — WILL MORE LIKELY BRING A SUIT AGAINST A JERK-OFFICER THAN THEY WILL ONE WHO TREATS THEM WITH RESPECT AND CONSIDERATION.

DILLON CALLS THE PHENOMENON OF A COP WHO IS FIRST LOOKED UPON AS A HERO BUT TREATS PEOPLE WITH DISRESPECT, ETC., AS **HERO-TO-ZERO!** DILLON CITES NUMEROUS EXAMPLES OF OFFICERS WHO ALWAYS TREAT OTHERS WITH RESPECT AND KINDNESS BEING IN SCUFFLES WITH BAD GUYS AND CITIZENS RISKING THEIR LIVES BY JUMPING IN TO HELP THE OFFICER. I, ON THE OTHER HAND, CAN GIVE YOU CHAPTER-AND-VERSE ABOUT JERK OFFICERS AND OTHERS WHO WERE INVOLVED IN FIGHTS WHERE

CITIZENS EITHER HELPED THE BAD GUY OR CHEERED THE BAD GUY ON FROM THE SIDELINES!

COPS AND CORRECTION OFFICERS WOULD BE WISE TO FOLLOW DILLON'S ADVISE TO TREAT PRISONERS, ARRESTEES, AND SUSPECT WITH RESPECT. DILLON POINTS OUT THAT HE HAS WITNESSED NUMEROUS SCENARIOS WITH BAD GUYS WHO ALWAYS LIKE TO FIGHT, EVEN WHEN BEING PRINTED AT THE STATION, SURROUNDED BY COPS.

"GOOD AFTERNOON, SIR (OR, THE MAN'S NAME). LOOK, YOU ACT LIKE A GENTLEMAN AND THINGS WILL GO SWELL HERE. I'LL GET YOU PRINTED NICE AND QUICK AND I'LL GET YOU OUT OF HERE BEFORE YOU EVEN KNOW IT. HOW'S THAT SOUND?"

DILLON SUGGESTS THAT OFFICERS CONSIDER OFFERING A STRESSED OUT SUSPECT OR SUBJECT A SANDWICH, OR SOME OTHER TYPE OF FOOD (CANDY?), A CUP OF WATER, EVEN A CIGARETTE. "YOU'D BE SURPRISED HOW A DRINK OF WATER, A SMOKE, MAYBE A REESE'S CUP, CAN CALM THE NERVES," HE SAYS.

AND I CAN ATTEST TO THAT. I HAVE SEEN IT AND I HAVE EXPERIENCED IT. WHICH IS WHY I WROTE THIS BOOK. AN OFFICER WALKS INTO A SITUATION BY HIMSELF — BACKUP STILL MINUTES AWAY — AND ENCOUNTERS A ROWDY AND HOSTILE CROWD. THE CROWD BEGINS TO CLOSE AROUND THE COP, AND THE BIGGEST THUG IN THE MOB STEPS UP AND STANDS NEXT TO THE BELEAGUERED COP AND SAYS TO THE ADVANCING MOB,

"ANYONE WHO WANTS TO ATTACK THIS COP GOTTA GO THROUGH ME FIRST!"

AS NAPOLEON ONCE SAID, "**AN IRON FIST IS BETTER SERVED UP IN A VELVET GLOVE.**"

RED FLAGS & SIGNATURES OF DANGER!

I DID NOT DELVE DEEPLY INTO SIGNATURES OF DANGER. RED FLAGS THAT OBSERVANT OFFICERS CAN PICK UP THAT CAN GIVE THEM AN "EARLY WARNING" THAT SOME SORT OF ATTACK MIGHT BE ON ITS WAY. EXPERTS CALL THESE "TELLS."

FOR INSTANCE. LET'S TAKE THE ALWAYS NERVE-RACKING VEHICLE STOP. PERRY HARRIS. AN OUTSTANDING PPCT INSTRUCTOR TRAINER AND SOUTH CAROLINA COP. SUGGESTS THAT YOU CAN TELL A LOT BY WHAT A DRIVER OR PASSENGER DOES WITH HIS/HER EYES. IT HAS BEEN A COUPLE YEARS SINCE HARRIS MADE THIS COMMENT. SO I AM PARAPHRASING: "NORMAL JOES HAVE NORMAL EYES. HARD TO DEFINE "NORMAL EYES." BUT YOU CAN TELL THEM WHEN YOU SEE THEM. THEY LOOK AT YOU AND REGARD YOU JUST LIKE ANOTHER NORMAL PERSON MIGHT IN A CONVERSATION.

"BUT. THEN. THERE IS THE ALREADY AGITATED PERSON. AS YOU APPROACH. YOU CAN SEE HIS HEAD MOVING. HIS

SHOULDERS MOVING, OR HIM DOING SOMETHING WITH A PASSENGER. HIS EYES LOOK AWAY, LOOK AT YOUR GUN, ETC. I CAN ALWAYS TELL WHEN THIS IS GOING TO BE A BAD STOP. PAY ATTENTION AND SO CAN YOU."

OTHER SIGNATURES THAT CAN SAVE YOUR LIFE INCLUDE:

> **THE MOTORIST OPENING HIS DOOR AS YOU APPROACH.** HE IS EITHER GOING TO ATTACK OR DOES NOT WANT YOU TO SEE SOMETHING INSIDE THE VEHICLE.

> **THAT SAME MOTORIST MOVES TOWARD YOU, MAYBE EVEN RUSHES!** DOESN'T WALK. DOESN'T OBEY COMMANDS TO STOP (SOUNDS LIKE A **SBC**. DOESN'T IT?).

> A PERSON APPEARS AGITATED AND NOW **HE CLAPS HIS HANDS TOGETHER!** READ THIS AS A DEAD-BANG **PRE-ATTACK DANGER SIGN!** EXPERTS SAY THAT THE HAND-CLAP IS A NATURAL FIGHTING ACTION BECAUSE IT GETS THE BLOOD FLOWING IN THE HANDS AND WRISTS. THE NEXT MOVE IS A PUNCH OR A GUN PULL!

> **THE THUMB-TWITCH.** IF YOU SEE THIS MOVE, DO SOMETHING, LIKE **NOW!** HIT COVER, USE YOUR TRAINING. BUT ALWAYS BE AWARE THAT THE SUBJECT IS INSTINCTIVELY PREPARING THAT THUMB TO WITHDRAW A SECRETED GUN AND BEGIN THE FIRING PROCESS.

> **BLADING THE BODY**, WHEN AN OFFICER APPROACHES IS USUALLY A SIGN THAT THE SUBJECT IS TRYING TO OBSCURE A GUN HE IS SECRETING UNDER A SHIRT OR ON HIS HIP IN PLAIN VIEW.

- *BILLOWING THE SHIRT. THIS IS ANOTHER MOVE A BAD GUY MIGHT MAKE TO OBSCURE THE OFFICER'S ABILITY TO DETECT A GUN OR KNIFE. HE WILL PULL THE BOTTOM OF A SHIRT, JACKET, OR JERSEY AROUND THE GUN.*
- *INDEXING THE GUN. OFTEN, A BAD GUY WILL SUBCONSCIOUSLY TOUCH THE AREA WHERE HE IS WEARING A GUN OR KNIFE TO REASSURE HIMSELF HE IS GOOD TO GO WHEN THE TIME COMES.*
- *SHORT-SIDING. WHEN A BAD GUY WHO IS WEARING A WEAPON ON HIS HIP WILL SHORT-STEP WITH THAT SIDE LEG AS HE ASCENDS OR DESCENDS STAIRS. WHILE WALKING OR RUNNING — ESPECIALLY IN THE RAIN — YOU WILL NOTICE A SHORT OR STIFF ARM SWING AND A SHORT LEG STRIDE.*

ON VEHICLE STOPS, LOOK FOR:

THIS *RED FLAG COULD SAVE YOUR LIFE: LOOK FOR A RISING SHOULDER, OR MOVING UPWARDS TO ALLOW THE BAD GUY TO SNATCH A GUN FROM HIS WAIST BAND.*

ANOTHER RED FLAG. BE AWARE WHEN YOU OBSERVE A MOTORIST BENDING OVER OR DIPPING A SHOULDER TO SECRETE A WEAPON UNDER A SEAT OR SOMEWHERE ELSE.

CLOTHING AND ACTIONS. Signs that may Save your Life!
- *DOES THE CLOTHING MATCH THE SEASON?*
- *IS THE CLOTHING LOOSE OR BAGGY?*

270

- *Does the clothing match the weather or conditions?*
- *In cold weather, is his coat unzipped or open?*
- *The individual is wearing only one glove.*
- *Guns have weight. When concealed in a jacket or coat, hood or bag, gravity will pull that weight down. The collar on the side of the weapon will be tight to a neck and the bottom of a jacket will flap open and the subject will hold it down!*
- *No belt loops on pants, but he is wearing a belt?*

You can contact the author and/or check out his web site to learn what he is training, where and when at:

www.ActionFightingArts.com
"A Total Threat Management Training System."
Email: harrywigder@rcn.com

ACKNOWLEDGEMENTS

I would like to thank the following people, whose assistance in this and other writing projects proved invaluable.

Thomas Moy, Manadnock DT & OC Instructor Trainer, Delaware University, Lewes, Delaware. Tom has been instrumental in the success of my first two books, and was even more helpful with this book. I feel indebted to Officer Moy for his moral support and for his seemingly unlimited supply of incredible knowledge about everything law enforcement and subject control. Tom is a graduate of the Delaware State Police Academy and a current senior Public Safety Patrol Officer for the University of Delaware.

Joshua Goldstein. Josh is my son-in-law, residing with my daughter Rachel in Pennsburg, Pa. He was enormously helpful with what I hope to be a successful book by helping me edit this work. His suggestions were so helpful.

"Marvelous Marvin" Wigder, my cousin, who resides in Chicago with his lovely wife Marilyn. The Marvelous one, as usual, did absolutely nothing to help me research and write this book. But, gosh-darnnit, Marv loved to see his name in print, and, not only that, he has always motivated me with his spiritual support!

Jeffrey Imboden, former board member, Pa. Board of Probation & Parole, also provided moral support, plus one or two stories from his experience as a probation/parole officer and hearing officer.

James O. Smith, former Direction of Staff Development, Pa. Board of Probation and Parole. As I noted in the Introduction, Mr. Smith, who was my direct supervisor at the time, first encouraged me to teach De-escalation Techniques and later taught me how to do it. For that, plus the fact that Smitty was easily the greatest training mentor a person could ever have, I will be eternally grateful.

Sergeant E.B. Bud Shull, Wilson Police Department. I am grateful for Bud's awesome contribution to this work. Relating his experience with *"Cooper"* in the ER was instrumental in my being able to personify and humanize the central theme(s) of de-escalating aggression and violence. As a result of Bud's story – he met with me three times to make sure I got it right – I researched further into how to manage and defuse suicidal and mentally disturbed people and discovered the **Third-Party Method** of calming the mentally ill and other disturbed people.

Ms. Tracy Medellin, Nurse, Gracedale Hospital, Nazareth, Pa. Ms. Medellin resides in Easton, Pa., and happens to be one of my three beautiful daughters. I only quoted Nurse Medellin once in this book, but the insights she has shared with me relative to her work with troubled people revealed before unknown gems on how to deal with, manage, and bring calm to all people under her care.

Ms. Helen Palmer, Retired Nurse. Ms. Palmer resides in Blairsville, Pa., and is the wife of Dr. Frank Palmer, now deceased. Ms. Palmer once worked at the Torrence State Psychiatric Hospital in the Pittsburgh, Pa. area. Helen shared with me some valuable insights on dealing with schizophrenic patients and others.

Thomas G. Coleman. Tom is a Technical Writer for a nuclear power concern in the Pittsburgh area. He is also my best friend and brother from a different mother, so to speak. I am grateful for Tom being my **writing muse.** His capacity for unimaginable patience with me has continuously inspired me to write and write and to relentlessly search for ways to write better.

Christopher Hertig is a former professor from York University in York, Pa. Chris has shared super-valuable information for both this book and for my second opus – *Super Secret Police Shit That Can Save Your Life.* I am indebted to Mr. Hertig for his exceptional insight into the importance of proxemics and "limited verbal interaction" relative to the art of bringing calm to chaotic environments.

Made in the USA
Middletown, DE
13 July 2018